RECOVERING OUR LOST THEOLOGY

RICK BROWNELL

RECOVERING OUR LOST THEOLOGY

THE SOVEREIGN GRACE OF GOD

TATE PUBLISHING & *Enterprises*

Published by Tate Publishing & Enterprises, LLC
127 E. Trade Center Terrace | Mustang, Oklahoma 73064 USA
1.888.361.9473 | www.tatepublishing.com

Tate Publishing is committed to excellence in the publishing industry. The company reflects the philosophy established by the founders, based on Psalm 68:11,
"The Lord gave the word and great was the company of those who published it."

Cover design by Blake Brasor
Interior design by Kellie Vincent

Published in the United States of America

ISBN: 978-1-61777-612-0
1. Religion / Christian Theology / General 2. Religion / Christianity / General
11.05.25

DEDICATION

Gratefully dedicated to my wife, Sheila Fesler Brownell. Long before the kitchen conversations we shared as I struggled to come to terms with how to think theologically, perhaps even long before that first day I decided I couldn't wait to talk to you any longer, God must have given you an inkling that marriage to a realist impassioned by theology and music might eventually reveal (if one were to examine the smallest nooks and crannies)...a romantic heart. What is more romantic than loving God, music, and you? You are the girl.

ACKNOWLEDGMENTS

To Glenn Zirkle, who had the interest (and nerve) to sit through my first Sunday school class in theology, actually reading Clark Pinnock *during* class, and still came through it acknowledging the ultimate value of struggling with biblical theology.

To Rob Martini, who read the manuscript, offering helpful critique, but more importantly, who listened cautiously from the very beginning to my theological wrestling, finally making many of my theological struggles his own, and whose passion for preaching and teaching I've always admired and strive to emulate whenever he gives me the opportunity.

To Bud Inman, who read the manuscript and whose heart for ministry and people makes him, in my mind, the kind of person who would be a sound "theological" pastoral blessing to any congregation.

To Dick Roberts, who read the initial musings of the manuscript, a gem of a human being whose thorough passion for studying the Word makes him a standout pastor, teacher, and mentor to his congregation.

To Ken Ramak, who read the manuscript and always impressed me with his openness to consider new ways of thinking about theology and whose passion for God in worship and evangelism is genuine. Don't ever stop searching the Word.

To Belinda VanVeldhuisen, whose helpful and detailed attention to the language of the manuscript showed me why I needed to say what I wanted to say better than I had thought I'd already said it; who questioned my theological meanderings with a friendly attitude and concern when necessary, and whose valued friendship and Christian spirit I will always appreciate and want to emulate.

To Dr. Jack MacArthur, the first pastor and theologian to get my attention and challenge my theological perspectives in the early days in Solvang, who put up with all those questions and helped steer my muddled thinking into a passionate faith in Christ.

To Grace and Helmet Bubetz: Helmet, who loves life and is more thankful for it than most Christians I know, and Grace, a wonderful, faithful woman to whom I apologize for upsetting her theological apple cart on more than one occasion.

TABLE OF CONTENTS

PART 2
EMPOWERING THE SOVEREIGN GRACE OF GOD IN EVANGELISM

PREFACE

Mark Twain said, "It's not the parts of the Bible that I don't understand that bother me; it's the parts that I *do* understand that bother me." Reading Scripture accurately and understanding it is one of the most difficult tasks under the sun, not only for atheists like Mark Twain, but for Christians as well. It's not necessarily difficult to understand because of the original languages that the manuscripts were written in, although knowing Greek and Hebrew does make a difference in interpretation. It's not difficult because the era and culture that it was written in are two thousand years removed from ours. It's not difficult because of the various translations available which affect interpretation and meaning to some degree. It's not difficult because of the numerous denominations or cults or liberal theologians that pepper the theological landscape with various persuasions of the historic Christian faith.

It's difficult, first, because we don't know how to think about what we're reading, and second, we've come to think it's more important to share some condensed, peanut-sized version of the gospel at the simplest, most juvenile, least thought-provoking level with our culture rather than let people wrestle with the theological difficulties and search out for themselves how they might be rectified logically.

I think I know how we got to the place where we began to think so shallowly and superficially about theology. I think it came through what were initially the good intentions of many theologians who wanted to impact our culture and world by bringing people to Christ. That is a fine motive, but how far from the theological truth are we willing to allow our "good intentions" to take us in order to achieve this end? We demonstrate our shallowness in understanding what Scripture means from the pulpit, in preparing for our sermons, in our LIFE group study guides, in our conversations with unbelievers, and in most all the available Christian writings on the market, but most prevalently in our own muddled thinking about God. The answer isn't that God should have made it easier for us to "get it." It's that "getting it" means having to think a little harder.

This defeatist attitude toward theology is clearly demonstrated even by Bible publishers in their notes on Scripture! The NKJV Open Bible with a Reader's Guide to Understanding the Bible that explains certain passages of Scripture, for example, writes in its second note on 1 Thessalonians 1:5: "We must be able to clearly give out the *simple* facts of the gospel without getting bogged down with profound theological concepts." (Translation: Don't get hampered, impeded, hindered, obstructed, and thwarted by profound, learned, intellectual, discerning, deep, knowledgeable thoughts about theology when you're sharing the gospel). Is that because the editors aren't smart enough to get it, or they think *you're* not smart enough to get it or that the *rest of the world* isn't? Or is it because they've decided that it's just too much work to think accurately and logically and nobody cares anyway?

It seems to me that every word in the book of Romans is a logical and orderly attempt to express the deeply profound and theological truths of the grace and mercy of God. Its intention is to walk us through the process of thinking about what God is doing in Christ. Yes, thinking theologically is difficult. Get over it. Some Christians who have read their Bibles for decades are incapable of thinking any deeper about God than that He's our Daddy and nothing He wrote to us is more important than this: what He wants us to do more than anything else is to climb up in His lap and hold His hand and listen to Him tell us He loves us. Don't think about the tough theological concepts; don't wrestle with the seeming paradoxes; don't try to put it together logically or, God forbid, intellectually. All that stuff just bogs you down. Just climb up in His lap and stop thinking altogether. Just *feel* the love. Such are the evangelical encouragements from the eminent theologians who put together our most trusted Bible study notes.

We Christians are essentially ignorant about the Bible and theology, and leadership, it seems, likes it that way and feeds us at that shallow level whenever the opportunity presents itself. I continue to be astounded at our lack of ability to systematically think about theological ideas and to explain even basic scriptural concepts and premises in a rational and logical fashion. And that inability to think deeply and rationally is having a huge impact on our understanding of salvation, evangelism, and theology. It is no wonder to me that we are so confused about what we should say to people about God and Christ because, frankly, we don't know ourselves! Or maybe it's worse. Maybe we don't want to know! And we won't want to know as long as we think that the deeper we go, the worse it gets.

The purpose of this book is to make this struggle in the areas of our understanding salvation, evangelism, and theology more comprehensive, more cohesive, and more beneficial without demeaning the process.

This book is divided into three parts, and in all of them we want to emphasize the grace of God in saving believers in Christ. In part one we will look at the grace of God in our salvation and at this incredible gift of new life in Christ in more detail as we consider the *way of salvation* that God has revealed in His Word and all that God has done to enable us to see the truth of his revelation and become and remain believers in Jesus Christ.

If God is the author of Scripture, and He resides in perfect majesty high above His creation, His revealed Word to us is also perfect. It tells us all we need to know about God and His relationship to the world. Before we look at each step of the *way of salvation,* we will explain two important principles that will help to better discern the significance of this revelation in His word regarding salvation.

The first principle is the inerrancy of Scripture. This means that Scripture is without error, and that the Word of God written by human beings is not merely a *human* matter, because Scripture's testimony of itself is that it proceeded from the Spirit through the words of men. It is a *divine* matter that has a *divine* origin in God Himself and can therefore be relied upon as truthful.

The second principle is the analogy of faith. This is an important foundation to the science and art of interpretation and means that sacred Scripture is its own interpreter. Because the source of Scripture originates in God, no part of it can be interpreted in such a way as to render any other part of it in conflict with itself.

Clarifying these principles will give you two important tools to use as you learn and formulate your understanding of what God has revealed in His Word.

Then we will look at the sovereignty of God. God's sovereignty should be the overarching grid through which you view, digest, and process all of Scripture. A firm understanding of God's sovereignty will have a critical influence on your understanding of Scripture; it will temper the events that come into your life; it will be the foundation of your view of salvation, prayer, and eternity. Here we will also examine how the Bible describes man's relationship to the sovereign God prior to and after this great work God does in our hearts to bring men to Himself.

The rest of part one will examine in detail this *way of salvation* by showing you how each step of the way is interrelated in biblical theology. Most importantly, we want to study and understand God's grace toward us because God wants us to be "established" believers in Jesus Christ, ones who "desire the pure milk of the Word that you may grow thereby" (1 Peter 2:2). When we understand what He has done for us in our salvation, we will have a greater appreciation for His sovereign grace and mercy in salvation. He wants us to have sound biblical knowledge of His eternal word, enabling us to grow in our relationship and love for Jesus Christ, so that we will ultimately become confident enough "to make disciples of all nations" (Matthew 28:19).

In part two we want to take what we have learned in part one and apply it to evangelism. Having understood what God has revealed to us about His merciful saving work on our behalf every step of the way, where do we begin the discussion of his grace and mercy with those who have no sense of it? We'll begin thinking about evangelism by approaching the problem from a theological perspective: How do we go about convincing an unbelieving world that is incapable of believing this revelation of the most improbable of possibilities—that the one, true God has really spoken to us in time in His Word and in His Son Jesus and has revealed "propositional truth" about his mercy and grace that we would otherwise never have known but for that revelation?

Then we will consider the significance of Bosch's amazing painting, *The Ship of Fools*. The *Ship of Fools* has been used in religious literature and art as a parody of the ark of salvation. It was an expression or image used in a metaphorical way to legitimate the reality of sin and evil in the medieval mindset. It depicts the criticism of frivolous and deranged passengers on a ship who are looking for the paradise of fools but are ignorant of their own direction, never finding what they are looking for. Why does the Bible teach that someone is a fool who has no knowledge of God? What is the difference between a fool's approach to living a joyful life and the biblical model for joyous living? How can we differentiate these two points of view for the unbeliever?

What is the task of theology as we consider discussing topics like the love and wrath of God? Why do we need to formulate and differentiate the details in understanding these complex ideas as we speak to an unbelieving world about them? How can God love the world and yet be justified in pouring out His wrath against the unbelief of its inhabitants? Can we speak about either the love or wrath of God without wrestling with the theological issues that surround them?

How did the Apostle Paul use theology to correct wrong notions about God? Why do we settle for articulating deep, theological issues to unbelievers in no more than lame clichés? Is there a biblical precedent to the evangelical madness of taking serious theological issues and stuffing them into simplistic concepts and calling that evangelism? Is there a biblical model for us to follow as we talk to an unbelieving world about salvation? What things are critical to include? How do we go about correcting the misunderstandings that the world has about God, man, and sin through Scripture? What kinds of things must we say and how do we know when to say them when speaking to someone about theology? How can we be truly effective in sharing the truth of God's mercy and love to a world that is blind to it without doing it from a theological reference point? Finally, in part two, how shall we discuss the difficult topic of the goodness of God with an atheistic world that is convinced that the Christian God often fails to demonstrate goodness? What if God demonstrated the supremacy of his goodness by allowing the greatest evil to occur?

In part three we want to look at why we often fail to see the grace of God in the pursuit of theology. Even though the interpretation and significance of certain theological ideas has been historically problematic for the church and has led to confusion, hostility, and division within the church, we cannot get any closer to interpreting revelation correctly by abandoning theology! The confusion, hostility, and division are a necessary part of the symbiosis. If the goal of theology is to think correctly about revelation and what God is intending to teach, then we must necessarily abandon the notion that there remain different ways to interpret that revelation.

Does God do what he wants to, or is he stymied by the apostate wills of unbelievers? If Scripture teaches that God, in his sovereignty, does whatever he pleases, and it also teaches that God desires to save everyone, then what are we to make of the fact that he clearly doesn't save everyone? What is keeping Him from doing what He desires? How can a correct view of theology help us to grapple with that issue? Did Christ's death make salvation possible for every existing individual or not? Did Christ actually save certain individuals on the cross, or did the cross only make salvation a possibility once they believed the gospel? Why does this matter theologically? How can a theological understanding of the grace of God help us to arrive at a correct understanding of what his revelation teaches about him theologically?

The overall scope of this book is intended to assist Christians at all levels of theological knowledge to develop a more thorough, thoughtful, and careful view of theology so that they might be better equipped to think through theological issues to better understand their own salvation and to be better informed as they speak to unbelievers about the grace of God. I urge you to carefully examine all of the scriptural passages that pertain to each section. Ask any questions you might have regarding those passages as you study the comments about them and do not hesitate to seek to answer them anywhere along the way as you study God's Word.

PART 1

EMPOWERING THE SOVEREIGN GRACE OF GOD IN SALVATION

INTRODUCTION

> To know God is at once the easiest and the most difficult thing in the world.
>
> —A. W. Tozer

While it is true that the main concern of Christian theology is the study of an eternal, infinite being of great mystery, a study that should become a monumental, life-long undertaking for every believer, it is equally true that what we need to know about the person of God and what He has done for us in our salvation can only be grasped sufficiently by a childlike faith. We know who God is and what He has done by believing what He has revealed to us.There are great biblical scholars who would say that they have spent their lifetime studying the Scriptures in an attempt to understand the complexity of the character of God and have only just begun to grasp who He is. In your lifetime, no one could, in any way, even begin to tell you all you could know about the person of God. And even if someone could tell you all that *he* knows about God, that would only be an infinitesimal part of who He is! While what God did for us in salvation is simple enough to be grasped by the faith of a child, many of God's actions are also challenging to us. As difficult as it can sometimes be for us to understand and articulate who God is by what He does, it is more difficult, if not impossible, to do so without a theological framework from which to proceed to make sense of that revelation.

In the following chapters, we will endeavor to demonstrate that a foundational appreciation of theology (which attempts to carefully distinguish and define what the Bible has proposed as the basis for our belief system) is critical to our interpretation of the meaning of any given text in Scripture. Having a sound theological framework from which we draw our conclusions about what God has revealed about Himself and His relationship to the world is critical to our personal understanding of all that God has done on our behalf as believers. It also allows us to comprehend the extent of His grace in our salvation.

But a strong theological foundation also teaches us what we should and should not articulate about the Christian faith to those who doubt its validity. Without this basic framework of theology as a systematic whole, our comprehension of any single part of Scripture that describes how we have come to faith in Christ or how we should articulate that faith to a non-believing world is, in the least, short-sighted and, at most, completely misunderstood. It is my hope that this book will help people to begin to think critically about God's grace in our salvation and give them insight into how we might articulate the theological importance of sovereign grace in our evangelism.

NEW LIFE IN CHRIST

As you begin to share with new believers about their new life in Christ through the use of this book, you can encourage them that a marvelous and mysterious event has occurred in their life! That new life in Christ, which was set in motion from eternity past, has been given to us because God loves us! God's love for us has been demonstrated to us by Him graciously opening our eyes to the truth and by turning us from the power that had kept us blinded to it.

If the person you are sharing the gospel with is *in* Jesus Christ, he is a new creation, a new person. That person now has a new vision not only of what God is like, but a new vision of what He wants to do in his life. All the things that once made him the person he was have passed away along with all the old ways of thinking about God (2 Corinthians 5:17). Because that person is now in Jesus Christ, God sees him in an entirely different way than He saw him before he was in Christ. Before he came to Christ, he was one of the children of God's wrath (Ephesians 2:3), living without Christ, an alien and stranger to God, having no hope and without God in the world (Ephesians 2:12). All he could do was to think incorrectly about God and Christ. His thoughts were darkened to truth. But now in Christ Jesus, all those who once were far off have been made near by the blood of Christ (Ephesians 2:13).

This new "spiritual" life is described by one theologian as "a free, mysterious exercise of divine power, not explainable in terms of existing human resources, nor caused or induced by human efforts or merits."[1] This new life came about because of what God has done through the work of the Holy Spirit exclusively, not because of anything that we did to earn His favor. We did not merit any part of this new life; we were awakened to it. Theologically, we call this new life "regeneration." It is also referred to as "being born again" or "being born from above."[2]

This regeneration is just one step in the process of what God has done to bring those He loves to Himself through faith in Jesus Christ. Theologians call this whole process of salvation from beginning to end the "Order of Salvation," or "The Way of Salvation."[3] We want to examine what that way of salvation is so that we understand more clearly what God has done for us. Once we understand what God has done in us, we will more readily understand how we can help others along the way as they question truth and their understanding of the things that happen in their own lives.

THE WORD OF GOD

> The truth, as it is contained in the Christian revelation, includes the recognition that it is neither possible for man to know the truth fully nor to avoid the error of pretending that he does.
>
> —Reinhold Neibur

The Bible does not have an answer to every single question in life. My eight-year-old son once wrote a note to the pastor of our church asking, "How did God get into heaven in the first place?" There is nowhere we can turn within the sixty-six books of the Bible to find that answer. In fact, there are many questions you could ask about God that the Bible will not answer for you. For instance, nowhere in the Bible is the notion of God having a "beginning" ever explained or defended; the very first words of the first verse in the first book of the Bible assume that God has always existed. Further study and understanding of Scripture infer that in order for anything to exist *now,* there must have always been *something* that existed, namely, God.[4]

The original documents of Scripture were written in a cultural setting far removed from the twenty-first century, and consequently, there are also some current social and ethical questions that are not addressed in the Bible. For instance, the Bible says nothing about watching television or smoking cigarettes or going to the movie theater. That does not mean that to God or to us these should necessarily be insignificant issues. Though He has not spoken directly about these modern issues, we can infer how He might respond to such things by learning what the Bible does say about His character in general and from there make inferences as to how we might be obedient to Him in areas He has not spoken to specifically in Scripture.

In a very real sense, the Bible is not concerned with explaining the vastness and complexity of this awesome universe or whether or not we should smoke cigarettes or watch television, or whether there is life on other planets, although unfortunately, many have chosen to make some of these questions a major concern in the life of the Christian.

Rather, the Bible is concerned with the beginning and end of one race of people on one planet. The Bible is particularly concerned with that few thousand years surrounding the earthly and eternal presence of one individual: Jesus Christ. Christ is the supreme focus of the Bible. He should enrapture our thinking beyond anything else.

Charles Hadden Spurgeon wrote:

> There is something exceedingly improving to the mind in a contemplation of the Divinity. It is a subject so vast, that all our thoughts are lost in its immensity; so deep, that our pride is drowned in its infinity...No subject of contemplation will tend more to humble the mind, than thoughts of God...Would you lose your sorrow? Would you drown your cares? Then go, plunge yourself in the Godhead's deepest sea; be lost in His immensity; and you shall come forth as from a couch of rest, refreshed and invigorated. I know nothing which can so comfort the soul; so calm the swelling billows of sorrow and grief; so speak peace to the winds of trial, as a devout musing upon the subject of the Godhead...[5]

Think of the volumes of pages that would be necessary to accurately describe the chemical, physical, electronic, and mathematical structure of a single atom of hydrogen. Yet F. A. Filby has written that the miracle of simplicity is at the heart of the biblical story of creation.

> It has been estimated that to give a complete account of the position of the groups and bonds in a single virus...would take a 200 page book...What hope is there of ever giving a scientific account of the creation of man and the universe? Yet Genesis 1 in its original form uses only 76 different root words...The scientific description of the "how" of the universe is beyond the understanding of any human brain, but Genesis 1 was written for all readers, not for none.[6]

Read on in God's Word to increase your faith. Read on to understand and obtain wisdom about our wonderful Lord. Prayerfully seek to grasp what God has said you should know. Read on to learn to continue loving Him and to share that love with others. And read on because Scripture alone is the divine revelation regarding the person of God.

THE DOCTRINE OF SCRIPTURAL INERRANCY

The doctrine of inerrancy means God and man so cooperated in the production of Scripture that the end product is "God's word in human language." The Word of God written by human beings in Scripture is not a *human* matter then, in spite of the fact that it proceeded from the Spirit through the words of men. It is a *divine* matter that has a *divine* origin. Because it has its origin in God Himself, it can be relied upon as truthful.

The following points help clarify what we mean when we say that Scripture is inerrant:

1. Inerrancy does not mean that God *dictated* Holy Scripture to men and that these men were obliged to write down every word that God spoke. Inerrancy implies that in the word of God, neither human personality nor divine authority is violated in the writing of Scripture.

2. Inerrancy means that all the words (and their verbal relationships, their positions in the sentences, grammar, etc.) in the original texts are inspired by God, including those verses that are seemingly no more than peripheral statements. Likewise, when we speak about inerrancy, we mean that the words spoken by Jesus are no more *inspired* or *authoritative* than any other words found in the Bible. All the words of Scripture are equally inspired by the Holy Spirit and authoritative for us, whether they came from the mouth of Jesus or the devil (see Luke 4).

3. Inerrancy is intimately tied up with hermeneutics, the science and art of interpretation of Holy Scripture. Though we maintain that the Scriptures are completely true, no *human* interpretation of them is infallible or free from error.

4. Inerrancy is related to Scripture's *intention.* For example, Christ said, "The kingdom of heaven is like a mustard seed, which a man took and sowed in his field, which indeed is the least of all the seeds" (Matthew 13:31–32). Today we know that the mustard seed is not the least or the smallest of all the seeds on the earth. Many believe that the orchid or tobacco seed is the smallest. Yet if Christ had mentioned either of these two types of seed in His illustration, His hearers would have wondered what kind of seed He was talking about, as none of those were indigenous to Israel. We can still hold to the doctrine of inerrancy in spite of Christ's statement because it was

not Christ's *intention* when He used that illustration to teach a botany class on which of all the seeds on earth are the smallest. It was His intention to use that illustration about the mustard seed to demonstrate how quickly and greatly the kingdom of heaven will grow.

5. Inerrancy applies only to the autographs, or the original documents, and not to scribal copies of documents, as any copy could contain some errors because they were copied by human beings.

The significance and importance of the doctrine of inerrancy is that Scripture speaks with exactitude on all the matters that it addresses, and divine teaching is communicated on all matters concerning Christian faith and living.

SCRIPTURAL INERRANCY EXPLAINED

There is a tremendous biblical passage in the second epistle of Peter chapter one, verses 16–21, which helps us understand that Scripture is inerrant because it is sourced in God Himself.

> For we did not follow cunningly devised fables when we made known to you the power and coming of our Lord Jesus Christ, but were eyewitnesses of His majesty. For He received from God the Father honor and glory when such a voice came to Him from the Excellent Glory: "This is My beloved Son, in whom I am well pleased." And we heard this voice which came from heaven when we were with Him on the holy mountain. And so we have the prophetic word confirmed, which you do well to heed as a light that shines in a dark place, until the day dawns and the morning star rises in your hearts; knowing this first, that no prophecy of Scripture is of any private interpretation, for prophecy never came by the will of man, but holy men of God spoke *as they were* moved by the Holy Spirit.

In verses 16 to 18, Peter gives the reader two motives that will serve as the basis for their diligent pursuit of the knowledge of God: the divinity of Christ's origin and the divinity of Scripture.

Peter writes to his readers that he was a witness to Christ's divine origin. What he has revealed in this epistle is not a cleverly devised myth or fable, but truth that is verified by personal experience. My more literal translation of what Peter writes in 1:16 is, "spectators we became of that one splendor."

Peter is speaking of the time when there were only three people—Peter, James, and John—who were among those privileged enough to be eyewitnesses of that momentary yet complete revelation of Christ's divinity. Peter writes that the day that Christ revealed the reality of Himself on the mount of transfiguration, we witnessed the power, coming, honor, and glory of God Himself (2 Peter 1:16–17)! That was undoubtedly for Peter an unforgettable, one-of-a-kind event. In fact, if you go back and read that passage, you see Peter's very human response to what he saw (Matthew 16:28–17:3). His response reflected confusion, bewilderment, awe, worship, and humility; and that is the kind of a response we would expect from anyone who had just witnessed the full glory of God in the person of Christ!

But he goes on to say that even though that event was an absolutely reliable experience in demonstrating to Peter, James, and John the reality and power of God in Christ, Peter says that the very words of Scripture itself that he is writing are "confirmed" (*made more sure*) than his apostolic experience of the perfect majesty of Christ at the transfiguration (2 Peter 1:19)!

Think about that statement! Peter contends that not only did the apostolic experience of Christ that day on the mountain reveal and utterly convince him of Christ's divine origin, but that the prophetic word he is writing to us that *describes* that experience is equally divine in origin! Indeed, that same God whom the apostles heard speak about Christ that day at the transfiguration is the same glorious, majestic God who has been speaking through the prophets in all of Scripture (2 Peter 1:17–18).

The point he is making in verse 21 is that the Old Testament prophets didn't just sort of arbitrarily unravel Scripture. The message and meaning of Scripture isn't just something that men "announce" in their own wisdom. Nor is the meaning of Scripture "born along" because men *will* it to be so. Scripture is a combination of men speaking and God speaking. Prophecy comes from both God and men, as they were "moved" (*driven*) by the Holy Spirit [cf. Acts 27:15, 17 where the New King James version says, "We let her drive" and "so were driven" respectively in 15 and 17, using the same Greek word (*phero*) that Peter uses in 2 Peter 1:21]. Peter says, "And so we have the prophetic word (which was not announced or born along by the will of men) confirmed (made more sure), which you do well to heed as a light that shines in a dark place, until the day dawns and the morning star rises in your hearts" (1:19).

Several English versions translate the Greek word *bebaioteron* as 'made more sure' as does the New King James version. Now, that begs the question: "The prophetic word is made more sure than what?" The answer is that the prophetic word is made more sure than that incredible experience we had that day on the mountain when we personally experienced that Christ was absolutely divine in nature. *The divine origin of Scripture is more reliable than that experience where we beheld the divine nature of Christ.*

Note that Peter is not concerned with informing his readers about the proper interpretation of Scripture, even though most every translation unfortunately says that "no prophecy of Scripture is of any private interpretation" when it translates the Greek words in 2 Peter 1:20.

If he were really interested in telling us about proper interpretation, he would not have finished his thought in verse 21 by telling us where it originated or who announced it or how it was born.[7] Peter's point was not to say that scriptural prophecy is disclosed or explained or has the sense of its meaning revealed to us because of some *private* interpretation men have devised. In fact, I think a very strong case can be made for the fact that, indeed, many different private interpretations *have* arisen from men's own opinions about Scripture. I think it is unfortunate, but natural, that men interpret Scripture oftentimes by their *own* private interpretations apart from the context. Rather, Peter was telling us that Scripture didn't originate in the thoughts and minds of men, but holy men of God spoke what God wanted to say when they were moved (carried along, driven) by the Spirit of God when they wrote Scripture. If that is the case, then indeed Scripture can surely be trusted because it originated in the heart of God Himself! The fact that the Spirit of God carried men along when they wrote Scripture has led to the doctrine we call the inerrancy of Scripture.

THE ANALOGY OF FAITH

There is a principle that aids us in the interpretation of Scripture called the "analogy of Scripture" or "the analogy of faith." That principle is taken from Romans 12:6 where Paul uses the word *analogia* when he writes, "Having then gifts differing according to the grace that is given to us, *let us use them:* if prophecy, *let us prophesy* in proportion (*analogian)* to our faith," or let us prophesy according to the *analogy,* the right relationship, the correct proportion to, or the measurement of faith. In other words, let us exercise prophesy "confining our activity modestly within the limits of the gift itself...let us exercise them by abiding simply in them, by not seeking to go out of them."[8] What this analogy of faith means as an interpretive principle or guide is that the whole of Scripture must be the limitation and boundary for our understanding any particular passage. This should be the guiding principle behind our hermeneutic.

In the strictest sense, the analogy of faith means that a more obscure text or passage will be illumined by other texts whose meaning is clearer. God is the author of Scripture and had in mind a specific, intended meaning when He authored the texts. Every verse in Scripture, then, is dependent not only upon the immediate context but upon the entirety of Scripture. We verify our understanding of each verse by understanding the verse within the context that it is used and by knowing that the whole of Scripture cannot contradict itself on the same subject. The principle of the analogy of faith is important because it is a way to safeguard our interpretations as we try to understand Scripture. Our goal is always to aim for a sound, God-honoring, consistent, harmonious interpretation of divine truth.

Sometimes, understanding how a word is used in context can be difficult. We can use this principle to show that the word *faith* does not always mean true, genuine belief when used in Scripture. When we look more closely at trying to understand what the Greek word for *to believe* (*pistuein*) means in all of its various uses, we see that it is used in the Gospel of John to speak of various degrees, levels, or states of faith, some of which are false and damning:

- It can refer to the juvenile, first beginnings of faith, its embryonic stirrings in the soul, as in John 2:23: "Now when He was in Jerusalem at the Passover, during the feast, many believed in His name when they saw the signs which He did." [9] They did not necessarily become "believers" in Christ at that time.

- It refers to a faith that does not yet recognize Jesus as the Messiah but as a prophet very like the Messiah, as in John 7:31: "And many of the people believed in Him, and said, 'When the Christ comes, will He do more signs than these which this *Man* has done?'" Here they are not yet seeing Jesus as the Christ.

- It signifies that a faith is preserved, strengthened, increased, and raised to the level that it ought to reach, as in John 13:19: "Now I tell you before it comes, that when it does come to pass, you may believe that I am *He.*"

- It is applied also to the faith by which one is persuaded that Jesus was raised from the dead, inasmuch as by that fact God declared him to be his Son and the Messiah, as in John 20:8: "Then the other disciple, who came to the tomb first, went in also; and he saw and believed." [10]

We see then that the word *believe* is used in several different ways to indicate different levels of faith and understanding about Christ in the Gospel of John.

Applying the "Analogy of Faith"

Using the analogy of faith can really help our understanding of the meaning of faith (*pistuein*), for example, in a problematic passage like John 8:30–59. Even if we can fully grasp what the intended meaning of the word *faith* is in a particular context, and even when we know the significance of using different tenses in Greek, a particular scripture may be difficult to understand without using the principle of the analogy of faith to assist us in greater clarification.

The Greek word *to believe,* or *pistuein,* occurs in the New Testament about five hundred times, about nineteen of those times in the perfect tense. The Greek perfect tense is the tense of completed action in past time with continuing results. As noted Greek professor at Dallas Theological Seminary Daniel B. Wallace comments in his *Greek Grammar Beyond the Basics,* the Greek perfect defines the action of the verb as "presented *externally* (summary), while the *resultant state* proceeding from the action is presented *internally* (continuous state)."[11] When we talk about faith in the perfect tense, we mean a "full-orbed" faith, one that has come to fruition or completion, one that necessarily exists in full assurance, the results of which carry on into the present.

An example of the use of *pistuein* appearing in the perfect tense is John 3:18: "He who believes (Greek present participle) in Him is not condemned; but he who does not believe (Greek present participle) is condemned already, because he has not believed (perfect tense) in the name of the only begotten Son of God." Hence, he is condemned because his faith is not the kind that is full-orbed, one that has come to fruition or completion with Christ as its object.

Another good example of the usage of this tense is in John 8:31: "Then Jesus said to those Jews who believed (Greek perfect tense) Him, 'If you abide in My word, you are My disciples indeed.'"

Note that in the John 8:31 passage, Christ is speaking to those Jews "who believed Him." John indicates by using the perfect tense of believe that this is a full-orbed faith and one that exists in full assurance. These Jews that Christ is speaking to in 8:31 are the same ones in 8:42–44 whom He calls sons of the devil. These are the same ones who say Jesus has a demon in 8:48. These are the same ones that want to stone Jesus in 8:59. There is no context change in the passage.

What is most troubling here is that John uses the perfect tense to describe their full-orbed, continuous state of belief. They believed in past time as a completed action, and they continue believing. This isn't a fly-by-night faith. It isn't dubious in its character. It's not a childish faith or one that is likely to fail in the near future. These Jews won't walk away from their faith. They are committed to what they believe. The language suggests that these Jews are among those who possess the fullest possible assurance of faith! These *believers* are totally committed to their faith. Do you see the dilemma? Why would Jesus call someone with this kind of faith the son of the devil? And why would they want to kill Him?

By Jesus's response to them we can see that they are not in a state of true, genuine faith that has Christ as its object! True, genuine, saving, life-giving faith must possess Jesus Christ as its object. John has never taught anything differently since the first words in his gospel. Make no mistake, these *believing* Jews believe in Abraham. They trust that physical relationship to a patriarch who is the father of Israel. These Jews mistakenly think that they believe in God just like Abraham did. That is the only sense in which their faith is complete, full-orbed.

And they believe they are right with God. They respond: "We were not born of fornication (*porneia*), we have one Father—God" (8:41). *Porneia* comes from the idea of a harlot who sells her body for sexual uses. "We don't fornicate with idols" is what they meant! We're not idolaters. We know Yahweh! We're monotheists. We believe that Moses wrote, "Hear O Israel, the Lord our God, the Lord is One." And these Jews are fully assured about their faith in God. But John wants the readers to be fully assured that they are *dead wrong* in their assurance because their faith has no room for Christ, and therefore, though in a sense it is a complete faith and full of assurance, it is not a complete, genuine faith in Christ.

You see, our mistake is that we think that when we see the words *faith* or *believe* in the book of John, it always means "genuine faith" or "genuine belief." As an interesting note, John uses the perfect tense with the word *faith* six times in his gospel, and twice in his first epistle, and every *other* time he uses faith in the perfect tense, it's always in the context of a saving faith that correctly sees Christ as the Son of the living God, *except* here in John 8:31.

These Jews Christ is speaking to in John 8:31 obviously don't have genuine faith. They don't believe that Christ is the Son of God at all. The faith they possess is a committed faith in the wrong object! They have an assured faith in something that cannot save them. And Jesus is treating their assurance in their misdirected faith as if it *proves* they are in a state of unbelief! Their solid assurance in Abraham and their assurance in their perception about their right standing with God have closed the door to genuine faith in Christ for them. While they are resting assured in a faith that they think is genuine, they are missing the thing that actually would make it complete: Jesus Christ.

The good Bible student will ask a question here: Are there any other occurrences of the word *faith* in the New Testament where it is used in this perfect tense where the ones who possess it are believing and trusting in the wrong thing? Yes, in Acts 15:5.

In Acts 15:5, "But some of the sect of the Pharisees who believed (Greek perfect tense) rose up, saying, "It is necessary to circumcise them, and to command *them* to keep the Law of Moses." We couldn't have asked for a clearer example, could we? These Pharisees had a faith that the language deems full-orbed, assured, and complete, but in this instance in the wrong thing! They are making the case that circumcision is deemed divinely necessary for salvation *as well as* possessing faith in Christ.[12]

So believing with full assurance in the book of John can mean that one has a genuine faith that trusts Christ as the Son of God the redeemer or that one has an assurance of their faith but in the wrong object as well. These Jews in John 8:31 have an assurance in what they believe, but that assurance is a false assurance because they don't have Christ as the object of their faith. We know how to interpret the difficult use of this word here because we have seen how the word can be used in more than one way.

The analogy of faith, then, as a general principle of interpretation, aids us in illuminating the true meaning of a common biblical word in any given context by showing us how the parameters of the meanings in any given word become clear after we understand the various uses of it in Scripture.

Since Scripture is authored and sourced in God, what is taught in one passage of Scripture cannot contradict what is taught in another passage. When a word like *believe* occurs in an obvious negative and condemning sense as opposed to how it is normally used, we need to understand that the meaning of that word in the difficult passage is established after careful consideration of the entirety of its use in other passages.

B. A. Demerest confirms that this principle of the analogy of faith assists us, for example, in understanding whether or not the occurrence of the word *law* should be seen in a positive or negative context depending on our understanding of its full range of meanings by writing that:

> Paul's negative attitude toward the law in Romans 10:4 and Galatians 3:13 is clarified by consideration of his positive endorsement of the law, as in Romans 7:12, 14, 16. When the full sweep of Pauline teaching is examined, it will be seen that the apostle repudiates law keeping as a means of salvation, although as an expression of the moral will of God the law's precepts serve as a universal standard of conduct.[13]

SOVEREIGNTY IN LIFE AND SALVATION

> If there is a single molecule in this universe running around loose, totally free from God's sovereignty, then we have no guarantee that a single promise of God will ever be fulfilled.
>
> —R. C. Sproul

The word *sovereign* means that God is the supreme ruler over all things. He is above, over, and beyond this world and all that is in it. The Bible clearly teaches that God knows all things. There are never any surprises for Him. There are no details He is unaware of. Carefully ponder the following verses as you are made aware that He knows everything because He is everywhere (Jeremiah 23:24; Psalm 139; Hebrews 4:13), and He is a God of knowledge (1 Samuel 2:3; Psalm 147:5). He not only knows the thoughts and intents of the hearts of all men (Proverbs 15:11; Hebrews 4:12–13), but necessarily knows all the details of inanimate particulars as well (Psalm 147:4; Isaiah 40:26). Furthermore, He has known these details from all eternity (Isaiah 46:10; Acts 15:18). He does not "discover" the truth, and His knowledge of all things arises from within Himself, they are not imparted to Him by those things He created. God did not learn about the intimacies of who you are by first needing to observe you (Proverbs 8:22; Isaiah 40:13).

By virtue of the fact that God has created everything that exists, He is the owner and final disposer of all that He has made. All that He created is His to do with as He chooses. He is under no obligation to men to move in any particular direction to please them. Regardless of how things might appear to us, God is controlling all things in undisturbed majesty. Even the sinful actions of men can only occur by His providence and permission and with the strength that He gives to them. All that comes to pass then must be, in some sense, in accordance with what He has eternally purposed and decreed. Coming to terms with the fact that God is sovereign in all details of life will change the way that you pray, think, and look at the world and the things happening around you.[14]

SOVEREIGNTY IN LIFE

THE SOVEREIGN CONTROL OF STORMS, LOTS, FISH, GOURDS, AND WORMS

The first chapter of the book of Jonah provides a good description of God's sovereignty in the details of everyday life. The Lord calls Jonah to go to Nineveh to cry out against its wickedness, but Jonah runs in the opposite direction (Jonah 1:1–3). In response, the Lord hurls a storm at the ship Jonah has used to attempt to escape God's command, causing the pagan mariners on board to wonder why this storm was upon *them.* How would they have known the storm was upon *them* in particular? Perhaps they saw that as the ship was tossed about on the ocean, the storm was obviously just hovering above their ship, and it may have been completely clear just beyond the sides of the ship! In search of answers, the pagan mariners cast lots to find out why this storm was upon them. Of course, God desired that the lots fall on Jonah (1:7). After these pagan mariners find out that the storm was upon them because Jonah was running from his God (1:9–10), the mariners muster all their strength and attempt to outmaneuver God's storm by struggling against it even more tenaciously, only to have the storm grow more tempestuous against them (1:13). In utter panic, these pagan sailors call out to the God of the Hebrews and beg Him not to bring judgment upon them for Jonah's sin. Even though they were completely taken aback by the experience they had encountered with God, these pagan sailors could only resign themselves to saying, "For You, O Lord, have done as it pleased You" (1:14).

Eventually, at Jonah's suggestion, they see no other recourse to escape the storm than to throw Jonah overboard, after which they sacrifice and make vows to God. The next line of the text says, "Now the Lord had prepared a great fish to swallow Jonah" (1:15–17). The Hebrew word used in Jonah for *prepared* is *mana*. It means to "weigh out, allot, appoint, prepare or set." It is not unusual to see that the book of Jonah attributes even such mundane things as Jonah's fish (1:17), a gourd (4:6), a worm (4:7), and the vehement east wind (4:8) as all being *under* the control of God. He appoints not only the time they are to appear, but how He will use them in the lives of men.

Elsewhere this word *prepared* is used in Isaiah 53:12 where the suffering servant is "numbered" with the transgressors, indicating God's sovereign role in *appointing* Christ's death to be among thieves. In Isaiah 65:12, "Therefore, I will number you for the sword" is a clear indication of God's ordaining the destiny of idolaters.

THE SOVEREIGN CONTROL OF HEARTS, HAIL, AND LOCUSTS

I think that much of this doctrine of sovereignty is difficult for us to accept carte blanche because of the extent to which Scripture says that God controls the natural world. Sovereignty is a biblical doctrine that God preserves and controls what He has created, and we should believe it because Scripture tells us that *is* the kind of a world that we live in! The famous nineteenth-century preacher Charles Spurgeon affirmed that God controls not only the smallest of insects but even particulate matter.

> I believe that every particle of dust that dances in the sunbeam does not move an atom more or less than God wishes—that every particle of spray that dashes against the steamboat has its orbit as well as the sun in the heavens—that the chaff from the hand of the winnower is steered as the stars in their courses—that the creeping of an aphid over a rosebud is as much fixed as the march of the devastating pestilence [for example, of God's plague of locusts upon Egypt (Exodus 10:13–14, 17–19)], and the fall of the sere leaves from the poplar is as fully ordained as the tumbling of an avalanche. He who believes in God must believe this truth.[15]

Why do so many Christians today doubt what most every Christian was convinced was true one hundred years ago? Why do we doubt that we *must* believe this truth if we believe in God? I think it is because rather than simply trust Scripture as a true revelation of God's power in the world that He created and sustains, we have insisted that we humans have power as well; we think we all possess a freedom that God won't even touch! If Scripture suggests that God indeed is sovereign to the extent that Spurgeon suggests, why would we want to deny it? Furthermore, to what degree does our denial of those details make it clear that we really do not believe Scripture? Why do we struggle with believing that God maps out the details in the path of "an aphid, or the drops of water, or the fall of a leaf" when Scripture teaches, for example, that God is providentially in control of the minute details of nature in Exodus 10? Note how Moses records how God uses His sovereign power in this chapter to bring about His desired ends: "Now the Lord said to Moses, 'Go in to Pharaoh; for I have hardened his heart and the hearts of his servants, that I may show these signs of Mine before him'" (Exodus 10:1).

The Lord has sovereignly prepared the hearts of not only Pharaoh but his servants as well to respond in a specific way to what He is about to do before them: He has hardened their hearts so that He might show them his signs. He doesn't want Pharaoh at the last minute to soften His heart and release the Jews to do what Moses has asked him to do because God is going to use this demonstration of power to convince all of Israel, their children and grandchildren (and the subsequent readers of the Bible) of something:

"'and that you may tell in the hearing of your son and your son's son the mighty things I have done in Egypt, and My signs which I have done among them, that you may know that I *am* the Lord'" (Exodus 10:2).

The Lord is at the same time demonstrating His sovereign power and making a record for all nations of His glory and grace to the future generations of Israel, so that He can be trusted in that power He has over creation.

> So Moses and Aaron came in to Pharaoh and said to him, "Thus says the Lord God of the Hebrews: 'How long will you refuse to humble yourself before Me? Let My people go, that they may serve Me. Or else, if you refuse to let My people go, behold, tomorrow I will bring locusts into your territory. And they shall cover the face of the earth, so that no one will be able to see the earth, and they shall eat the residue of what is left, which remains to you from the hail, and they shall eat every tree which grows up for you out of the field. They shall fill your houses, the houses of all your servants, and the houses of all the Egyptians—which neither your fathers nor your fathers' fathers have seen, since the day that they were on the earth to this day.'" And he turned and went out from Pharaoh. Then Pharaoh's servants said to him, "How long shall this man be a snare to us? Let the men go, that they may serve the Lord their God. Do you not yet know that Egypt is destroyed?" So Moses and Aaron were brought again to Pharaoh, and he said

to them, "Go, serve the Lord your God. Who *are* the ones that are going?" And Moses said, "We will go with our young and our old, with our sons and our daughters, with our flocks and our herds we will go, for we must hold a feast to the Lord." Then he said to them, "The Lord had better be with you when I let you and your little ones go! Beware, for evil is ahead of you. Not so! Go now, you *who are* men, and serve the Lord, for that is what you desired." And they were driven out from Pharaoh's presence. Then the Lord said to Moses, "Stretch out your hand over the land of Egypt for the locusts, that they may come upon the land of Egypt and eat every herb of the land—all that the hail has left."

Exodus 10:3–12

In verses 3 through 12, Moses says that Pharaoh must let all the people go or there will be total devastation like has never been before in Egypt. This is controlled devastation, if you will, that God promises; it is controlled, specific, sovereign, providential devastation. Only Egypt will be devastated. The locusts are so well governed that they don't sort of wander off into the next country by accident. They aren't going to go into the houses of the Israelites, only into the houses of the Egyptians. They observe without choice the "boundaries" set for them by this particular sovereignly ordained circumstance. Note also that the previous hail must not have been able to destroy everything so as to leave enough food for this devastating locust population to finish off.

We begin to see the traces of softening in the hearts of Pharaoh's servants when they suggest to Pharaoh that only the men be let go to worship the Lord, leaving their possessions and the rest of Israel behind. Pharaoh thinks he relents just enough by telling the men *only* to go, revealing the evidence of his heart's refusal to submit to Moses's request to free the entire nation of Israel. As if operating on some kind of cosmic timer, only when Moses stretches out his rod are the locusts permitted to begin their assault on the land of Egypt.

> So Moses stretched out his rod over the land of Egypt, and the Lord brought an east wind on the land all that day and all *that* night. When it was morning, the east wind brought the locusts. And the locusts went up over all the land of Egypt and rested on all the territory of Egypt. *They were* very severe; previously there had been no such locusts as they, nor shall there be such after them. For they covered the face of the whole earth, so that the land was darkened, and they ate every herb of the land and all the fruit of the trees which the hail had left. So there remained nothing green on the trees or on the plants of the field throughout all the land of Egypt. Then Pharaoh called for Moses and Aaron in haste, and said, "I have sinned against the Lord your God and against you. Now therefore, please forgive my sin only this once, and entreat the Lord your God, that He may take away from me this death only." So he went out from Pharaoh and entreated the Lord. And the Lord turned a very strong west wind, which took the locusts away and blew them into the Red Sea. There remained not one locust in all the territory of Egypt.
>
> Exodus 10:13–19

God's control of the natural world is evident in that the Lord brings in an east wind all day and all night. In His sovereignty, he controls the necessary physical elements and features of the world in a specific manner to fulfill His promise. His control over the wind never gets out of His control. It is being governed to serve His greater purposes. He controls it in exactly the way He knows He needs to: to bring in the locusts that are also going to serve His purposes.

Apparently, the Lord brought in some locusts that were not indigenous to Egypt with the east wind so that there was suddenly a variety of locust there that had never been there before and would never be there again. After the locusts fulfilled what God had intended they do, in His sovereign control again, the Lord brought in a west wind that blew the locusts away from Egypt and into the Red Sea. After they had served their purpose, He didn't simply send them back to where they came from. He arranged for their departure into the Red Sea. But the Lord wants us to be very sure that we understand His attention to detail. Moses could have simply written that the west wind blew and the locust plague was *eventually* over.

Note that our sovereign, all-powerful, all-preserving, all-governing, amazing-regardless-of-the-circumstances God needs to make one final thing clear before the story is finished. He's not finished until He says that there remained *not one* locust in all of the territory of Egypt. He's not done with the demonstration of His complete sovereignty until every single locust is gone. God wants to make it clear that not *one* locust in billions is left over or has strayed from His sovereign control.

And isn't it curious that we struggle when we read that Spurgeon said, "The creeping of an aphid over a rosebud is as much fixed as the march of the devastating pestilence." I think we struggle with that because we don't really believe Scripture when it says that God is sovereign over even the tiniest details.

All of Scripture teaches that God is *sovereign.* He created this world, He owns it, and He is running it according to His own sovereign, good pleasure. Any theology that teaches that the serious intentions of God can in any way be defeated or thwarted by the will of sinful apostate creatures is in striking contrast to the biblical idea of His immeasurable exaltation and power to do as He pleases.

Though we have seen only a very small segment of what the Bible teaches about God's sovereignty, I do not in any way want to suggest to you by its brief review here that how we perceive the sovereignty of God is not *critical* to biblical theology. How you view the extent of the sovereignty of God in the world will have a tremendous effect on how your theological interpretations are colored. It will affect your prayer life, your walk with God, your desire to do His will, and every thought you have about Him and the people you interact with. The way you understand how His sovereignty interrelates with mankind can completely alter your perspective of theological issues. I urge you to reflect often on this aspect of God's power and authority while you meditate on Scripture.

SOVEREIGNTY IN SALVATION

Since the Bible clearly teaches that God is all-powerful and all-knowledgeable, and all things come to be through the power of God, then God can convert a sinner to Jesus Christ when He so chooses (Acts 16:14). He can also change the character of the creatures He has created. Though many would disagree, God can and does control the human will (Daniel 4:35; 11:36; et al.). He alone is able to cleanse the soul from sin. He could raise a myriad of ministers and missionaries who, through His spirit, could convert the world in a very short time. Likewise, if He had so desired, he could save all men so that no one would ever be lost.

Another critical aspect of God's sovereignty involves His ability and desire to choose lost sinners from among the multitudes and bring them to Himself in spite of the fact that they are slaves to sin, who, in their unregenerate state, really want nothing to do with Him. When theologians speak of man's spiritual condition, they often use two words to describe the nature and extent of man's fall into sin. They speak of man's depravity and of his inability.

Depravity means that there is an inherent spiritual corruption within the heart of each human being that extends to every part of his nature, and that there is within him no spiritual good in relation to God whatsoever, only perversion. It does not mean that an atheist is so depraved that he cannot do a good deed for his fellow man or that he has no regard for anything true or good in the world. Nor does it mean that mankind is as bad as it can be all the time. What it does mean is that man is beyond all self-help; in his natural state he is not capable of doing anything or desiring anything pleasing to God; in his depravity he is completely incapable of discerning truth.[16]

Inability means that the natural sinner can perform acts of kindness and be deserving of the approval or gratitude of his fellow man, yet all things that he does in relation to God are utterly defective because they are not prompted by love or any regard for the desire to please God or to do His will. Man's inability keeps him in this spiritual condition and plight until God chooses to remove him from it. Man cannot through some ability of his own change his natural preference for sin to a desire to do God's will, nor can he realign his will to no longer be enslaved to sin. In his natural, physical life, every single person is said to be totally depraved and totally unable to choose God, even by using what some say is his "free will."[17]

THE SPIRITUAL CONDITION OF THE HEART

Ephesians 2:1–3; Romans 3:10–19

The condition of our heart prior to God's regeneration is that it is spiritually dead. These two passages speak of the depth of our human depravity. Ephesians 2:1–3 teaches that God made us alive, we didn't make ourselves come to life; we were (spiritually) dead in trespasses and sins. Before God made us alive to spiritual things, all of us were continuously under the power of the spirit of this age that the devil controlled. We conducted ourselves in accordance with Satan's God-opposing will. We were by nature disobedient children deserving of God's wrath.

Romans 3:10–19 is one of the clearest passages in Scripture that truly reveals the character and the total, universal depth of depravity and sin in all aspects of the human nature. Verses 11 and 12 speak of the universality of this sinfulness in every human being. Verses 13 through 18 speak of death, deceit, defilement, violence, destruction, despair, conflict, and unrestrained irreverence. Only by the mercy of God does anyone escape so great a burden of sin.

Romans 6:16; 7:23; 8:6–8

We were hopelessly bound to this condition of death, unable to escape from the previously described hopeless condition by our own efforts. When we presented ourselves as slaves to obey sin, we could do nothing more than be obedient to sin. Even as regenerated Christians, the struggle still continues, and if not for Jesus Christ, we could not be delivered from this body of death, so great is its hold on our lives. The unregenerate mind is "hateful, hostile, in a state of ill will, an *enemy*" against God (Romans 8:7). It is not able to be subjected to the law of God. Those living only in the flesh cannot please God spiritually.

John 3:18; 2 Corinthians 4:3–4

Before faith, we were in a state of condemnation before God. Those who are not in a state of believing Christ have already been judged by God. That judgment is completed, and they continue to live in that judgment, as do all unbelievers, until the Spirit of God moves upon them to come to Christ for salvation. Those persons who are not regenerate have a veil that prevents them from understanding the Gospel. They are perishing because the minds of the unbelieving are blinded by the devil (the god of this age), so that they might not see the light of the truth of the Gospel of Christ (2 Corinthians 4:3–4; Acts 26:18).

In the Bible, the heart is regarded as the center or focus of a man's desires, motives, behaviors, emotions, feelings, thoughts, and choices. Due to the condition of the hearts of natural men, the divine appeal in the Bible is concerned with and addressed to the hearts of men (Psalm 44:21; Jeremiah 12:3; Romans 10:10). Because of the severity of man's heart condition and his total inability to put his own heart right with God by his own efforts, the heart must be changed so that a man is able to believe in the "good news" of Jesus Christ (Matthew 15:18–19). The heart is so deceitfully wicked in its natural state that it must be radically altered so that it is able to choose for the good that exists alone in Jesus Christ.

Genesis 6:5; Jeremiah 17:9–10

The extent of the wickedness of men, due to the invasion of evil, was great upon the earth, so great, in fact, that God decided to destroy man and beast. The depravity of the heart was evidenced in the fact that the hearts of men were dwelling upon evil continuously.

Jeremiah writes that God knows full well the depth of the deceitfulness of man's heart, and that the heart is incurably sick. There is no natural cure for such a condition; there is only the supernatural cure of a new heart bestowed upon men by God Himself.

Romans 2:5

The condition of one's heart is what brings about God's displeasure toward men. Here in Romans 2:5, it is because of the obstinacy, stubbornness, and hardness of the heart, as well as admitting no change of mind concerning the heart's unrepentant nature, that men are actually storing up for themselves wrath in the day of wrath.

Ephesians 4:18

This is an interesting yet complex passage. In 4:17, Paul instructs the believer to not walk as unbelievers do, in the "emptiness of their minds." The understanding of the minds of unbelievers (verse 18) is in a state of continuing darkness, and they remain alienated from the life of God for two reasons: (1) The ignorance that continues to be in them, and (2) the hardening (callusing) of their hearts. The ultimate problem with this condition is that it renders them being *past* any feeling of pain, which leads to an insatiable greediness, which should be different than what Christians have learned (verses 19, 20).

Matthew 5:8; 22:37

We have seen what Scripture teaches regarding the condition of the hearts of unregenerate men and the extent of that defilement. Christ taught and clarified in the Sermon on the Mount what true righteousness is. True righteousness begins in the heart. Jesus had already stressed that the spiritual kingdom is made up of people who have right knowledge of the heart. The regenerate hearts of men recognize their spiritual poverty apart from God (5:3). They see themselves in reality as ones who are lost, helpless, and sinful. They see their total spiritual destitution. They properly mourn for their sin and their spiritual condition (5:4). Because of this understanding of their sinfulness, truly spiritual people are made humble and meek because they see how righteous God is (5:5). They hunger and thirst for righteousness because they see that they have no righteousness of their own. They have a spiritually prompted desire for salvation from the true God who is able to give it to them (5:6). The truly spiritual person sees God's mercy in his own salvation and desires to be merciful to others (5:7). When God regenerates the heart, the heart is purified, and we begin to see God and comprehend His wonder through a new heart that has been spiritually opened to the truth. The pure in heart not only now desire to be holy in light of God's revelation of the sinfulness of men's hearts and God's holiness, but they are enabled to be.

The first part of the greatest commandment is that we should love the Lord our God with all of our heart. In order for that to happen, the heart must be enabled to love Him. In its natural state, without regeneration, it remains in rebellion and hatred toward Him.

Psalm 66:18; 1 Peter 3:15

The range of meanings of the Hebrew word for *iniquity* in Psalm 66:18 is wide because it covers the *progress* of sinfulness. Its root meaning probably stresses the idea of "trouble" that moves on to being "acted out in wickedness."[18] The word may also imply the whole range of progression of sin from planning it out in the mind and heart to expressing the plan through deception, pointing even to the painful aftermath of the consequences of sin. The Psalmist is saying that the regenerate heart does not regard or hold this sinfulness in esteem because he knows it separates him from the Lord.

First Peter 3:15 tells Christians to "sanctify (set apart) the Lord God in your hearts." Where the heart was previously the home of sin, enmity, and rebellion toward God and His Son, now it is a place that is "consecrated" or "purified," a place of "holiness" that sets Him apart as Lord in our hearts.

Matthew 6:12–15; 18:35; Luke 8:15

The regenerated heart understands the extent to which God has forgiven our wickedness and sinfulness. We are expected to forgive our brothers from our hearts. We are to take God's forgiveness so seriously that it will cause us to respond in forgiveness toward others. The thrust of Matthew 5:12–15 is that when we pray to God to forgive us our trespasses, the basis for that forgiveness we receive from Him is because we forgive those indebted to us (5:12). A regenerated heart understands how much God has forgiven him and so longs to forgive the brethren, which is the basis for God's continuous forgiveness toward us.

In Luke 8:15, the regenerated heart is enabled to hear the word of the gospel, and the Word is consequently enabled to bear abundant fruit in their lives. A "noble and good" heart in Luke 8:15 is a heart that is excellent in its nature and characteristics, made that way through regeneration by the Holy Spirit, and enabled to understand the word of the Gospel. Without that prior work of God, the wicked and sinful heart is not able to respond to the Gospel.

HOW DOES FAITH COME TO BE IN AN UNREGENERATE HEART?

The Westminster Confession of Faith clarifies the impossibility of man coming to faith generated through his own "free" choices, apart from God performing the miraculous work of regeneration in his heart. Describing the result of man's fall into sin in the garden of Eden, the Confession says that

> Man, by his fall into a state of sin, hath wholly lost all ability *of will* to any spiritual good accompanying salvation (Romans 5:6; 8:7; John 15:5); so as a natural man, being altogether averse from that good (Romans 3:10, 12), and dead in sin (Ephesians 2:1, 5; Colossians 2:13), is not able by his own strength, to convert himself (Titus 3:3–4), or to prepare himself thereunto (italics mine).[19]

The Bible explicitly declares man's inability to exercise faith in Christ or to do any spiritual good which originates within him. And while it remains true that an atheist can do "good things," such as acts of kindness and mercy, he cannot "do any spiritual good accompanying salvation." Indeed, the conversion of a lost sinner to Jesus Christ is the work of the sovereign God alone (Ezekiel 11:19, 20; 36:26, 27; Jeremiah 31:33), who changes the heart and opens the spiritual eyes of men to see the truth.

We understand that many teach incorrectly that men are endowed with a free will to choose God or not to choose Him, and that when man supposedly "turns over a new leaf," so to speak, or puts into action this supposed will and ability to choose or not to choose God, God is suddenly obligated to rescue him. But this is not the view of orthodox, historical, or biblical theology as expressed in the creeds and confessions that have been written in the last five centuries to not only clarify specific theological teachings, but to refute theological error.

To illustrate how common this error regarding free will is and how frequently it is expressed, one theological writer has actually written that "election is more than just foreseeing who would eventually believe; it is action of choosing those who would believe."[20] Some theologians believe that men have free wills to do as they please, and therefore, God, seeing in advance those who will freely bring themselves to faith in Christ, chooses to elect those particular individuals once they have exercised that will to believe. However, if this is true, then God's election is not from the foundation of the world as the Scriptures teach (Ephesians 1:4). Rather, in this view election must take place temporally, "in time," when a man chooses to will himself to believe in God. In fact, in this instance, salvation is not based on the grace of God at all, but rather on the free-will choice of men whom God is then obligated to save.

This view errs in that it teaches that election takes place *after* a man believes. This view asserts that man must first move his own apostate will to believe God, and then God moves His will to choose him. In this view, the sovereignty of God has no power over the will of men.

But the Bible clearly teaches that men are spiritually dead in trespasses and sins (Ephesians 2:1–3). Spiritually dead means that in their natural state, people are unable to choose to come to God.[21] They are blind to truth and dead to spiritual realities. This is why the word *regeneration* is used to describe what God does on their behalf. Men must be given a new spirit because the spirit within them is dead to God. They must be regenerated. When sinners come to Him, it is only because He has begotten them anew so that they might have a new life unto the glory of God.[22]

From a personal e-mail correspondence from the proprietor of Pilgrim Publications dated Saturday, April 08, 2006, Bob L. Ross wrote:

> 1 John 5:4 says "For whatever is born of God overcomes the world: and this is the victory that has overcome the world, our faith." This verse affirms that faith is born of God, and

> is the victory that overcomes the world. The person who has experienced this faith which is "born of God" has experienced the new birth; the person who has not experienced this faith which is "born of God" has not experienced the new birth. There is therefore *no new birth* (being "born of God") unless and until faith has been born of God...
>
> Faith is said to be "born of God" because it comes by "hearing the Word of God" (Romans 10:17); it is given or created by the gracious influence of the power of God (1 Thess. 1:5; Eph. 1:13–18); the Word of truth begets us (James 1:17); we are born again by the Word of God (James 1:23); it is the work of God that we believe (John 6:29); it is God that works faith in us (Phil. 2:13); it is given unto us to believe (Phil. 1:29; Eph. 2:8–10); and it is the Spirit who quickens the Word unto life (John 6:63); etc. The faith that saves is born of God by the instrumentality of the Word and Spirit; it is not of blood, nor the will of the flesh, nor of the will of man, but of God (John 1:12). The Seed is the Word of God (Luke 8:11), and when it is sown in the heart, the fruit of faith is the result (Luke 8; Matthew 13; Mark 4).

Before we look at the tremendous work God has done on our behalf to bring us to Him, we have to first see the seriousness of our plight without Him. One reason some people wrongly perceive of the necessity of God first working in the hearts of men to regenerate them so that they might come to Christ is because they do not grasp the depth of the depravity and inability of the souls of men. The Bible teaches that in man's state of depravity he is unable to respond to any offer of grace in and of himself. This condition is all-pervasive and involves moral corruption and liability to guilt. There is no aspect of man untouched by sin; intellect, loves, desires, and will are all equally affected. In his natural state, man is totally unable to come to Christ. It is never said in Scripture that man has the power to change his own life (Jeremiah 13:23). The Holy Spirit of God is necessary for salvation (John 3:3–7; Zechariah 4:6).

All are considered condemned by God already who do not believe in Him because they are separated from Him by sin and are indifferent toward His Son and will not decide for Him, even though many of them may even recognize that the Bible teaches that there is only one solution for sin: forgiveness (John 3:18). And there is only one person who can forgive it: Jesus Christ. Now, if all must believe Christ and yet are not able to come to Him without God first regenerating that spiritually dead person, you will probably ask, "How then can that spiritually dead, unable soul be responsible for his condition if there is nothing he can do to change it?"

One theologian helps us to understand this supposed problem more clearly by writing:

> A man is not saved on the ground of his virtues, but he is condemned on the ground of his sin...while some men are saved from their unbelief and disobedience, in which all are involved, and others are not [saved], it is still the sinner's sinfulness that constitutes the ground of his reprobation[23]...It is a travesty... to say that because God elects to save a man irrespective of his character or deserts, that therefore He elects to damn a man irrespective of his character or deserts.[24]

The biblical answer to this seemingly unfair situation is that a man is condemned and held responsible for his own sin. The sin that makes a man sinful and rebellious to God and unable to come to Christ by his own free will is still his *own* sin (John 12:48)!

PREDESTINATION AND ELECTION

> The New Testament dares to declare that the origin of human existence and, indeed, human salvation is prior to the creation of the world itself...The God Who calls us into being also elects us to be His people. God's grace precedes our decision. God chooses us before we choose God. This is the well-known doctrine of predestination. The doctrine presupposes human sin, but even if we had not sinned, God's gracious calling would precede our decision. The Christian life is a gift before it is a human achievement.
>
> —John Leith

The word *salvation,* in its broadest sense, is really best defined by several different terms. Determining how those terms interrelate and overlap in meaning and sequence has historically been the daunting task of theologians. Though it is preferable to avoid being dogmatic as to whether these terms must always take place in one *particular* order or not at all, preparing an "order" of salvation is really just man's way of clarifying, understanding, organizing, and applying our understanding of biblical theology in describing God's grace to the individual. Clearly, all theologians do not agree to the position or sequence in which each aspect of this order of salvation occurs.

By saying that, however, I do not mean to suggest that on the one hand there is such a thing as man's point of view about the meaning and sequence of steps in salvation or, on the other hand, that God always works in the same way theologically with each individual. Scripture teaches us a systematic view of theology from God's point of view, and our aim must be to interpret carefully what Scripture teaches about theology, never exchanging our point of view for God's, coming to terms with the scriptural teaching about salvation in spite of our limitations and preconceptions of God's actions.

Many scholars say that regeneration and faith happen simultaneously, as do justification and at least one part of our sanctification. Yet part of sanctification also involves a process. We study these processes and events separately in an attempt to fully grasp what is occurring in our salvation, though in a sense they work together sequentially and interchangeably. All of the following terms viewed together properly define the word *salvation.* Some aspects of salvation are judicial, or legal, others concern moral and spiritual renewal. Some are instantaneous and some continuous. If one or two of these terms are removed from the process or the order of salvation, our understanding of all that occurs in salvation is incomplete.

PREDESTINATION

The first step in the process of salvation whereby God brings us to Christ and saves us begins in eternity past and is called predestination. The Oxford American Desk Dictionary and Thesaurus defines predestination as "determined beforehand, or to be ordained in advance by divine will." It is because God determined this order by Himself before the existence of anything that it is called *pre*destination. Predestination is the *sure determination of the order of means for the end* in man's salvation. In other words, God determines the means by which He will accomplish what he predestines, as well. Furthermore, predestination does not only *presuppose* that the end in sight shall occur; it causes it to occur and it *orders* that it should be, as a result of firm deliberation. Predestination is an act of the divine will toward a certain object that it determines to bring to a certain end by certain means.[25]

The Greek word for predestination is *prooridzo.* The root word, *oridzo,* occurs eight times by itself in the New Testament. The word *prooridzo* occurs five times in the New Testament: Acts 4:28, Romans 8:30, Ephesians 1:5, 11; 1 Corinthians 2:7. Virtually all the Greek lexicons unanimously agree on the definition: It means "to predetermine, decide beforehand or ahead of time, to foreordain, appoint beforehand."[26] *Prooridzo* is derived from combining two words, *pro* (before) and *oridzo* (determine, settle, decree, to bind oneself with a pledge, appoint, declare, ordain). The idea of foreordaining is also derived from the Latin translation *praedestino,* predestine.

The subject of predestination is not an obscure, inaccessible doctrine, nor is it one derived only through inference. It permeates the Bible. The Scripture reveals to us all that we *ought* to know about the subject of predestination. God predestines with a clear purpose and in an apparent theological sequence so that predestination is not an end in itself, but for the purpose of fulfilling His ultimate goals of calling, justifying, and finally glorifying those individuals He predestines. The point of predestination was to lead men to the stages of Christian life; it was an invitation to sinful and anxious men that they should begin their pilgrimage of faith, and it was assurance that they had been placed on their pilgrimage by God.[27]

The difficulty with this doctrine for most people is twofold: On the one hand, they cannot conceive of God's fairness in choosing to forgive the sins of some while choosing not to forgive the sins of others, and on the other they struggle trying to balance, theologically, verses that appear to suggest that God loves everyone with verses that say he chooses only some, leaving the rest to condemnation.[28]

> We call predestination God's eternal decree, by which he determined within himself what he willed to become of each man. For all are not created in equal condition, rather, eternal life is foreordained for some, eternal damnation for others. Therefore, as any man has been created to one or the other of these ends, we speak of him as predestined to life or death.[29]

As difficult as this doctrine may be to the Christian, "We cannot form just and becoming ideas of God without it. Foreknowledge, perfection, omnipotence, and sovereign grace must be abandoned if predestination is denied...[and] by the preaching of predestination, man is duly humbled and God alone is exalted."[30]

Interestingly, predestination does not take any special preeminence among the other theological topics regarding salvation within the creeds of Christianity, even though the creeds teach that the will and intentions of God govern *all that exists.*

Theologians have been perhaps too concerned with attempting to articulate the order of the decrees of God in the decision to save men and what role the fall of men into sin played in God's electing purposes. Consequently, the writers of the historical creeds and confessions of Christianity found it necessary to place predestination and election in one of two sequences in their theological discussions: either *prior* to the discussion of the fall of man[31] or *after* the discussion of the fall of man.[32]

Infralapsarians (*infra,* "after," and *lapsus,* "fall") favor the view that in predestination, God first decreed to create, then decreed that man should fall into sin, and then decreed who from among all of sinful humanity He would save. This view tended to see the purpose of God's salvation as a reaction to sin.

Supralapsarians (*supra,* "before," *lapsus,* "fall") favor the view that the logical and temporal orders of God's purposes were reversed; election and reprobation were both decreed from all eternity without respect to the merits or demerits of persons by first decreeing who among sinful men he would save, then decreeing that men fall into sin, and finally decreeing that he would create them. This view sees salvation as God's primary purpose in predestinating men but saw sin and evil as necessary elements in God's overall plan of salvation. Consequently, it also tended to accuse God of being the author of sin, making him appear to create men with the intention of condemning.[33]

This predestinating will of God affects us at a very human level. Non-response to the gospel, or unbelief, is rooted in the will of God just as is belief. Human beings do not believe in God by their own efforts but as a result of the outreaching and predestinating grace of God. It is God who initially confronts the individual with the truth of His reality. Faith is first and foremost, then, a result of the act of God that elicits the human response to God. It is for this reason that the historical creeds of Christianity never left the human failure to respond to the gospel to mystery. It is for God's glory and in His justice and perfection that He passed over some people and in condemning their sin rather than forgiving it, He ordained them to their condemnation.

All of human life is rooted in the will, purpose, and intention of God. No human life is ever the simple result of the forces of biology, human will, or history. Every person, as the result of sin, is self-centered when he ought to be God-centered. And there is no way for a self-centered, spiritually dead person to become *un*self-centered by trying hard, anymore than he can forget himself by trying hard. Trying hard does not make us grateful, nor does it make us love someone, nor does it make us folly-proof. Gratitude, self-forgetfulness, and love are always elicited by something that happens *to* us. So it is with faith. Human beings do not believe in God or change their tune from folly to servant by their own efforts, but as a result of the outreaching grace of God, which elicits trust and confidence.[34]

THE PRACTICAL IMPLICATIONS OF PREDESTINATION

1. Predestination is a source of great comfort to believers because all aspects of our salvation are motivated by the mercies of God and do not depend on human effort for their successful outcome. This is one important reason why theology is critical to the overall view one has of the meaning of Scripture.

   For instance, if God is the one who predestines us, elects us, and effectually calls us to himself with his irresistible grace; if it is God who regenerates us, gives us our faith to believe in Christ, and causes us to repent; and if it is God who freely justifies us and adopts us, sanctifies us, and finally glorifies us, why would we accept a theological position as biblical that teaches that we can somehow ultimately lose our salvation in spite of what God has done?

   > Predestination is set down as a hopeful promise. Election to salvation is sure and, therefore, one can rightly expect the "application" of the work of Christ. God's election is *pre*-destining; it does not follow, confirm, or depend upon anything. [It is not] depicted...as a sequence or as a result of man's faith or good works. But election is always prior in the sense that it sets before us our destiny. By virtue of God's decree we are made ready to become what we were intended to be from eternity.[35]

2. Those predestined are elected to a life of service and a fruitful walk. William Ames considered the topic of predestination best discussed as a transitional theme between the work of Christ on our behalf and the description of the Christian life. Likewise, John Calvin located his theological discussion of the doctrine of predestination *after* his discussion of the Christian life, signifying that he felt that it was best

understood at the conclusion of the life of faith, not the beginning. Scripture teaches that "God from the beginning chose you for salvation *through sanctification* by the Spirit and belief in the truth, to which He called you by our gospel, for the obtaining of the glory of our Lord Jesus Christ" (2 Thessalonians 2:13–14). In our salvation, we were called from eternity to ultimately obtain the glory of Christ, but through the sphere of sanctification where the Spirit works in bringing about fruitfulness and service in our lives.

3. Predestination must never become a source of arrogance or presumption in the hearts and minds of Christians. We may not ever rashly judge who God does or does not elect, but must rather humbly acknowledge that our election proceeded purely from the gracious goodness of God to us who are undeserving of it. Aside from that, we must remain hopeful and never become judgmental toward the actions of others and decide in ourselves who we think God has or has not called to Himself. Like the doctrine of the perseverance of the saints, the doctrine of predestination is a source of comfort and hope to the believer. Calvin once said that predestination is nothing less than the knowledge of the adoption of God, a love that persistently and invincibly pursues the distraught and the alienated.

ELECTION

The second step in the process of God bringing you to Christ is called election. Election is defined as:

> The *unchangeable* purpose of God whereby, *before* the foundation of the world, out of the whole human race, which had fallen by its own fault out of its original integrity into sin and ruin, He has, according to the most free good pleasure of His will, out of mere grace, chosen in Christ to salvation a certain number of specific men, neither better nor more worthy than others, but with [the rest of humanity] involved in a *common misery* (all italics mine).[36]

Note these particular ideas in this paragraph:

a. The purposes of God in electing are unchangeable. God does not choose to elect based on anything we *do* since the elect were chosen *before* the foundation of the world; nor can we lose our election by something that we do.

The decision to choose you was not based in time, but in eternity past. It was based on the will of God, not on some condition of merit on your part either before or after your election. He did not choose you because He saw that you would someday believe in Him. There was no condition that you could meet that could make you one of the elect or cause you to become reprobate once you were elected! Since you were elect in salvation *before* you believed, then your faith could not be the basis for your election, nor the loss of faith the condition of your reprobation. [37]

If there could be something you must first do to be elected, namely believe in God, then you not only would have good reason to boast in your election, but you would have helped in the process. But the Bible says that your being saved by faith is the gift of God, not of your own works, "lest anyone should boast" (Ephesians 2:8–9). Election is His choosing of us, not our choosing of Him, and it is all by and because of His sovereign grace.

b. The purpose of election finds its meaning not in intellectual secrecy but in salvation *in* Christ. Wendel quoted Calvin as saying that

> "Reduced to his own resources, man is incapable of either accepting or refusing the message of Christ. The reason why some accept and others reject it is to be sought only in God, in a decision of His will which is incomprehensible to us and which we must not even seek to penetrate." Calvin finds no difficulty in declaring: "I confess this decree [of election] ought to appall us." At least, that is how it is when we think of it according to

human reason. But in reality that judgment cannot be unjust, because by definition every manifestation of the will of God is the expression of righteousness itself.[38]

c. The elect are neither "better nor more worthy than others, but [you were] with them involved in a *common misery* [i.e., the same misery of sin and separation from God as the rest of mankind]."[39] Indeed, so miserable is the plight of man in his natural condition without God and so saturated by sin in every facet of his life, that the only way man could escape is if God enabled men to see that there is a way out provided by God Himself.

There is a lot of testimony regarding God's purposeful election in Scripture. In the New Testament, the word for *elect* is *eklektos,* which, along with its derivatives, is used twenty-two times and is interpreted in the New King James as both *elect* (fifteen times) and *chosen* (seven times). It occurs in 1 Peter 1:2 in the phrase, "elect according to the foreknowledge of God the Father, in sanctification of the Spirit, for obedience and sprinkling of the blood of Jesus Christ: Grace to you and peace be multiplied." Here it is tied in with the idea of receiving salvation in Christ according to the foreknowledge or prearrangement of God the Father [that is, God's prior disposition to favor certain ones].[40] The elect are chosen "in the sphere of" sanctification (setting apart from sin) by the Spirit for the purpose of, or unto, obedience. Here we see clearly that God's choosing is purposed in the very real, practical aspect of living a life of personal purity and obedience to God.

Psalm 65:3–4 says, "Iniquities prevail against me; *As for* our transgressions, You will provide atonement for them. Blessed *is the man* You choose, And cause to approach *You, That* he may dwell in Your courts. We shall be satisfied with the goodness of your house, Of Your holy temple." The word for *choose* is *bāhar* and means "to choose, elect, or decide for." The root and its derivations occur one hundred ninety-eight times in the Old Testament, meaning "to take a keen look at...always involving the idea of a careful, well thought-out choice."[41] With only a few exceptions, every instance of those one hundred ninety-eight times refers to "that choosing that has ultimate and eternal significance." Note in Psalm 65 that God provides atonement for those He chooses so that they may dwell with God in His courts.

In Ephesians 1:4, "just as He chose us in Him before the foundation of the world, that we should be holy and without blame before Him in love," the elect are chosen by God in Christ before the foundation of the world to become more and more holy through His power and grace. Since He chose you before the foundation of the world, His choosing you was not based upon anything you did, but rather was purposed in Himself (Ephesians 1:9) because of His mercy (Titus 3:5 and 1 Peter 1:3) and not based on any works you might do to earn it (Romans 9:11).

Often times people are inclined to ask, "Why is it that only *we* were chosen?" The answer is because God is merciful (1 Peter 1:3; 2:10). But how, you ask, can God be merciful to some and not to others, and yet still be "all-merciful?" Indeed God, in reality, would be cruel if He were to reject sinners pleading to be forgiven. That is why Christians have understood that historically, anyone pleading for forgiveness for his sin is forgiven because God is merciful. The pleading for forgiveness is an indication of one's election. It is not that God is bound so rigidly to His decrees that He would not save some particular person pleading with Him for forgiveness because he or she is not among the elect! It is only the elect, chosen by God, who want to come! Only the elect see their need for forgiveness of sin.

The fact of the matter is that it is not a biblical principle that people in general seek His mercy and forgiveness (Romans 3:11–18). Rather, sinners dead in trespasses and sins are content in their apostasy and do not seek Him until their hearts are softened and they comprehend the depth of their own depravity. But anyone who does desire forgiveness receives it. Sinners convicted of sin have nowhere to run except to Jesus. And when they run to Him, they are forgiven and receive the mercy of a loving God (Matthew 11:28).

Even though the language in Scripture may suggest to us that election is a random selection of sinners on God's part, God had something specific in mind, some very special purpose, when He chose the elect. [42] In 1 Peter 2:9–10, believers are a *chosen* generation, a royal *priesthood*, a *holy* nation, and God's *special* people. They have a distinct reason for being chosen. God has chosen the elect for the specific purpose of proclaiming the praises of Him to the world. The ones God rescues from eternal damnation are the only ones who are capable of singing of His great mercy and saving power!

The unregenerate world, still lost in sin, has no interest or ability in singing the praises of such a God! Indeed, as yet they do not even believe that there is a God who is worthy of having His praises proclaimed! (Prior to your coming to Christ as your personal Savior, how often did you praise God for His mercy in the salvation of others?) In a sense then, God blesses Himself by choosing the elect to bless His Name (1 Peter 1:3).

In 1 Peter, God is further qualified as the One who "called us out of darkness" and "into His marvelous light" (1 Peter 2:9). When we proclaim the praises of Him to the world, we are to share the fact that God was merciful to us. He shed the light of the Gospel on our hearts, which separated us from a lost world of sin and darkness! The Scriptures teach that "men loved darkness rather than light, because their deeds were evil" (John 3:19). No one loves the light until God makes them see the beauty and truth of His presence in it. And He has provided tremendous eternal promises and blessings for us who come to the light (2 Peter 1:4).

EFFECTUAL CALLING AND REGENERATION

> In the N. T. Epistles, only those are spoken of as called by God who have listened to his voice addressed to them in the gospel, hence those who have enlisted in the service of Christ.
>
> —Joseph Thayer

There may be a gap of time between hearing the gospel call to salvation and being regenerated by the Holy Spirit. We don't know how long a time there can be between when the Holy Spirit regenerates a person, making him or her able to come to Christ, and when that person hears the call to come to Christ for salvation and then comes! It may be seconds or it may be years! But whoever is regenerated by the Spirit will hear the call to come in the gospel and then respond by coming.

Once the Holy Spirit regenerates the elect person, He never departs from that individual. He will not regenerate you only to leave you on your own.

I remember listening to a woman tell me that it was possible for a person to be regenerated by the Holy Spirit and genuinely converted to Christ and yet walk away from Him after years of apparently living a "Christian" life! I referred her to Romans 8:29–39, which clearly taught that that was not the case at all. I showed her that that passage closes with the astounding assurance that "neither death nor life, nor angels nor principalities nor powers, nor things present nor things to come, nor height nor depth, nor any other created thing, shall be able to separate us from the love of God which is in Christ Jesus our Lord" (Romans 8:38–39). Her response was, "Nothing can separate me *except* myself!" Apparently the sovereignty of her own will is more powerful than the sovereignty of God's will.

This calling by which God brings us to Himself is spoken of as being either general or specific. The following examples depict that the *general* call is God's summoning persons all over the world to Himself, by His Word; and the specific call is to those whom He has elected.

THE GENERAL AND SPECIFIC CALL TO SALVATION

Who are to come to the waters in Isaiah 55:1? Everyone who thirsts. Who does Christ bid to come to Him in Matthew 11:28? All who are weary and heavy laden. These are examples of a *general* calling of persons to the truth of the gospel. Christ is freely offered to everyone in the general call to the gospel. But certainly even in these examples of the general call, the implication is that there must be something that the person *thirsts* for, some acknowledgment that they are *weary and heavy laden* by sin before they respond to the offer to come to Christ.

There is also a *specific* call to the elect, whereby God *effectually* lays hold of their hearts by the power of His Word and Spirit. God does this to bring them out of that state of sin and death in which they are by nature, to recognize that state of grace and salvation being offered in Jesus Christ, so they may play a part in and enjoy the benefits of His gracious redemptive purposes. All those He enables to come, do come (John 6:37). This *particular* call can only be responded to by the elect whom the Holy Spirit always regenerates, resulting in their conversion. God's sovereign action secures a positive response to His summons of repentance, faith, salvation, and service, through the secret operation of the Holy Spirit, who unites men to Christ according to God's gracious purpose in election.[43]

In Romans 8:30, who are the ones who were effectually called? Those whom God predestined, justified, and glorified. In Galatians 1:15, Paul writes that he was called from his mother's womb, and the agent of that calling was God's grace. Paul tells the Thessalonians that they were called by the Gospel for the obtaining of the glory of our Lord Jesus Christ in 2 Thessalonians 2:14 and that they were chosen from the beginning in 2 Thessalonians 2:13.

Note that in Matthew 22:1–14, at the end of the parable of the wedding feast, in verse 9, as many as His servants could find were invited to this feast. That is the general call. Yet verse 14 clearly states that though there is a general call to the many, there is also a specific call to the few who are chosen.

This effectual calling has been termed *irresistible grace.* It means that God, in His own mercy, gives life to whom He chooses. The living, human spirit, which is born of God, now finds the call from the living God wholly irresistible. The lost remain irresistibly drawn to the god of the dead (Satan) unless the God of the living sees fit to give them the gift of faith and life.[44]

In speaking of God's irresistible call, theologians mean that God's particular or effectual call to salvation may be resisted at certain points, but that the sinner who is called will not be able to *ultimately* resist God's call. In Acts 2:39, to whom are the promises of repentance and receiving the Holy Spirit in (Acts 2:38) made? To as many as the Lord our God will call to Himself. In Romans 9:23–24, to whom did God make known the riches of his glory?

Even us, whom He has called, not of the Jews only but also of the Gentiles. In Romans 9:23, what had God already prepared them for beforehand? Glory. In Acts 13:48, who were the ones who believed? All those who had been appointed to eternal life.

REGENERATION

The fourth step in the order of salvation that we will discuss is called regeneration, or "being born again." We have seen this idea already in 1 Peter 1:3 in the words *begotten us anew.* Regeneration is defined as that work of the Holy Spirit whereby He initially brings us into a living union with Jesus Christ and changes our hearts so that we who were spiritually dead become spiritually alive. Man's spiritual condition is so bent on sin that if left to himself, man would continue in his state of rebellion and refuse all offers of salvation if not for the work of the Holy Spirit in this step.

Jesus said in John 3:3 that in order to experience or participate in or be able to understand that there is a kingdom of God, we must be "born from above."[45] Being born from above is not an option. Being born again is an essential work of the Spirit of God in the heart of the sinner (John 3:6, 8). There is nothing you can do to help God in this process. Nor is there any way one could ever pretend that this has happened. Theologically, the implication made by some theologians that we actually help Him bring about this new birth while we were dead in sin by first coming to Christ in faith and then being born again is staggering!

Being predestined, elected, effectually called, and regenerated are the first steps to being converted to Christ. Only those "born from above" can receive Christ and become children of God (John 1:12–13). In 1 Peter 1:3, being born anew is the proof we are chosen by God as elect!

In the First Epistle of John, God's regeneration by the Spirit is said to issue forth in "spiritual fruit." For example, the regenerate:

- practice righteousness (1 John 2:29; 3:10).
- do not and cannot [continue to live a life of] sin (1 John 3:9; 5:18).
- continue to love their brothers (1 John 3:10; 4:7; 5:1).
- continue to know God (1 John 4:7).
- continue believing Jesus is the Christ (1 John 5:1).
- continue loving God (1 John 5:1).
- overcome the world and experience faith's ultimate victory over the world by continuing to believe Jesus is the Son of God (1 John 5:4–5).
- continue to guard themselves and the evil one does not touch him (1 John 5:18).

The signs of being born again, or begotten of God, are that those who are regenerate continue to live a life that demonstrates their "begotten-ness." The new birth given to us from God is not for a season only. A genuinely born-again person will continue on in the faith and practice of being a Christian to the end of his or her Christian life. Faith and fruit persevere in his life because genuine faith perseveres.[46]

This does not mean that we have entirely mastered the power of sin in our lives so as to never sin again; nor does it mean that we may never again commit acts of unrighteousness or never again experience doubts about what God is doing in our lives. But it does mean that the regenerate Christian lives a life that persists in dedication and consecration to God.

First Corinthians 15:1–2 says, "Moreover, brethren, I declare to you the gospel which I preached to you, which also you received and in which you stand (Greek perfect tense), by which also you are saved, if you hold fast that word which I preached to you—unless you believed in vain."

> *Holding fast,* etc...[is the] condition on which hangs the truth of the words *you stand* and *are being saved.* It is therefore a warning suggesting self-examination and is an appeal to the readers' inner consciousness that their spiritual erectness and victory are in proportion to the firmness with which they hold fast Paul's teaching...unless they have relaxed their hold upon Paul's teaching, they now stand firm and are now in the way of salvation, for otherwise, the faith they formerly exercised is an empty thing. And that it is not such, their innermost heart proclaims.[47]

WHY GOD IS BLESSED IN OUR BEING BEGOTTEN ANEW

First Peter 1:3 says that God is blessed because He has "begotten us anew" to a hope that is living, through the resurrection of Jesus Christ from the dead.

The Greek word for "begotten anew" is *anagennao* and occurs only here in the New Testament. It means "to produce again, beget again, beget anew." It is used in a metaphorical sense to "thoroughly change the mind of one, so that he lives a new life, [a life] conformed to the will of God."[48] In 1 Peter 1:3, it appears in the passive voice, which means that the recipient of this new birth did not beget himself. Rather he was "begotten" by an outside source. People need to be begotten anew because in their natural state they are neither able nor willing to come to God. They are spiritually dead.

This hope of a resurrection like Christ's is our hope, our expectation, our life. It is a hope shared only by the ones God has chosen. This hope is living because we look for the same immortality that Christ has (Romans 8:11).

First Peter says that we have been begotten anew to an inheritance that is *incorruptible* (untouched by death), *undefiled* (untouched by evil), and that *does not fade away* (untouched by time), which is reserved in heaven for us (1 Peter 1:4). These are tremendous words, and we will benefit by looking at them more thoroughly.

The word *corruptible* is the word *phtheiro,* which means "to corrupt or destroy." The root word is used eight times in the New Testament. This is a word Peter liked to use, and it appears three times in 2 Peter 2:12. "But these men, as natural animals without reason, have been begotten for capture and *corruption,* blaspheming in the things they are ignorant of; in their *corruption* indeed they will be *corrupted*" (2 Peter 2:12).

Peter's use of *incorruptible, aphthartos,* is a strong word whose root, *phthora,* also appears in 2 Peter: 2:12, 19 and 2 Peter 1:4. In 2 Peter 1:4, "having escaped the *corruption* that is in the world through lust," means moral decay, perishing, or total depravity. It is used elsewhere in the New Testament five times to refer to "ruin, destruction, the loss of salvation, and eternal misery." The promise that our Christian hope is something that is the opposite of ruin, decay, corruption, destruction, or perishing is a wonderful assurance! In the Greek language, *corruption* is a word in opposition to the concept of eternal life in salvation. Our natural birth leads ultimately to a state of corruption, which, as Peter states, we are saved from when we are begotten anew by God.

Defiled is the word *miaino,* which means "to dye or stain; to defile or soil" in both a physical and moral sense and appears five times in the New Testament. The word Peter uses in 1 Peter 1:4 is *amiantos,* "not defiled, unsoiled; free from that by which the nature of a thing is deformed and debased, or its force or vigor impaired."[49] Here Peter informs us that in spite of the fact that we are naturally stained and defiled by sin, our eternal inheritance is free from the stain of sin through Christ's work on our behalf. This promised inheritance is ours because of God's work of regeneration in our depraved hearts; consequently, our inheritance is completely unlike ourselves, one that is undefiled.

The English translation, "that does not fade away," is a very interesting, single Greek word, *amaranton.* It only occurs here in the New Testament and it is from the root word *marainomai*, "to extinguish, to render arid, cause to wither, make to waste or pine away, have a miserable end." *Marainomai* occurs only in James 1:11.

An amaranth is a perennial flower that has the distinct characteristic of not withering or fading away when plucked from its stem if it is moistened with water. Peter uses it to describe our immortal inheritance, one that will never wither away once God plucks us from our physical life.

These three words are rich in their description of the wondrous mercy God bestows upon our defiled, depraved, and mortal lives. Peter adds that this inheritance is *reserved* in heaven for us (1:4). In the Greek text, *reserved* is in the perfect tense and might be better translated as *being kept* in heaven. The perfect tense speaks of the permanence and resulting continuance of this inheritance.

This inheritance already exists and is reserved for those whom God is guarding. The word *guarding* is literally "continuously being guarded" by the power of God, through faith unto salvation, ready to be revealed at the last time" (1 Peter 1:5). This continuous guarding (Greek present tense), or being protected or watched over, is the guarantee of the final victory we will obtain because of the power of God's mercy upon us. We could never in our own strength and power ever guarantee such a thing. Surely these verses in 1 Peter are a marvelous description of God's mercy and love upon those whom He regenerates and preserves for an immortal inheritance with Him.

The Apostle Peter states that God is blessed because He has begotten us again to a living hope, a hope we never could have had had He not begotten us anew! This living hope is never altered or changed because of the circumstances in our lives. Without the grace of God, what we would have inherited would have been death and separation from God. As slaves defiled by sin, we had earned, and deserved, death (Romans 6:17, 22–23; 7:4–5; 8:1–2). Everyone who does not believe the good news of Jesus Christ has a hope that is only corruptible, defiled, and fading away (1 Peter

1:4). We have not earned our new inheritance. It was freely given in grace, "according to His abundant mercy" (1 Peter 1:3). And that is why we are to proclaim the praises of Him to the world! Because our God is a God of mercy and grace!

EXPLORING TWO VIEWS OF REGENERATION

The understanding of what takes place in regeneration theologically can be somewhat confusing. Even Nicodemus, the teacher in Israel who came to Jesus in the night in John chapter three, was *clueless* about it...to Jesus's amazement! Nicodemus wonders, "How can a man be born when he is old? Can he enter a second time into his mother's womb?" (John 3:4). He was wrestling with a practical truth on a very theological level in much the same way that we do today.

Theologians have sought to articulate their understanding of what happens in the regenerated man's life in two general ways. One view believes that after regeneration there are two distinct natures that exist in men. One is the "old (spiritually dead) man" who existed before regeneration and the "new, spiritual sinless self." According to this view, the old man and the new man live side by side for the rest of the person's life, perpetually struggling against each other. In this view, the old sin nature that remains in man is necessarily left unchanged and unsanctified in regeneration.

The opposing view that we believe best suits biblical theology teaches that

> Regeneration consists in a divine implanting of the principle of the new spiritual life in man, in a radical change of the governing disposition of the soul, which, under the influence of the Holy Spirit, gives birth to a life that moves in a Godward direction...and is made holy and the first holy exercise of this new disposition is secured.[50]

Anthony Hoekema, who was professor emeritus of systematic theology at Calvin Theological Seminary, writes that this second view is fundamentally different from the first view of two distinct natures residing in the individual.

> Regeneration is a radical change from spiritual death to spiritual life, brought about in us by the Holy Spirit–a change in which we are completely passive. This change involves an inner renewal of our nature, is a fruit of God's sovereign grace, and takes place in union with Christ...at the moment of regeneration [when] the dead sinner becomes spiritually alive, that resistance to God is changed to non-resistance, and hatred for God is changed to love...The person who was outside Christ is now in Christ. Hence this is a radical, not superficial change...it is the giving of a new heart...it is the fountain of thinking, feeling, willing, believing, praying, praising, that is renewed.[51]

At a minimum, Scripture teaches that to become a Christian is to experience the power of Christ in the forgiveness of sin and in the receiving of a new life. We see then that this second preferred view teaches that our entire fallen human nature is enlivened or renewed by the Holy Spirit during regeneration. It is not that there are two distinctly *different* natures that must now struggle against each other within the individual. The idea is that the entire person that we were before regeneration took place has now been made spiritually alive.

The Westminster Confession of Faith states that this is a change in the entire person.

> Effectual calling (regeneration) is enlightening their minds spiritually and savingly to understand the things of God; taking away their heart of stone, and giving them a heart of flesh; renewing their wills, and by His almighty power determining them to that which is good, and effectually drawing them to Christ Jesus...[52]

Included in this regeneration is a new capacity, love for and affinity with truth. This statement by the Westminster Confession is suggesting that there is a changing of our human mind about God, Jesus, and the Gospel through the enlightenment of the Holy Spirit in this effectual calling. Our new birth, or regeneration, means God replaces our hardened heart with a new heart and our old spirit with a new spirit while our human will is renewed so that it will become one that is continuously drawn to Christ (Ezekiel 36:26).

On the surface, it may appear that this discussion between two distinct natures that remain after regeneration versus one nature that is entirely affected in regeneration is a non-issue.

The reason that Reformed theologians do not agree with the view of two distinct natures existing side-by-side in the regenerated believer is because it suggests that the old nature is *entirely unaffected* by regeneration. Additionally, this has led to a view and subsequent teaching that there are three kinds of individuals: regenerated Christians, unregenerate unbelievers, and "carnal" Christians.[53] The most troubling aspect to this carnal Christian view is that a new heart and new spiritual life are considered *optional* in regeneration, and hence, those who hold to this view are not able to make a distinction between a counterfeit faith and a saving faith. Furthermore, this view implies that by merely *saying* that one has invited Jesus into his or her heart, one is in possession of a genuine saving faith and a new regenerated spirit. The "carnal" Christian can supposedly find solace in justifying a life exactly like the natural man (while claiming to be a Christian) because that old nature was never affected by regeneration.

But should we be trying to make a distinction? Iain Murray, prolific Reformed theologian, pastor, and founder of the Banner of Truth Trust Publishing House, asks a good question in light of our understanding of regeneration:

> Is it not offensive and intolerant to suppose that anyone can distinguish true Christians from others? Are there not, it is said, many kinds of followers of Christ and does not love

> demand that we regard them all as 'fellow Christians'? This objection often proceeds on the basis of another argument—usually unstated—namely, that the New Testament itself does not give us enough light to be definite. And if Scripture does not resolve the question, 'What is a Christian?' then we must tolerate and justify a breadth of opinion on the subject. But if the New Testament *does settle the question,* then we have no liberty to redefine 'Christian' in terms which neither Christ nor his apostles ever authorized. Evangelicalism has historically been distinguished by its conviction that Scripture speaks plainly on this fundamental issue; it gives us all the light we need to discern between the true and the false, between the nominal and the real.[54]

At the conclusion of the article from *Evangelicalism Divided,* Murray writes that "saving faith requires the power of the Holy Spirit—and His presence or absence in an individual is to be known by their response to God's word" (1 John 4:5–6). This is perhaps the *only* valid test and the biblical boundaries upon which we might base a person's state of regeneration.

Blatant sin should be corrected for the good of the church and for the good of the believer. But since we all suffer from a multitude of sins and we all have many areas of weakness and ignorance in our lives, should we judge that those persons claiming to be Christians *genuinely are* only after we establish some subjective set of rules they need to follow to prove it?

Isn't it prideful for us to suggest that we should create rules that we impose upon the Spirit to purify and sanctify a fellow believer in one way or another, all according to *our* set of sanctified spiritual demands? Isn't it wrong for us to set up unbiblical categories to determine how genuinely "Christian" someone is, categories like not smoking, not going to movies, not drinking alcohol, not dancing, not playing cards, attending every church service, etc? These are all artificial categories that only the spiritually proud would seek to establish and maintain to prove the validity of someone's claim to regeneration. None of us are in a position to qualify another person's walk with the Lord by determining how genuine their claim to being Christian is from our human perspective.

If the agent in regeneration and sanctification in the life of the Christian is the Holy Spirit, should we create some arbitrary superficial rules to impose upon the life of another person to remedy what we suppose to be their carnal weaknesses? It is the Spirit's role to convict us of the sin that remains in our life and provide the true motivation to get free from sin. Shall I decide that someone is a different class of Christian because the Spirit is taking His time to convict him of a particularly sinful area that needs attention in his life, oftentimes an area that the Spirit helped someone else conquer with relative ease? And you thought theology was easy? I hope I have illuminated some of the difficult areas in this issue for you.

The most important consideration in regeneration is that all aspects of the believer's life are *permanently* affected by the Spirit of God. If the old nature that supposedly remains in the believer after regeneration is never sanctified by the Holy Spirit and does nothing but sin, it *is* utterly unaffected by regeneration. If that is the case, then many other aspects of the order of salvation are seriously and negatively impacted because of this view. It necessarily follows then, that this new life, given in regeneration, may or may not be lived out by the Christian. In this view, the believer may not persevere in holiness while in the one-nature view the believer is called by the Spirit in the sphere of sanctification and the Spirit must persevere in him in holiness to the end of his life.

This view of two natures living side by side is inadequate because even if the person continues to choose incorrectly between the old man and the new divine nature, his salvation is secure because how the old nature behaves cannot be indicative of his regeneration. To the contrary, the view that there exists after regeneration one new nature states that the regenerated person will strive after holiness, without which no man will see the Lord (Hebrews 12:14). If he does not do so, it is manifest that he has not been regenerated. John Owen, brilliant Puritan scholar and theologian, said, "The sin that indwells the believer was killed in principle on the cross; Christ's death will in time be its death. It was dethroned in fact by regeneration, and now, with the Spirit's aid, the Christian is to spend his lifetime draining its lifeblood."[55]

CONVERSION, UNION WITH CHRIST, JUSTIFICATION, AND ADOPTION

> If the doctrine of the Trinity really presents us with the true God of creation and redemption; if Jesus Christ really is God from God, Light from Light, very God from very God; and if original sin is as pervasive and debilitating as we believe it to be, then the doctrine of "justification by faith alone in Christ alone" is the only faithful interpretation of the New Testament promise of forgiveness, pardon, and new life in Christ.
>
> —Timothy George

CONVERSION

Conversion is closely tied to faith, repentance, and regeneration. The word translated as "converted" in Acts 3:19 is *epistrepho* and always means "to turn," occurring some forty times in the New Testament. But it is only translated with the sense of turning toward God in worship, obedience, or the true faith after salvation about thirteen times.[56]

Only the regenerate can become converted to Christ because salvation involves a profound change of heart. None entrenched in sin are able to change their own heart about Christ. That heart must first be changed by God. Perhaps conversion could also be expressed as a coming over from one's former ignorance, or error, or infidelity, or sin, to the true faith. Synonyms for the word conversion include *change, metamorphosis,* and *transformation.*

Conversion is a two-sided coin. In historical Christian theology:

> Conversion was understood as the human response to regeneration, the infusion of new life into the soul. Conversion was held to be dependent on grace; it was seen as an act empowered and directed by divine grace. Calvinism was inclined to portray this grace as irresistible, with the result that conversion became a virtually spontaneous turning of the one who was elected to receive grace [once the gospel was heard]... Conversion has two sides, divine and human. It represents the incursion of divine grace into human life, the resurrection from spiritual death to eternal life...We are active only on the basis of grace, and only through the power of grace...Conversion is the sign but not the condition of our justification, whose sole source is the free, unconditional grace of God.[57]

One difficulty in describing what conversion is theologically is that there are many very articulate theologians who envisaged the whole Christian life as one of conversion! John Calvin, for instance, had an amazing career as a scholar, preacher, and pastor, yet "his inner life showed few signs of the progress which he associated with godliness; he was, [much like the Apostle Paul's comments of his own struggles in Romans, chapter seven], still wrestling at the end of his life with the self-doubt, confusions, and contradictory impulses that had been with him from the beginning."[58] It is interesting to note that as analytical as Calvin was about his own Christian walk, he attached very little, if any, significance to conversion as a precise event in his discussions of the Christian life or in expressing it in the context of the way of salvation. He emphasized it in terms of gradualness rather than suddenness, even as a mere shift and quickening of his interests. He wrote, "We are converted little by little to God, and by stages."[59]

Conversion involves repentance, that is, turning from sin as an event in time (Acts 26:20), and it involves the action of the Holy Spirit moving upon us so that we are inclined to initially respond to God and Christ in faith (Acts 11:21; 15:19; 1 Thess. 1:9, 10). It also causes us to repent and cling to Christ in ongoing repentance as we continue to turn to God regularly. One theologian said that "repentance means turning from as much as you know of your sin to give as much as you know of yourself to as much as you know of your God, and as your knowledge grows at these three points, so our practice of repentance has to be enlarged."[60]

In order for conversion to take place, the heart must have recognition of sin's destructive character and the guilt incurred through it. First, God must open the heart of the sinner to recognize his or her sin, producing a disposition whereby the individual despises that sin. Then the individual's will is exercised to turn from it. To be saved, you must agree with God and confess that you are sinful and turn to Christ in faith as the only remedy for that sinfulness. This *turning* is known as conversion. Again, this faith in the fact that Christ alone can save you from sin is the evidence of regeneration, not the cause of it.

There is no denial of the fact and necessity of conversion. There is, however, some question, at least in the mind of some scholars, whether the term *conversion* is indispensable because where the word would be thought to be used in Scripture, it is avoided altogether or another word is substituted for it in preference.[61]

> We encourage you to be cautious in your application and use of this term, as some in the past have insisted upon [conversion] as universally necessary in order to a state [sic] of salvation—when preachers divide their hearers, being believers

> in a common Christianity, into the two classes of "converted" and "unconverted"—when the former class are led to cherish overweening ideas of their acceptance with God, and of their assurance of eternal salvation; and the latter are either driven to despair of their spiritual state, or else, without any real change of heart, to adopt the phraseology and exhibit the outward signs and badges of the "converted"...[62]

If someone said to me, "Tell me all that I need to know so that I can be saved," I would never respond by saying, "Be converted," as if that satisfied all that is required. It would be as silly to respond with "be converted" as it would be to answer with, "All you need to know to be saved is: And she gave birth to her first-born son; and she wrapped Him in cloths, and laid Him in a manger, because there was no room for Him at the inn" (Luke 2:7)!

Just as this statement about the birth of Christ only begins to inform us about all there is to know about Christ for salvation, the words *be converted* only begin to sum up all of what the Bible means when it asks, "What must I do to be saved?" Understanding what it means to be saved is multifaceted and deeply layered.

The first part of 1 John 5:1 teaches that everyone who continues believing that Jesus is the Christ is, in past time, born of God. The action of our being born of God has been completed, and the things that result from that being born again continue to take place.

Likewise, we should never answer the question, "What I must do to be saved?" with "All you have to do is believe today, in this moment, and you are saved for eternity!" To really answer the question, we must answer with the totality of Scripture.

Being converted means "believing" (Acts 16:31); "receiving Christ" (John 1:12); "repenting and turning to God" (Acts 3:19); "obeying the truth" (Galatians 5:7); "being childlike in your faith" (Matthew 18:3); "getting free from the love of possessions" (Luke 14:33), and more.

UNION WITH CHRIST

Union with Christ is complete identification with the work of Christ on our behalf and is accomplished by the baptism of the Holy Spirit of the believer. It is a single act of divine grace and power. Union with Christ is the precondition of any enjoyment of the benefits that the Son has acquired on our behalf.

Union with Christ is essential to the entire program of grace. The believer is interpenetrated and empowered by the spirit of Christ. When we are in union with Him, we are identified with His death (Romans 6:3), burial (Romans 6:4), resurrection (Romans 6:5; Colossians 3:1), life (Ephesians 2:5), heavenly position (Ephesians 2:6), reign (2 Timothy 2:12), suffering, and glorification (Romans 8:17).

This identification of a believer with Christ results in two things. First, because we are in union with Christ, God declares us to be justified. Secondly, because we are justified and declared legally pardoned, we stand in a new relationship with God the Father because He has adopted us into His family.

Before we look more closely at the practical results that ensue from our being united to Christ, our justification and adoption, it is important to understand what union with Christ is *not*.

As close as our relationship to Christ becomes, both Christ and men keep their own characteristics. To be in union with Christ does not mean to somehow mystically *mingle* the divinity of Christ with our humanity (otherwise known as panentheism or Gnosticism), as this would abase Christ's purity. As Christians we should be revolted by the notion that God mingles himself with us with such a mixture as do the foods we eat. Our union with Christ is purely legal and spiritual.

> Whence we also gather that we are one with the Son of God, not to say that he transmutes his substance into us, but because by virtue of his Spirit, he communicates to us his life, and all the benefits he has received from the Father. This union with

> Christ is, then, the indispensable condition for our access to the spiritual life. Neither justification nor sanctification, nor perseverance nor the final perfection [glorification] is possible without that insertion into [union with] Christ that the Holy Spirit effects through faith. It renders us pleasing to God: He begins to love us uniquely when we are united with the body of his well-beloved Son...We are not otherwise included in that love, except that Jesus Christ is dwelling in us.[63]

This union is not accomplished by us, nor did it begin with us. What ends in spiritual union with Christ goes back to Christ Himself, who works in us through the Holy Spirit. That union is obtained only by faith. The way in which we know of this union is by Christ "infusing his life into us by the hidden virtue of his Spirit...the Holy Spirit is the bond, as it were, by which the Son of God unites us to [God] effectually."[64] Both justification and adoption are results of our being in union with Christ.

JUSTIFICATION

Justification is an interesting theological notion in reality. Most every Christian would tell you that he or she does not "feel" righteous twenty-four hours a day. But being justified is not something that we feel physically or emotionally or even spiritually. In fact, being justified has nothing to do with feeling anything! Justification is a legal pronouncement on our behalf that God accepts and treats believing sinners as "just."

Justification is the cardinal principle of the Reformation and the heart of the Evangelical Christian faith. It refers to the divine act whereby sinful humans who are worthy of condemnation are freely made acceptable before a God who is holy and righteous. Justification is *forensic* (that is, relating to lawyers and law courts). We are declared, counted, or reckoned to be righteous when God imputes the righteousness of Christ (an "alien, extrinsic righteousness") to our account. In other words, the judge of all the earth declares us not guilty when we believe because Christ was pronounced guilty for us on the cross (as our substitute). We are not *first* made righteous and then *declared* righteous (as is implied repeatedly in the theology of Catholicism); we are declared righteous by grace alone through faith alone in Christ alone and then become righteous through the process of sanctification.

Keeping justification and sanctification distinct and separate from each other is critical to the Christian doctrine of justification. When we believe, God imputes Christ's righteousness to us as if it were our own. However, it is forever *His* righteousness that justifies us, which is necessarily followed by a faith that demonstrates its validity through good works. That is why Paul says in Romans 1:17 that there is a righteousness that has been revealed from God, a righteousness *not of our own,* but one revealed from God. The theological tenant of justification is the revealed righteousness of Christ imputed to us through faith.

Justification means that the righteousness of Christ has been attributed to believers in Christ based on the biblical fact that God pardons believing sinners (cf. Acts 13:38–39; Ephesians 1:7; Colossians 1:14). Justification's legal basis is related to Christ's life and death fulfilling the requirements of God's law. It is God's *legal* declaration, acceptance, and treatment that the one who has been effectually called and has believed in Christ now stands "declared" as righteous. It means that in God's legal system, believing sinners are acquitted and so are forever excluded as to any possibility of condemnation from the law. It forever settles our legal status before God. We are declared legally "righteous" (cf. 1 Corinthians 1:30; Titus 2:14; Galatians 2:16, 21; 3:10–13; Colossians 2:13–15; Romans 3:28; 5:1, 9–11; 8:28–30).

Justification includes the pardon, remission, and non-imputation of all the sins of the believer who is in union with Christ. It includes our being brought back into the family of God, our reconciliation to God. It means that when we are justified before God, there is an end to His wrath and hatred toward our sin. Being justified means that to us has been bestowed a righteous man's status and entitlement to all the blessings of that status.

THE BIBLICAL EVIDENCE

In Romans 4:3–11, eight times Paul uses a form of the Greek word *logizomai,* our root word for *logic,* which means to "reckon, count, or impute." It is used some twenty-seven times in the various epistles of Paul (excluding quotations from the Old Testament), and only four times in the rest of the New Testament. This reckoning is not because of works (Romans 5:18). *Logizomai* carries the idea of "having the like force and weight of something."[65]

In Romans 4:3, Paul wrote "Abraham believed God, and it was accounted to him [*logizomai,* imputed] as righteousness." Abraham's faith (in the promises of God) was "having the like force and weight" of righteousness. God didn't suddenly make Abraham a righteous person by taking His own righteousness and infusing it into Abraham. Paul meant that from God's perspective, Abraham's faith in the promises of God had the same force and weight as being righteous from God's point of view.

Again, in Romans 4:4, Paul wrote, "Now to him who works, the wages are not counted as grace, but as debt." If our justification (being pardoned and accepted) before God was based (legally) on what we *did,* then our being declared right before God couldn't be based solely upon His grace. Biblically, justification is based completely upon God's grace. We cannot be made "just" by what we do because doing right means keeping the perfect law of God perfectly. But by grace alone, God imputes Christ's righteousness to us because Christ kept the law perfectly.

Paul reiterates in Romans 4:5, "But to him who does not work, but believes on Him who justifies the ungodly, his faith is accounted for righteousness." Clearly, our own works could never make us righteous before a Holy God. Biblically, it is *faith* in the finished work of Christ that has the "like force and weight" of righteousness. The early Reformers had a statement that applies here: "Salvation by grace alone through faith alone in Christ alone."

The graciousness of justification is that we are guilty, but our sins are pardoned. We deserve the condemnation that the law of God brings against erring sinners, but God cancels that condemnation by grace for those persons who have faith. The faithful are now accepted as righteous because righteousness has been credited to their account. Their faith is having the like force and weight of Christ's righteousness. And Christ was righteous because He kept the law perfectly.

After justification, the believer is accepted because of his faith, based on God's declaration of Christ's righteousness. Justification equals peace with God. We have peace because God cannot pour out His wrath on our sin because He already poured it out on Christ, whose righteousness is imputed to us through faith.

The basis for our acceptance as justified sinners is not our faith. Our acceptance is never *because of* faith. We are not accepted because we believed. If we were accepted because of our faith, our faith would then be a work by which God would be indebted to pay us. The basis of our acceptance is Christ's having satisfied every requirement of God's perfect law.

WHAT SHALL WE DO WITH THE LAW?

Many Christians continue to struggle with how they should understand and respond to God's moral laws, the Ten Commandments, and how that relates to our justification. To those who have been pardoned from the sinful consequences of falling short of God's perfect moral law, what purpose does the law serve for those who have been justified by faith? Does the law still condemn Christians? Can it really be true that we are at peace with God because of someone else's work that has been imputed to us?

Justification is the most important canon to Christian theology. It is the one doctrine that makes Christianity different from all other religious beliefs. All of orthodox belief hinges on this theological concept. Virtually every cult group or aberrant religious belief system will either pervert or fail to consider clearly this Christian distinction, and the reason is because they do not understand that there is *nothing* they can do in and of themselves to be righteous before a Holy God. Virtually every cultic group fails to understand that faith alone in Christ alone imputes Christ's righteousness to our account. There is nothing we do that earns that righteousness. This is the heart of what it means to say that God is gracious to us.

The third article of the Articles of Faith of the Church of Jesus Christ of Latter-day Saints reads: "We believe that through the Atonement of Christ, all mankind may be saved, by obedience to the laws and ordinances of the Gospel."[66] You see, it isn't Christ's work *alone* imputed to your account in Mormon theology that justifies you before God. It's Christ's work *plus* your obedience to the laws and ordinances of the gospel that justifies the Mormon! James Edward Talmadge's *The Articles of Faith: A Series of Lectures on the Principle Doctrines of the Church of Latter-day Saints* provides clear evidence of the habitual Mormon inclination to associate works with the justification of salvation. In Talmadge's lengthy commentary on Article 3 of The Articles of Faith, he quotes President John Taylor as saying

> [Christ] bore the weight of the sins of the whole world, not only of Adam, but of his posterity; and in doing that, opened the kingdom of heaven, not only to all believers and all who *obeyed the law of God*...and thus [they] participate, *according to their capacity, works and worth,* in the blessings of His atonement (italics mine).[67]

This is essentially identical to the Roman Catholic doctrine of justification as well, which has also clearly departed from the orthodox understanding of justification by faith alone in Christ alone. But in Catholicism, this departure from the orthodox understanding of justification is much more subtle and difficult to discern because the Catholic Church realizes the problem their theological position posits with the historical orthodox Christian view of justification and works hard to make it appear as if its doctrine is orthodox. Let me explain this subtlety briefly.

According to the Catechism of the Catholic Church, 'Our justification comes from the grace of God' (1996) and 'Justification is the *most excellent work of God's love* made manifest in Christ Jesus and granted by the Holy Spirit' (1994).

Now, on the surface of it, these appear to be very good quotes suggesting that there is no difference between the Catholic view of justification and the Christian view of justification. They both appear to be by God's sovereign grace alone. And yet, in the same document, point 2019 states: "Justification includes the remission of sins, *sanctification,* and the renewal of the inner man (italics mine)." [68] Catholic theology combines sanctification and justification together, making it nearly impossible to distinguish God's saving work in justification by faith alone in Christ alone as separate from our work in sanctification.

Point 2025 similarly verifies the difference between the Catholic view of justification and the Christian view: "We can have merit in God's sight only because of God's free plan to associate man with the work of his grace. Merit is to be ascribed in the first place to the grace of God, and secondly to man's collaboration. Man's merit is due to God." Merit for man's justification is in the first place subscribed to God's grace, but secondly to our cooperation with God.

One need only look a bit farther to understand how divergent the differences clearly are. The Council of Trent on Justification (1545–1563) is the Roman Catholic doctrinal response to Protestant doctrine. Trent is the foundational doctrine upon which the Catholic Church's theology is built. Canon IX states clearly that "if anyone says, that by faith *alone* the impious is justified; in such wise as to mean, that *nothing else is required to co-operate in order to the obtaining the grace of Justification,* and that it is not in any way necessary, that he be prepared and disposed by the movement of his own will; let him be anathema (italics mine)." Likewise, Canon XXIV states, "If anyone says, that the justice received is not preserved and also increased before God *through good works;* but that the said works are merely the fruits and signs of Justification obtained, but not a cause of the increase thereof; let him be anathema (italics mine)." Below is a brief summary of how the two views differ from the orthodox perspective.

The Roman Catholic View:

- Justification is by infusion
- Justification is based on inherent righteousness
- Justification is by faith plus works
- Justification is by grace plus merit
- Justification is on the basis of Christ's righteousness and my righteousness

The Historical Christian View:

- Justification is by imputation
- Justification is based upon an alien, extrinsic righteousness (Christ's)
- Justification is by faith alone, in Christ alone, by grace alone

This declaration of our righteousness is a positional righteousness, not an experiential righteousness. It is not an infused righteousness; it is an imputed righteousness.[69] God does not take His righteousness and put it into our human souls. He takes the righteousness of Christ and places all of His righteousness in our account. This is the righteousness of all Christians.

Orthodox and historical Christian morality, then, is not law keeping as a means to salvation, but law keeping out of gratitude to the Savior whose gift of righteousness made law keeping needless for our acceptance. Biblical righteousness is imputed, not earned, deserved or inherited. Christians strive to keep the law because we see that Christ's perfect life showed that only He could keep it perfectly. By grace, God imputed Christ's righteousness to sinners who were not able to keep the law. Not only did God graciously spare believing sinners from His holy wrath for not keeping the law perfectly, but He imputed to their account a righteousness that was completely foreign to them. And God passes to us the verdict that Christ's obedience merited perfect righteousness. It is because we know of God's graciousness to us that we walk in a way that respects and cherishes God's moral law.

To think that we can keep the moral law through our own efforts proves that we really do not understand its function in the first place. The function of the moral law was to multiply and aggravate sin in the human heart so that we might see it more clearly in ourselves, and turn to the only remedy for it: Christ the Savior. This is aptly illustrated, even in its use of archaic expression, in one section of John Bunyan's *The Pilgrim's Progress:*

> Then he took him by the hand, and led him into a very large parlor that was full of dust, because it was never swept; the which, after he had reviewed it a little while, the Interpreter called for a man to sweep. Now, when he began to sweep, the dust began so abundantly to fly about, that Christian had almost therewith been choked. Then said the Interpreter to a damsel that stood by, "Bring hither water, and sprinkle the room;" the which [sic], when she had done, it was swept and cleansed with pleasure.
>
> *Christian:* Then said Christian, What means this?

Interpreter: The Interpreter answered, This parlor is the heart of a man that was never sanctified by the sweet grace of the Gospel. The dust is his original sin, and inward corruptions, that have defiled the whole man. He that began to sweep at first, is the law; but she that brought water, and did sprinkle it, is the Gospel. Now whereas thou sawest, that so soon as the first began to sweep, the dust did so fly about that the room by him could not be cleansed, but that thou wast almost choked therewith; this is to show thee, that the law, instead of cleansing the heart (by its working) from sin, doth revive (Romans 7:9), put strength into (1 Corinthians 15:56), and increase [sin] in the soul (Romans 5:20), even as it doth discover and forbid it; for it doth not give power to subdue.

Again, as thou sawest the damsel sprinkle the room with water, upon which it was cleansed with pleasure, this is to show thee, that when the Gospel comes in the sweet and precious influences thereof to the heart, then, I say, even as thou sawest the damsel lay the dust by sprinkling the floor with water, so is sin vanquished and subdued, and the soul made clean, through the faith of it, and consequently fit for the King of glory to inhabit (John 15:3; Ephesians.5:26; Acts 15:9; Romans 16:25, 26).

ADOPTION

Adoption is another legal transaction whereby God makes us a part of His own family, giving to all who believe the privileges, benefits, and responsibilities that are attached to being a true son or daughter. Adoption as sons includes "the redemption of our bodies" (Romans 8:23), and is thus something hoped for as well as already possessed.

The Greek word for adoption appears only in biblical literature written by Paul. In Scripture, the word for adoption, *huiothesia* (*huio* = sons; *thesia* = to arrange as), occurs in the New Testament six times: in Romans 8:15, 19, 23; 9:4; Galatians 4:6; Ephesians 1:5.

In the N. T. it is used to denote a) that relationship which God was pleased to establish between himself and the

Israelites in preference to all other nations: (Romans 9:4). b) the nature and condition of the true disciples of Christ, who by receiving the Spirit of God into their souls become the sons of God (Romans 8:15; Gal. 4:5; Ephesians 1:5); it also includes the blessed state looked for in the future life after the visible return of Christ from heaven; hence, [it means], *to wait for adoption,* i.e., the consummate condition of the sons of God, which will render it evident that they are the sons of God (Romans 8:23, cf. Romans 8:19).[70]

Look at verses 4–5 in Ephesians chapter one. Before the very "throwing down" [foundation] of the world, we had been chosen in Christ, "picked out" to be holy and without blame before Him. In His love He predestined us, He "separated" us (marked us out with a boundary, appointed us) to adoption as sons by Jesus Christ, according to the good pleasure of His will. The process of our adoption as sons is begun in the past and continues into our future.

> As in Galatians and Ephesians, adoption is connected to the Spirit in Romans as well. It is those who are "led by the Spirit" who are sons, who have received the "spirit of sonship," not that of slavery (Romans 8:14–15). Again, the Spirit produces the cry "Abba!" and indicates by his presence the reality of the coming inheritance...the consummation of the adoption awaits the future, because the adoption as sons includes "the redemption of our bodies" (Romans 8:23). Thus adoption is something hoped for as well as already possessed. Adoption then is deliverance from the past (similar to regeneration and justification), a status and way of life in the present (walking by the Spirit, sanctification), and a hope for the future (salvation, resurrection).[71]

God does not adopt us because of our original, created relationship to Him as children who bear his image. Like the rest of the words affiliated with our salvation, adoption is another term that demonstrates that God freely granted His grace to believers to become his children. Scripture makes a clear distinction between "natural sons" and "adopted sons." An important distinction to remember is that Christ is *uniquely* the Son of God while believers are sons *and* heirs, neither by the uniqueness of our natural relationship, nor by our natural heritage of being created in the image of God. Before God enabled us to become "adopted" sons of His, and though created as the image of God, we were "natural" sons of His. In this natural relationship we conducted ourselves in the lusts of our flesh and mind and were by virtue of this natural relationship His children only in the sense that He created us; we become his spiritual children in adoption, without which we would be children of His wrath (Ephesians 2:3).

SANCTIFICATION

> Sanctification is a neglected priority in today's church everywhere and a fading glory in the evangelical world in particular. Today, the concern for holiness that was once so striking a mark of evangelical people is largely a thing of the past. To listen to the sermons and read the books we publish today, you would never know that once the highway of holiness was clearly marked out for Bible believers, and that ministers and people knew it well and spoke of it with authority and confidence.
>
> —J. I. Packer

SANCTIFICATION

First and foremost, sanctification is a continuation of our regeneration. God not only begins the Christian life with regeneration, he brings it to completion *through* the process of sanctification. Its completion is not *in* the sanctification; the process of us being set apart from sin to holiness is finally completed in the one-time act of glorification. Sanctification is defined as "to make holy, to set apart." It indicates both our spiritual status and the process by which our character is changed.

Our spiritual *status* before God is one that is bestowed upon us in that we have been set apart from sin by grace *positionally* once we have come to Christ. This is also called *definitive sanctification.* Definitive sanctification is conclusive, decisive, or final sanctification. It is seen as a completed act. It means that at the point of conversion (for lack of a better term), believers have been set free from sin's dominion in their lives because of Christ's work on our behalf, and we now *stand* sanctified in Christ as people who have been set apart from sin.

Yet while the dominion of sin is broken, there will be constant guerilla warfare until the believer is finally united with Christ. Some may question whether or not they have ever really trusted in Christ because they continually struggle with specific and problematic sins. The struggle itself is the very sign that God is indeed continuing to sanctify them.

One of the main ways we determine that sanctification is *definitive* or completed is by the use of the perfect tense in Greek, the tense of completed action. In several instances, the Greek perfect is used in reference to sanctification. The progress of the action has reached its culmination and the finished results are now in existence. It can have reference to the past action and the state that results from that action or only to the resulting state. Unlike the English perfect, which indicates a completed past action, Greek perfects indicate the continuation and present state of a completed past action. [72]

> To open their eyes, *in order* to turn *them* from darkness to light, and *from* the power of Satan to God, that they may receive forgiveness of sins and an inheritance among those who are sanctified by faith in Me.
>
> Acts 26:18

"To open," "to turn," and "to receive" in the original Greek language of Acts 26:18 are aorist infinitives that describe actions that happens at one point in time; the phrase "among those who are *sanctified* by faith in Me" describes action that is completed with continuing results because in Greek, sanctified is in the perfect tense. Note that Paul doesn't say among those who are *justified* by faith in Me. Justified is a one-time event as well. This particular use of sanctification is a completed act as a result of justification, so definitive sanctification in Christ is a for-all-time act that exists because we are justified (see also Acts 20:32).

> To the church of God which is at Corinth, to those who are sanctified in Christ Jesus, called *to be* saints, with all who in every place call on the name of Jesus Christ our Lord, both theirs and ours.
>
> 1 Corinthians 1:2

Note that they are called to be saints because they are sanctified (perfect participle) in Christ Jesus. As the sanctification is completed, so is the expectation of "saint-ness."

> But you do not continue to believe, because you are not of My sheep, as I said to you. My sheep are hearing My voice, and I continue knowing them, and they keep following Me. And I am giving them eternal life, and they shall never perish; neither shall anyone snatch them out of My hand. My Father, who has given (perfect tense) *them* to Me, is greater than all; and no one is able to snatch *them* out of My Father's hand. I and *My* Father are one.
>
> John 10:26–30

The Father is described as "having given" the sheep to the Son in past time. Their being given to the Son is a completed action, and the results of that action carry on into the future. They have been set aside as sheep. In the past the Father gave them to Him, and they continue to be His, and no one has the ability to snatch them out of the Father's hand.

The *process* of our changing character is called *progressive sanctification* and comes about by the continuous operation of the Holy Spirit, along with the believer's resolve and effort, to bring about increasing victory over sin's influence and increasing holiness and love. This changing in character is the growth within us in holiness that should gradually begin to follow conversion. Because this aspect of sanctification is not static, it is often referred to as our "progressive," ongoing sanctification, a sanctification that is advancing steadily by increments.

Our being declared righteous before God, our being adopted as sons because of our union with Christ, and our positional (definitive) sanctification are relative changes that take place *outside* of us in the will of God. Our changing character (progressive) sanctification happens *within* us as a result of what God has willed in us.

Note in 2 Thessalonians 2:13 that the believer was chosen "from the beginning for salvation *through* sanctification by the Spirit and belief in the truth." In other words, here we were chosen for salvation by God from the beginning through *the process* of sanctification. God does not justify believers without also sanctifying them.

There have been many throughout Christianity who have proposed that our sanctification will eventually be perfected by us in this life. Hoekema assures us that no perfection is possible in this life because all believing men live under sin and grace. There is a statement from the Reformation that applies here: "*Simul iustus et peccator*" (simultaneously just and sinner). We Christians are people who are sinful but declared righteous by God. First John 1:8 warns that "If we say that we have no sin, we deceive ourselves, and there is no truth in us." Yet 1 Peter 1:15 says, "But as He who called you is holy, you also be holy in all your conduct." Even the most faithful of saints struggle with sin to be like him in holiness.

> Sanctification does not allow any separation from ordinary practice nor does it admit of "consecration to some special use." The believer can never bask outwardly in his righteousness, if indeed there be any; he may never have a holier-than-thou attitude—he is rather to manifest a joy over the love and promises of God. Furthermore, on a practical note, the faithful should be far too busy with their own inner struggle to make outward declarations.[73]

If it's true that our justification (being made right before God) is entirely based on the imputation of Christ's righteousness to us by God and is not based upon any works we do, can we say with any real validity that we as Christians *ourselves* ever become "more righteous" in our sanctification? If we all have the same righteousness imputed to us, and we say theologically that "our" righteousness is not ours in the sense that it is "extrinsic, alien, or foreign" to us, do we ever become "more righteous"? It seems that Calvin was convinced we could not become more righteous when he wrote:

> The logical consequence of [the] doctrine of the imputation of the righteousness of Christ is that never, not even after the remission of our sins, are we really righteous. On the contrary, we have noted that the sanctification which accompanies justification, or at least begins with it, enables us to become precisely more and more aware of our sin.[74]

For Calvin, our sanctification doesn't amount to tallying up righteous deeds; it amounts to a greater awareness of our sin. The pressing question for believers is, "Is there anyone more righteous than the man who says he has *no* righteousness?" Or, better yet perhaps, can one *be* more righteous than admitting that he has no righteousness of his own? If we are nevertheless justified, that is because we have been grafted into Him and have received His righteousness.

A man cannot ever be more righteous than the righteousness that he possesses by faith in Christ because that is a perfect righteousness. And it belongs to him by faith alone. Our righteousness, the thing that makes us righteous before God, is not what we do; what makes us righteous is Christ's righteousness. That is why Reformed theologians are so adamant about making the distinction with regard to sanctification and justification. We are declared perfectly righteous because He is, and His righteousness is accounted to us when we believe. That is the true righteousness of every believer. That righteousness was never merited. It is not accounted to us ever because of anything that we do. I think the most righteous thing we can do is to realize that our righteousness comes from Christ. And that realization always comes on the heels of understanding that I have no righteousness inherent in me that makes me righteous before God.

Below is a quick, practical synopsis of the differences between justification and sanctification.

JUSTIFICATION

- Nature: relative change of status
- Order: precedes personal holiness
- State of Relationship to God: from condemnation to complete reconciliation
- Theological Form: a judicial act
- In Relation to Time: perfected at once in all believers
- Answers the Question: how do we gain a right standing with God?

SANCTIFICATION

- Nature: real change of the whole person
- Order: succeeds forensic justification
- State of Relationship to God: from impurity to growth in grace
- Theological Form: status conferred and process begun
- In Relation to Time: different degrees of advancement in different individuals
- Answers the Question: how are we conformed to Christ inwardly?

WHY THE CONFUSION BETWEEN JUSTIFICATION AND SANCTIFICATION?

Sanctification rightly follows justification and adoption. So while sanctification is distinct from justification, it is nevertheless a necessary adjunct. This means that no one who is justified remains unsanctified, and no one will be sanctified apart from prior justification. There has historically been real confusion between justification and sanctification in Catholicism, Mormonism, and many cultic groups, but these groups aren't the only ones who confuse the biblical doctrines of justification and sanctification. There are entire movements and denominations within evangelical Christianity, from the Vineyard Movement and the church growth movement to the political and social crusades, televangelism, the Promise Keepers movement, Billy Graham and Jerry Falwell, to Wheaton College presidents, all tending to combine justification and sanctification theologically and failing to maintain them as separate doctrines.

Charles Finney, the father of "make a decision for Christ" theology had the audacity to promulgate the utter rejection of this classic, historical, orthodox understanding of the doctrine of justification.

> The doctrine of imputed righteousness, or that Christ's obedience to the law was accounted as our obedience, is founded on a most false and nonsensical assumption." After all, Christ's righteousness "could do no more than justify himself. It can never be imputed to us...it was naturally impossible, then, for him to obey in our behalf." This "representing of the atonement as the ground of the sinner's justification" has been a sad occasion of stumbling to many.[75]

The most important thing we can do to be sanctified is to read and meditate on the Word of God. Sanctification is directly connected to the Word of God and to the indwelling Holy Spirit. The operation of the Holy Spirit brings the power of Christ to us by the reading of the Word. Therefore, man-made rules and techniques for increasing personal holiness from men like Finney are not only useless in bringing about true sanctification, but they are hindrances to it since they must obscure the primary means of sanctification, that is, the Word of God.

Our focus should be on the meaning of sanctification rather than on applications and practices to attain it. Some perfectionist schemes argue that only a few of God's people, spiritual elites, can attain the level of holiness expected by God. *But the promise of sin's broken dominion is for all Christians.* Our sinful nature is steadily weakened and diminished in "progressive sanctification." But the Bible expressly refers to all Christians as "saints" (Romans 1:7) since it is at our initial conversion, in definitive sanctification, that the dominion of sin is completely broken and every Christian is set apart from sin (1 Corinthians 6:11).

Sanctification is God acting on our behalf (definitive sanctification) and God acting in us (progressive sanctification) through specific means. Historically in church doctrine there has been no list of things that we *must do* to sanctify ourselves, and the many things that American evangelicals have claimed to be evil for us are not prohibited in the Scriptures. I would submit to you that even some seminaries are still trying to establish man-made rules to make us more sanctified such as not playing cards or not dancing or the like.

Sanctification extends to the entire person. There is no part of us that God leaves unsanctified. God not only sanctifies the soul, he sanctifies our minds, emotions, and wills as well. There is no radical dichotomy in our sanctification where God supposedly sanctifies the spiritual part of the Christian but leaves the rest of the person completely corrupted by Adam's fall. Since God indeed sanctifies the entire person, new birth and progressive sanctification inevitably manifest themselves in a cooperative effort with the grace of God. A. A. Hodge makes the point nicely:

> It must be remembered that while the subject is passive with respect to that divine act of grace whereby he is regenerated, after he is regenerated he cooperates with the Holy Ghost in the work of sanctification. The Holy Ghost gives the grace, and prompts and directs in its exercise, and the soul exercises it. Thus while definitive sanctification is a grace, it is also a duty; and the soul is both bound and encouraged to use with diligence, in dependence upon the Holy Spirit, all the means for its spiritual renovation, and to form those habits resisting evil and of right action in which sanctification so largely consists.[76]

The fruits of sanctification are good works because God has changed us in regeneration, as it were, from a bad tree that can only produce bad fruit into a good tree that can begin bearing good fruit. There is a corresponding change from someone completely unwilling and unable to cooperate into someone who does. By sanctifying the entire person, God continually works in us so that the full understanding of sanctification is that it is both the work of God and the work of man assisted by supernatural grace.

Here is an excellent synopsis to the topic of sanctification:

> I believe it is more true to Scripture to say that we who are in Christ are at various points on the pathway of sanctification. We experience neither total defeat nor total victory over sin. We are in Christ, but we need to grow up into Him more and more. We are indwelt by the Spirit, but we need to be more consistently filled with the Spirit. We have yielded ourselves to Christ as Lord, but we need to surrender more fully. We try to resist known sin, but we do not always succeed, and we are not always sure what is sinful and what is not. We continue to struggle against the "lusts of the flesh" in the strength of the Spirit, but we sometimes give in. We live a life of victory, but it is a qualified victory. We are not yet what we shall be. We are not yet totally like Christ (1 John 3:2). We live in the tension between the "already" and the "not yet." We are genuinely new persons but not yet totally new.[77]

PERSEVERANCE AND GLORIFICATION

> The perfection of Christ's work of salvation—from the reality of God's eternal decree, the deadness of man in sin, the effectiveness of His substitutionary death in behalf of the elect, to the application in time by the Spirit of God—is the sole and only basis of any consistent doctrine of perseverance or "eternal security."
>
> —James White

PERSEVERANCE

Someone has said that perseverance is defined as "this new life that is bestowed by irresistible grace and is lived out the rest of the regenerate person's life." Or to put it another way, true believers "can neither totally, nor finally fall away from a state of grace; but shall certainly persevere therein to the end, and be eternally saved."[78] They may fall into grievous sins from time to time and continue therein temporarily, but they will turn from sin once again to Christ.

But note also that this is also called "perseverance of the saints," not "preservation of the sinner." The perseverance to which Reformed theologians plead is perseverance *in holiness* to the end. Part of Robert Shaw's exposition of *The Westminster Confession* states:

> The certainty of the saints' perseverance affords no encouragement to any to neglect the means which God has appointed for their preservation. "Watch and pray," said our Savior, "that ye enter not into temptation." "Beware lest ye fall from your own steadfastness," said His apostle...God works in believers both to will and to do; but He requires them to do their part while He is doing this.[79]

The main reason for stating this element in the process of salvation is because there are many examples in the New Testament of false professions of faith as well as genuine ones:

1. In the Gospel of Matthew, Christ teaches about apparent receptions of the gospel message that appear to be false, where unconverted people, are at least temporarily involved with the kingdom of heaven (Matthew 13:4–9; 18–23; 24–30; 47–50).
2. There are also examples of false brethren: 2 Corinthians 11:26; Galatians 2:4; Jude 4; Matthew 7:22–23.
3. There are many warning passages to continue on *in the faith:* Romans 2:3–10; 11:22; 1 Corinthians 15:2; Colossians 1:23; Galatians 5:19–21; Mark 13:13; Hebrews 6:4–8; Matthew 10:22; 1 John 5:1.

True faith perseveres to the end through the trials and tribulations that accompany life. The element of *preservation* is equally important in the perseverance of the saints.

Theologians true to the doctrines of grace have historically maintained the importance of this continued preservation and perseverance in the faith. Of late, many things have been written to the contrary that suggest that Christians need not necessarily persevere in the faith to be saved.

Our perseverance is never dependent upon our own good works or our own ability to persevere, but rather, like all the definitions in the order of salvation, we are dependent on the grace of God. We never deserved that grace that saved us in the beginning, and there is nothing we could do to cause God to withdraw His grace from us. Yet at the same time, we remain faithful to God, in *His* strength, if for no other reason than because He is the author and source of our faith!

DENYING THE NECESSITY OF PERSEVERANCE

Let me describe to you how some theologians teach that we can actually remain *faithless,* that is, that there is no need to persevere in our faith, because, regardless of what we do *after* we once believed, God is still obligated to save us. In fact, the following example is a complete denial of the teaching of "perseverance of the saints."

In 2 Timothy 2:11–13, there is a faithful saying written by the Apostle Paul:

> For if we died with Him,
> We shall also live with Him.
> If we endure,
> We shall also reign with Him.
> If we deny Him,
> He also will deny us.
> If we are faithless,
> He remains faithful;
> He cannot deny Himself.

Note the pattern Paul has written. He makes a statement in the first sentence upon which the following sentence is conditioned. If the first statement is true, then the next statement is true. If we die, we shall live; if we endure, we shall reign; if we deny Him, He will deny us. Now, see if there is any difference to you when you read this if we write out the verbs with their appropriate Greek tenses, so as to clearly understand what was written:

1. For if we ourselves, in reality, died (to sin and the old, sinful self) with Christ when He died, we will, in reality, in the future, live with Him.

2. If we persevere under misfortunes and trials, holding fast to our faith, we will, in the future, reign with Him. If we, in our own interests, keep on disowning Him, He also will deny us at the end. [80]

3. If we continue on without faith, He is not faithless. It is impossible for Him to disown Himself.

Some scholars have taken verse 13, "If we are faithless, He remains faithful; He cannot deny Himself," to mean that a so-called believer in Jesus Christ can actually deny Christ continuously and yet God still promises to save that individual because God is incapable of denying Himself! It seems remarkable that a theologian would actually write that God must remain faithful in saving those who continuously deny Him.

There really are two problems here in this incorrect interpretation of the text in 2 Timothy 2:11–13. First, the New Testament teaches that faith is not a momentary decision for Jesus Christ! *Genuine* faith occurs in a moment's time, but it is a seed that, once germinated, lasts for the believer's entire life and into eternity. Genuine faith is not some flimsy "guess" at God born from the hearts of unregenerate men. Faith is an eternal gift from God to the hearts of sinful men that allows us to see the reality of the wonder of God's grace and the depravity of self.

This faulty understanding of the text in 2 Timothy suggests incorrectly that men somehow muster up faith from within themselves, which can therefore be subject to shallowness and failure. Furthermore, to imply that God would save someone for eternity based strictly on a one-time verbal acknowledgment that sprang from a spiritually dead, depraved heart, which cannot result in spiritual fruit, denies the clear biblical teaching that God has been working in the genuine believer's heart every step of the way from eternity past, through the moment he believed, and on into the believer's eternity. Like much of modern evangelicalism, this scholar's interpretation puts the weight of salvation on the momentary *decision* for Christ rather than upon the power of God to complete to the end of glorification what He started in regeneration.

Secondly, this faulty interpretation is simply illogical. Consider this question: If Paul really meant that someone could live a life of apparent faithlessness (on an ongoing basis) and *still* be secure in God's salvation, why would he then caution the believer to "be diligent to show yourself approved" two verses later (2 Timothy 2:15)? In other words, why would it be necessary to show ourselves approved when two verses earlier Paul actually meant, as this errant view suggests, that we can even stop believing in God and God must save us because He cannot deny Himself? If God will save us no matter what, why do we need to be cautioned to "show ourselves approved"?

And again, why would Paul write, "The Lord knows those who are His," and "Let everyone who names the name of Christ depart from iniquity" (2 Timothy 2:19) if God really meant that those who make a one-time verbal confession of faith but never bear fruit can stop believing and still be assured of salvation? Why even mention departing from iniquity if we are guaranteed salvation? Why should we bother to "show ourselves approved" if God accepts us even if we remain in total denial of Him, still thinking we can be saved?

Remarkably enough, the theologian quoted above would have us believe that Paul meant that the faithless are the ones that belong to the Lord! And what iniquity is worse than unbelief?[81] Paul clearly says that those who are believers must depart from iniquity, not "get saved" in spite of the iniquity of their faithlessness.

Surely it is nearly heretical to teach that the perseverance of the saint is not critical to salvation. Perseverance is the logical culmination of all that we have already said regarding God's work of salvation in us. It is God's work that regenerates us, changes our hearts, and brings us into union with Christ. If God is the author and finisher of our faith and it is by His grace that we become enabled to believe the gospel message, then it is also His power that enables our faith to grow and develop in our Savior Jesus Christ unto the end!

WHY BE "MORE DILIGENT"?

"Therefore, be even more diligent to make your calling and election sure, for if you do these things you will never stumble" (2 Peter 1:10). If you have been following along with my reasoning, this one sentence from 2 Peter may have made you want to ask, "If God does the calling of individual sinners to Himself and God chooses the elect to come to Him, why did Peter write 'be more diligent to make your calling and election sure'"? Is there anything about the calling and election of God that could ever be unsure if God is the one who is the source for all these things taking place in us? What could *we* do to make *sure* what God has done? And what could Peter mean when he says that "you will never stumble" (1:10) when everyone knows that Christians continue to stumble sometimes long after God has brought them to Himself?

This verse in 2 Peter is teaching us that the Christian walk is not all up to God. I had a professor in seminary who loved to say that the Greek word for *diligent* in 2 Peter 1:5 and 10 means "bust a gut." Another adequate translation is to "be earnest." Peter is saying, "Do these things earnestly, and you will never fail." If we add the qualities of virtue, knowledge, self-control, perseverance, godliness, brotherly kindness, and love to the faith that God has given us, Peter says three things will happen. And he poses these three items as two positive things and one negative thing.

The first *positive* postulate is that "if all these things (qualities) are ours and abound in us, we will neither be barren nor unfruitful in the knowledge of our Lord Jesus Christ" (1:8). Having these qualities present in the Christian life is the demonstration of the fruitfulness of the Spirit that regenerated you and made you alive to faith. Verse eight states the result of having these qualities. This knowledge you have received about Christ through the Spirit will not fail to produce fruit. A true, living faith is not a momentary human whim that merely says, "I made a decision for Christ," and I am therefore saved for all eternity based upon that decision. A true, living faith desires to persevere to the end.

The *negative* postulate is that if these qualities (virtue, knowledge, self-control, perseverance, godliness, brotherly kindness, and love) are not evident and nurtured in our lives after we come to faith, then we are "short sighted, even to blindness, forgetting that we have been purged of our old sins" (1:9). Literally, verse nine could be translated, "For in whom these things are not continuously present, he continues to be blind, being short sighted, taking forgetfulness of the cleansing of his past time sins." Genuine faith produces a faithful *lifestyle.* If these qualities are not present, then it is clear that you cannot even see back far enough to understand that your sins have been purged, which necessarily must change the outlook you have for the rest of your life.

Another *positive* postulate is "be even more diligent to make your calling and election sure, for if you do these things you will never stumble" (1:10). Because you don't want to act blindly and forget that your sins have been washed away, you will want to do everything in your power to make the demonstration of God's work in calling you and electing you just as firm as you can!

We're not talking about waltzing through the Christian life here, *acting* as if you were saved. Peter tells us to be diligent and sure. Don't be barren and unfruitful. Don't be shortsighted and forgetful, because you will want to make sure that "an entrance will be supplied to you abundantly into the everlasting kingdom of our Lord and Savior Jesus Christ" (1:11). And no one has the right to say they are sure unless they can demonstrate their calling and election by the fruits of a new life in Jesus Christ. In other words, Peter is speaking of the perseverance of the believer here in 2 Peter. The Christian life isn't just "believing in Jesus today and doing whatever I want tomorrow." It is persevering in genuine faith.

The ultimate end of perseverance is that the saints will one day be glorified in heaven. Peter couldn't have meant in verse 10 that we would never stumble along the way in our Christian walk or never see any failure. It would be particularly silly for *him* to have said such a thing, considering his own propensity for failure. Rather, it is clear that he meant that if we are diligent to do all of these things, then we will never fail to reach our final destination of being *glorified* in God's kingdom.

GLORIFICATION

Glory is an interesting biblical word. But it becomes a fascinating word when we realize that that is the end that God has in mind for those who were once rebellious sinners. *Glory* is a word that speaks of a characteristic that belongs to God alone. Its meaning carries with it the sense of "complete otherness." We Christians often think that glory is the limited idea of "splendor" or "illustriousness" depicting the light that emanates from God's person. But the essence of glory is far removed from a mere human understanding of light and majesty. Glory not only represents the character of God and Christ as being completely "other" than we are, but it is used to describe the reasons why the Father and Son do what they do here on earth as they interact with people.

In John 17, Christ speaks to the Father about glory. Christ, aware of His impending, brutal death on the cross, gives the Father permission to glorify Him in that death, so that in that death, the Son might glorify God in return (John 17:1, 4). But even more incomprehensible is Christ's desire that Christians behold Christ's glory that the Father gave Him (John 17:24). Glory belongs to Christ and the Father alone because when Christ completed all He set out to do here on earth, He completed the perfect eternal will of God, thereby bringing ultimate glory to him.

The word *glory* means "brightness, radiance, splendor."[82] Everything in heaven is said to have this splendor: the radiant bodies in the sky (1 Corinthians 15:40); the cherubim (Ezekiel 10:4; Hebrews 9:5); angels (Luke 2:9); and God (Exodus 24:17; 40:34; Numbers 14:10; Acts 7:2; 2 Thessalonians 1:9; 2 Peter 1:17). What is even more difficult to comprehend is that believers will one day be glorified as Christ was glorified prior to His incarnation. There is this sense in glorification of the culmination of all that God has designed for Christ and mankind being finally fulfilled by Christ and in us that bring to completion all that God has desired and set in motion from eternity past.

Like the other aspects of the order of salvation we have looked at, glorification is a gift from the Father to us and is the final completion of all that we have inherited as Christians. J. K. Grider, a professor of theology at Nazarene Theological Seminary in Missouri, wrote, "Glorification, therefore, is only for believers, and it consists of the redemption of the body. At that time 'this perishable' will put on 'the imperishable,' and 'this mortal,' (the body), will 'put on immortality' (1 Corinthians 15:53)."[83] Glorification, then, is synonymous with *immortality,* which is the "glorification" that believers will ultimately receive. We who believe must be glorified in order to live in eternity with Christ, and we participate in the radiance or glory of Christ (Colossians 3:4; 2 Thessalonians 2:14; 2 Timothy 2:10; John 17:22; 1 Peter 5:1).

The Old Testament refers to God as the glory of Israel. There is a wonderful passage in the book of Jeremiah where the prophet chastises the people of Israel for their failure to recognize God as *their* glory. Speaking to Israel as a nation through Jeremiah's words, God's first charge of their iniquity comes from their failure to see God's glory. They fail to see that His glory utterly differentiates Him from any other god.

In Jeremiah 2:9 God says through the words of Jeremiah, "Therefore I will bring charges against you, and against your children's children." The charge? God says, in effect, "Look at every other nation on the face of the earth and see if they have done such a thing with their false gods, as you, Israel, have done with the true God. No other nation has ever changed its idols, which are not even gods, for other gods! But you, My people, have changed your Glory for other gods that do not profit!"

Paul speaks of God's glory in terms of riches (Ephesians 1:18; 3:16) and might (Colossians 1:11). In Hebrews 1:3, the author expresses the importance of understanding the glory of God. Christ is a reflection of "the brightness of His glory and the express image of His person." The Greek word translated as "express image" is where we get the English word for *character.* Christ reflects the very character of our divine and glorious Father.

Glorification, in theological terms, for the believer is the complete and final perfection in holiness of the whole person, when God's people in body and spirit are conformed altogether to the image of the risen Christ. This will be a wonderful day for all believers in Jesus Christ. This hope for the future is based upon Scripture, which speaks of our becoming like Christ at His return (Romans 8:23–25, 29–30; 1 Thessalonians 5:23; 1 Corinthians 15:35–58; 1 John 3:2). To God be the glory!

PART 2

EMPOWERING THE SOVEREIGN GRACE OF GOD IN EVANGELISM

INTRODUCTION

Evangelism and theology for the most part go separate ways, and the result is great loss for both. When theology is not held on course by the demands of evangelistic communication, it grows abstract and speculative, wayward in method, theoretical in interest and irresponsible in stance. When evangelism is not fertilized, fed and controlled by theology, it becomes a stylized performance seeking its effect through manipulative skills rather than the power of vision and the force of truth. Both theology and evangelism are then, in one important sense, unreal, false to their own God-given nature; for all true theology has an evangelistic thrust, and all true evangelism is theology in action.

—J. I. Packer

The battle is much greater than simply out-performing our neighbors in kindliness. The battle has to do with propositional truth, with whether God the Creator has communicated his revelation to his creation, and whether we, his creation can know and recognize what he has communicated from what is counterfeit...If we believe and are convinced that what we say

> is true, then certainly we should be prepared not only to define it adequately but defend it passionately. Otherwise it is a truth not worthy of our time and energy, and certainly not worthy of our life's calling.[84]

The difficulty in challenging people to believe in the God of the Bible is that our ultimate hurdle is convincing them that what is written as revelation in the Bible comes to us as a propositional truth. Revelation comes to us as a statement subject to proof or disproof. The battle is much greater than simply being nicer than our friends and neighbors (even though I've heard somewhere that Christians are supposed to be the nicest people on earth!) or being better at outperforming them in kindliness or winning them to Jesus with overly simplistic platitudes. It's not about throwing people random, creative one-liners that reduce deep, theological issues to trivial statements in an attempt to avoid deep, theological discussion about serious issues.

Winning them to Christ or gaining their ear long enough for this propositional truth about what God has done so that the Truth can begin to "get" them, is difficult. You have to cover a lot of ground. No matter where you begin, it will always lead to other questions that need further clarification. "Getting" what God has done on our behalf means challenging them to reconsider and reevaluate all that they *thought* was previously true once they discover it no longer is! It's about convincing them of the most improbable of propositions: that the one, true God has really spoken to us in time in His Word and in His Son Jesus and has revealed truth that we would otherwise never have realized but for that revelation! The battle we have as Christians, theologians, and evangelists has to do with our putting forth as graciously as we can muster the proposition that the statements Scripture makes are subject to your proof or disproof. It simply will not do for you to ignore any longer whether the Bible reveals Truth that is over against all other truth claims which are necessarily utterly counterfeit if what the Bible reveals to be Truth *is* true. A good friend once wrote to me that he couldn't spend time reading the Bible because he was convinced that it was bunk! I said it was only bunk if it *wasn't* true. But that's why he needs to read it—reading it is the only way the proposal "gets" you.

Take the atheist, for example. Interestingly, my conversations with atheists almost always end up with them ultimately desiring to remove the theological veil from *my* eyes; they are convinced that as Christians we are blind and that we cannot comprehend that God doesn't exist. This is most fascinating in light of the fact that a cursory reading of the Bible clearly demonstrates that it is one's failure to believe this revealed, propositional truth that demonstrates that *they* are blind, having a veil over *their* eyes! They cannot even begin to get that truth without reading or hearing it.

The Apostle Paul is recorded telling Agrippa in Acts 26 about his account of coming to terms with his own failure to see this propositional truth. Paul's own testimony demonstrates that he was utterly convinced that his eyes were wide open to the truth prior to God opening them to his revelation. In Acts 26:5–11 he recalls:

> They knew me from the first, if they were willing to testify, that according to the strictest sect of our religion I lived a Pharisee. And now I stand and am judged for the hope of the promise made by God to our fathers. To this *promise* our twelve tribes, earnestly serving *God* night and day, hope to attain. For this hope's sake, King Agrippa, I am accused by the Jews. Why should it be thought incredible by you that God raises the dead? Indeed, I myself thought I must do many things contrary to the name of Jesus of Nazareth. This I also did in Jerusalem and many of the saints I shut up in prison, having received authority from the chief priests; and when they were put to death, I cast my vote against *them.* And I punished them often in every synagogue and compelled *them* to blaspheme; and being exceedingly enraged against them, I persecuted *them* even to foreign cities.

Paul was completely convinced that his persecution of the Church was justified and that all he had committed himself to being and believing was true, living as the strictest Pharisee persecuting Christians who had come to Christ. His conviction led him to do many things against God's promised Christ, the very One who was actually God's promise to the twelve tribes of Israel! On the one hand, Paul was the staunchest of servants to Israel's God as a faithful Jew who believed in the promises of God, yet in reality, his beliefs were completely in opposition to God's propositional truth that the Messiah had arrived in the person of Jesus Christ. Paul's blindness led him to persecute the one hope he was in reality living for! So far removed was Paul from God's truth that he cherished the shutting up of the saints in prison on the authority of the chief priests. He lived a religious, legalistic life, believing that he was doing everything in honor of God's promises to Israel, yet was completely unaware of his blindness that prevented him from doing what God really desired of him.

In his recollection of his Damascus-road experience, he says that God had sent him to the Gentiles "to open their eyes, *in order* to turn *them* from darkness to light, and *from* the power of Satan to God, that they may receive forgiveness of sins and an inheritance among those who are sanctified by faith in Me" (Acts 26:18).

How many of us today are theologically fit to handle the challenge of persuading and convincing ignorant men that they have their eyes closed regarding Truth? That there is a reality that the world has bought into that is fundamentally in opposition to Jesus Christ, the Savior of the world, and that failing to believe this revealed, propositional truth means that their eyes are not open? That their failure to recognize this propositional truth as Truth means that they are living in darkness and under the power of Satan? Their failure to address this propositional truth necessarily supposes that those who do not believe God's revelation have their senses ensnared. They are empirically bound, so to speak, so much so that they cannot, through any power of their own, see the truth.

Their failure to believe is evidence that they have been completely deceived.

This is the problem set before us. In one of the letters to the Corinthians, Paul teaches that "even if our gospel is veiled, it is veiled to those who are perishing, whose minds the god of this age [Satan] has blinded, who do not believe, lest the light of the gospel of the glory of Christ, who is the image of God, should shine on them." In a very real, spiritual sense, the very same gospel that has the power to save for eternity those who believe it is veiled to those who are perishing in unbelief, whose minds are blinded to the truth.

Knowing this, how can we not be as concerned as Richard Baxter in reaching the world with this propositional truth when he wrote:

> Alas! How few know how to deal with an ignorant, worldly man, for his conversion! To get within him and win upon him; to suit our speech to his condition and temper; to choose the most proper subjects, and follow them with a holy mixture of seriousness, and terror, and love and meekness, and evangelical allurement–oh! Who is fit for such a thing?...All these difficulties in ourselves should awaken us to holy resolution, preparation, and diligence.[85]

So perhaps the first consideration for us in terms of speaking to a world about this truth—a truth that they cannot yet see and do not yet believe—is, "How do we convince them that it really is as bad as the Bible is proposing?" What sound, practical, and theological evidence can we offer them that will incline them to consider their present condition in light of that proposition, including the way in which they have formulated their world view, in order to bring them along to believe that the only solution for the condition in which they live is to be smothered in the sovereign grace of God? What can we say that will encourage them to reconsider their point of view in terms that this truth is articulating?

IS EVERYTHING REALLY ALL THAT BAD?

The truth is a snare: you cannot have it, without being caught. You cannot have the truth in such a way that you catch it, but only in such a way that it catches you.

—Søren Kierkegaard

In Hieronymus Bosch's painting entitled *The Ship of Fools,* Bosch is imagining that the whole of mankind is represented as a small ship voyaging through the seas of time. Sadly, every one of the representatives is a fool. This is how we live, says Bosch—we eat, drink, flirt, cheat, play silly games, pursue unattainable objectives. Meanwhile, our ship drifts aimlessly, and we never reach the harbor. The fools are not the irreligious, since prominent among them are a monk and a nun, but rather, fools are all those who live "in stupidity." Bosch laughs, and it is a sad laugh. Which one of us has not sailed in the wretched discomfort of the ship of human folly? Eccentric and secret genius that he was, Bosch not only moved the heart but scandalized it into full awareness. The sinister and monstrous

> things that he brought forth are the hidden creatures of our inward self-love: he externalizes the ugliness within, and so his misshapen demons have an effect beyond curiosity. We feel a hateful kinship with them. *The Ship of Fools* is not about other people, it is about us.[86]

Did you notice that the writer did not suggest that we are at times merely foolish, but rather that we are fools? What is it that makes us fools? Is it that we do foolish things or is it that we are possessed by an unfathomable ignorance about the purpose and reason for living?

Biblically, a fool is a fascinating person, and the Hebrew language has several words for *fool.* The Arabic cognate of one Hebrew derivative, the word (kāsal), seems to have an original meaning of "'to be sluggish," referring to that which is thick, plump, or fat (BDB).'[87] Another source suggests that this word is from an Arabic word meaning "be thick," and therefore refers to someone who is "thick-brained" or "stupid."[88]

The words for *fool* imply a dullness and obstinate thinking process, with a propensity to make wrong choices. A fool in his folly is described as someone whose way of life is enticed by immature choices that eventually lead to his destruction and ruin. Folly is as far away from wisdom as light is from darkness. Wisdom is said to lead one into the brightness of the full day while folly leads one to the way that leads to darkness. The fool is unable to see the proper way to conduct himself as he makes his way through life. He cannot concentrate on what is right, yet somehow he seems to be convinced that he can obtain wisdom by purchasing it, while in reality he has no inclination for it.[89] As Bosch has accurately portrayed, the fool roams the seas of time, seeking the right way to go but misses it completely because he cannot escape from his life of folly.

Calvin condensed the theological problem as succinctly as anyone, I think:

> For there is no one who anticipates the Lord; but we [believers] are all, without exception, delivered by his free mercy from the deepest abyss of death, when there is no knowledge of him, no desire of serving him, in a word, no conviction of his truth
>
> (*Commentary on Romans,* 315).

Theologically, we are fools because we exist in a state of ignorance and darkness about God, a state likened in the Bible to existing in an abyss of spiritual death. Aren't Calvin and Bosch saying the same thing: though we are physically alive, we are all at the same time spiritually dead, living as fools who have no knowledge of God, no desire to serve Him, and no conviction of His truth in our lives?

The painting of *The Ship of Fools* and an old famous adage both capture in a magnificent way the reality of what it means to live life like a fool: "Eat, drink, and be merry, for tomorrow we die."

Bosch's painting depicts a fool's view of life: gluttony, drunkenness, and a reckless and irresponsible abandonment to pleasure simply for the sake of pleasure alone. It speaks to the reality that people live haphazardly in and for the moment only and for all the emptiness that can be gained in the mere pursuit of pleasure, with no thought toward the knowledge, service, or conviction of God's truth or attention to His providential hand in any part of life.

Ironically, the sentiment "eat, drink, and be merry, for tomorrow we die" was most likely first memorialized in the actions of a famous Assyrian king renowned for his effeminate characteristics. According to A. T. Robertson's *Word Pictures,* "At Anchiale near Tarsus is a statue of Sardanapalus with the inscription: 'Eat, drink, enjoy thyself. The rest is nothing.'"

Here you have the fool's entire motive for living. His ultimate purpose is to take from life what he can, to eat, drink, and enjoy all that he can; everything else matters not. There is no divine judgment, no eternity, and no consequence to any action worth mentioning or reflecting upon. There is just living, and all that really matters about it is our enjoyment of it.

Sardanapalus, whose actual identity remains a mystery, was believed to be the last of the Assyrian kings, dying in 626 BC. He was apparently notorious for his excessive wealth and sensuality. When Nineveh was attacked by the Medes, he emerged from his foolhardy stupor and sloth long enough to fight bravely, though in the end, in defeat, spurned his own advice about life, set fire to his palace, consuming himself and his court in flames. That action hardly seems consistent with one who purportedly held to such a reckless philosophy of abandonment to pleasure. Henry Howard wrote of him in "Of Sardanapalus' Dishonorable Life and Miserable Death."

> ...Who scarce the name of manhood did retain, Drenched in sloth and womanish delight. Feeble of spirit, impatient of pain, when he had lost his honor, and his right, (Proud time of wealth, in storms appalled with dread,) murdered himself, to show some manful deed.[90]

The motto "Eat, drink, and be merry, for tomorrow we die," memorialized by Sardanapalus and captivatingly elucidated in Bosch's painting, speaks to a spiritual condition manifested in the lives of more than just the glutton, sloth, and drunkard. "Eat, drink and be merry" taken by itself, and in the context that Bosch says we live in, speaks to a deep-seated, abysmal, and crippling spiritual blindness that is manifest in *every* human life. It speaks to the natural response to being aware only of the self only for the moment and living only as a fool with no thought or care for the providential hand of God in life.

The creeds of church history would have more accurately expressed this sentiment we have been examining in this way: "You eat, drink, and seek merriment alone like a fool because you're *already* dead."

Though we are ignorant of this truth until we are made alive, Scripture teaches that all men are physically born into a state of spiritual death and destined to live life as a fool.

MATTHEW 8:19–22

> Then a certain scribe came and said to Him, "Teacher, I will follow You wherever You go." And Jesus said to him, "Foxes have holes and birds of the air have nests, but the Son of Man has nowhere to lay His head. Then another of His disciples said to Him, "Lord, let me first go and bury my father." But Jesus said to him, "Follow Me, and let the dead bury their own dead."

These have always struck me as astonishing verses, but not because they speak to the urgency, priority, and difficulty of following Christ. One can hardly miss the amazing comment that Christ makes to a scribe weighing the value of a life of discipleship when He tells him to "let the dead bury their own dead." In a sense, He asks this scribe, "Are you spiritually alive?" "The sentence is an oxymoron, by which the burial of the dead is assigned to those who are spiritually dead...It also alludes to the goal and end of those who are spiritually dead—their last and highest aim here is to bury one another."[91]

Think of it. The immediate urgency and priority of those who are spiritually alive is to follow after God. It takes a higher precedence than burying a dead body, a task to be left to those who are spiritually dead! Spiritually dead people are dead in sin and dead to life while the spiritually alive get on with life by following after God! The obvious distinction being made is that those persons who follow Christ are spiritually alive as opposed to being dead!

LUKE 15:24, 32

> "For this my son was dead, and is alive again; he was lost and is found." And they began to be merry. "It was right that we should make merry and be glad, for your brother was dead and is alive again, and was lost and is found."

These verses occur within the context of the parable of the lost son. Jesus is telling a parable that depicts the Father's generosity and mercy exhibited in His receiving those who have gone astray and then returned to Him. The human father in this parable has two sons. One of them leaves the family and asks for his inheritance as he departs. The father gives it to him. That son proceeds to squander his inheritance, realizing finally that many of the swine that he has to feed are better fed than he himself! As a desperate resort he returns to his father and Luke records that the father "saw him and had compassion, and ran and fell on his neck and kissed him. And the son said to the father, 'Father, I have sinned against heaven and in your sight, and am no longer worthy to be called your son.'" In his great mercy, the father acknowledges that his son leaving him was a demonstration of spiritual death ("For your brother was dead," he explains to the elder son), but that coming back to the father in faith and repentance is a demonstration of spiritual life ("and is alive *again,* and was lost and is found"). Wandering and existing with no relationship to the Father is illustrative of a fool's life of folly.

EPHESIANS 2:1–5

> And you *He made alive,* who were dead in trespasses and sins, in which you once walked according to the course of this world, according to the prince of the power of the air, the spirit who now works in the sons of disobedience, among whom also we all once conducted ourselves in the lusts of our flesh, fulfilling the desires of the flesh and of the mind, and were by nature children of wrath, just as the others. But God, who is rich in mercy because of His great love with which He loved us, even when we were dead in trespasses, [He] made us alive together with Christ (by grace you have been saved). [92]

The theological import of these verses must not be overlooked. They describe as a theological truth that trespasses and sins have resulted in *all* people living in a state of spiritual death and being chronically bound to live life as a fool. All believers in Christ were in this state when God mercifully saved us. The extant powers that our trespasses and sins had over us that had kept us in this state of spiritual death required God's power, Spirit, and Word to free us from our captivity as fools. We *were always* (in the past, imperfect tense in Greek), by nature, children of wrath. We were always living in a state of spiritual death, bound to live life as a fool, unable to be anything other than our nature would allow us to be: fools, and consequently, sons of disobedience. Believers alone are liberated from the bondage of living as fools by virtue of Christ's victory; unbelievers are unable to conduct themselves in any other fashion than in accordance with the devil's God-opposing will. It is natural and customary for unbelievers to exist in this state of spiritual darkness and folly. Being in this state makes one a child of God's wrath.

This same truth is clarified in 2 Timothy 2:25–26:

> In humility correcting those who are in opposition, if God perhaps will grant them repentance, so that they may know the truth, and *that* they may come to their senses *and escape* the snare of the devil, having been taken captive by him to *do* his will.

Note also that the purpose of God granting them repentance is so that they might come to their senses. In their natural state of spiritual darkness and folly, men are not *in their senses!* If they were, they would know the truth of their spiritual condition, enlightening and enabling them to escape the snare of the devil, who has taken them captive.

Worse yet, this state that men exist in is not one that they can will themselves out of. The language Paul uses is that men are in a finished or completed state of folly and darkness (*having been taken captive* is perfect tense in Greek). They are neither able nor interested in rescuing themselves because they have not yet recognized the problem caused by their folly and spiritual darkness;

they wouldn't know that there was a problem, or that it was fixable, until it was fixed!

The unregenerate have no hunger for following after Christ. They may talk a good game at times, use vocabulary that sounds "spiritual," speckled with a smattering of spiritual buzz words, and muster up all kinds of reasons why the truth of Scripture does not apply to them *individually.* But the reality is that "they see the Bread of Life as loathsome until God grants them repentance. They drink iniquity greedily like water (Job 15:16), but the water of life does not appeal to them...The will of this natural man is totally depraved. Without regeneration, the sinner cannot will or even *will to will* spiritual good."[93] He does not receive spiritual things because he *cannot* know them (1 Corinthians 2:14). The carnal mind of the natural man living in an abyss of spiritual darkness and folly is enmity (hostility) against God. The carnal mind cannot be subject to the law of God nor does it desire to be (Romans 8:7).

Finally, Paul writes in 2 Timothy 2:26 that the spiritually dead have been taken captive by him (the devil) to do *God's* will.[94] Verses like this serve as an appropriate reminder that all of our theology stems from and is built upon a proper understanding of who our sovereign God is.

God is a dynamic, active, forceful, willful, intentional, governing God. This means that in keeping with a proper understanding of how God operates in His universe, we are to remember that the origin of faith is found in God's action (as is everything else) and not in human effort. The life of faith and the life of the church are not found first in the decisions of the individuals or the community, but in the action and counsel of God. The spiritually dead who live in an abyss of darkness and folly do not just sort of finally "get it" on their own. They don't just wake up one morning and flick on the light switch of spiritual life.

Spiritual darkness, unbelief, and a fool's commitment to folly then are all rooted in the will of God. You cannot ignore this truth in your attempts to share the gospel with unbelievers.

Consequently, those who choose not to believe God's truth are not merely mistaken; they have not merely made an intellectual error in judgment; they are wrong. They cannot be right about anything else they do or believe if, at the very core of their belief system and all they are convinced about and motivated by, is that God is not true. The focus of the propositional truth we have been talking about is that God Himself is ultimate reality. To be separated from God is to be separated from the truth itself. To be separated from truth or God is to be mired in spiritual darkness, falsehood, and corruption; it is to live life as a fool without discernment or direction. It means that all of our actions that proceed from this mindset have hanging about them the stench of death and futility.

Living life apart from any consideration of God with abandonment to utter worldliness is a spiritual and religious matter. In the book of Ecclesiastes, this abandonment to worldliness is the unbelieving person's *alternative* to God. The world is the home of his alternative allegiance; it is what he offers himself to instead of God. It provides meaning to him, albeit superficial and counterfeit meaning when viewed alongside this revelation; it is "meaning" bereft of truth. James 4:4 speaks boldly to this worldly commitment unbelievers have: "Do you not know that friendship with the world is enmity with God? Whoever therefore wants to be a friend of the world makes himself an enemy of God."

But don't confuse the world's motives with motives that are foundational to living with a view to propositional truth. The unbelieving world's motivation is to live life as if there were no such animal as Truth. A Christian worldview demands that we live life fully! It demands that at the center of our life we see life as graciously coming from God. This challenge is repeated to us numerous times in the book of Ecclesiastes.

> There is nothing better for a man *than* that he should eat and drink, and *that* his soul should enjoy good in his labor. This also I saw was from the hand of God.
>
> Ecclesiastes 2:24

And I know that *there* is nothing better for them than to rejoice, and to do good in their lives, and also that every man should eat and drink and enjoy the good of all his labor—it is the gift of God.

Ecclesiastes 3:12–13

Here is what I have seen: *It is* good and fitting *for one* to eat and drink, and to enjoy the good of all his labor in which he toils under the sun all the days of his life which God gives him; for it is his heritage.

Ecclesiastes 5:18

So I commended enjoyment, because a man has nothing better under the sun than to eat, drink and be merry; for this will remain with him in his labor *for* the days of his life which God gives him under the sun.

Ecclesiastes 8:15

Go, eat your bread with joy, and drink your wine with a merry heart, for God has already accepted your works.

Ecclesiastes 9:7

How do these verses penned in great wisdom, albeit from a biblical book that also seems to subscribe to an apparently deep sense of philosophical despair in grasping the meaning to life, differ from this common colloquial adage we have been considering: "Let us eat, drink, and be merry, for tomorrow we die"?

Here is the difference: Our Christian life is to be a thing of great joy that arises out of the truth that God Himself has initiated our awakening and rescued us from our abyss of spiritual blindness, folly and death; He has rescued us from a foolishness that motivated us to live as if there were no truth to guide us. Life is not intended to be a Godless, reckless, and haphazard pursuit that seeks only to "eat, drink, and be merry" at every opportunity.

It is, rather, to be a deep-seated, joyous experience tempered and overshadowed by judgment and the mysterious providence of God. One of the ways we put our praise into action is to *be* thankful to our providential God for all that He has provided! Live life in the truth, being thankful for the life He has given you even in the midst of the mysterious providences, providences that at times may even bring a desire to despair them as unfair and insoluble mysteries. The verses penned in Ecclesiastes are to be understood in combination with an immoveable faith in the sovereign *goodness* of God despite our frequent failure to interpret all things in the light of that goodness.

> I believe a prejudice has been created against the [theological] system of Ecclesiastes...by the repeated occurrence of such words as "eat and drink," "mirth," "be merry"; and [many] have felt that its philosophy can be summed up in the saying, "Let us eat and drink, for tomorrow we die'...[but] the phrase "eat and drink" is [the author's] regular formula to express not only what is sensuous, but all appreciation of what life brings. This... becomes indubitable where the expression "eat and drink" is applied to riches and to labor, and even to honor...There is throughout [Ecclesiastes] no note of abandonment to the revel, but the thought is always of simple satisfaction with the play of life: and this is what the Preacher considers the special gift of God...[the] one duty of life is happiness, and that nothing in religion can be higher than praise.[95]

The spiritual life that has God as its foundation and reason for everything doesn't prohibit the enjoyment of life one bit! Rather, it necessitates, enables, motivates, and encourages true and meaningful enjoyment! It relishes our God-given life in light of our being rescued from the alternative. And that enjoyment and heartfelt celebration in Him as the provider of all things is what the Giver of Life expects from us as our way of thanking Him! Our celebration in all of life is the recognition that all that has been given to us is from the hand of God. Abandoning ourselves to *this* truth pleases Him because it always leads to our praise and thankfulness *to Him* for His providential provision.

What the Bible prohibits and what is profoundly misunderstood by a world that cannot see the reality of God, is the reckless and misguided revelry of the fool who cherishes nothing except his own fulfillment and momentary satisfaction simply for the sake of satisfaction itself. Living with a view to this provisional truth prohibits the kind of spiritually blind celebration one exhibits while a passenger on the ship of fools. And because we cannot know through our experiences what God is ultimately doing providentially, the only reliable solution for everyone living in this world is to begin to recognize that God is the Giver of Life and that the enjoyment we have for life begins and ends with Him and all that He has provided. That is how we live a life thanking a providential God. His reality is our motivation for celebration and praise. Without Him we wander aimlessly on the ship of fools.

HOW DO WE FORMULATE CORRECT THINKING ABOUT GOD?

> Theology's critical task can be greatly disillusioning to persons who attach strong emotional commitments to inadequate or false interpretations of biblical texts or who center their devotional lives on songs and choruses or around teachings of television evangelists that turn out under examination to be misleading if not downright heretical. The theologian that brings these things to light is not often thanked for it!
>
> —Stanley Grenz and Roger Olsen

In an e-mail conversation with an associate at work, I once wrote: "Historically, the church has maintained that the central trait to God's character has been His holiness." I think that many Reformed Christians, myself included, like the idea of some single, dominant attribute that serves as an umbrella for God's other attributes. I had always thought that the one great attribute that defines and directs the other attributes is God's holiness. My friend in the office wanted it to be His love.

Many Christians tend to prefer that either God's grace or His love or His mercy or His holiness be the central character of God, supposedly in order to manage some other attribute or characteristic that they can't quite seem to fit into their "God package" in a logical way.

For example, many Christians believe that God equally loves every individual in the world eternally (from their understanding of John 3:16) and that He desires to save all men (from their understanding of 1 Timothy 2:4). How do we include within our understanding of the person of God another scriptural teaching that the Lord sent Saul on a mission to "utterly destroy the sinners, the Amalekites, and fight against them until they are consumed" (1 Samuel 15:18)? Is the destruction of the Amalekites a demonstration of His eternal love for them? Is this how the God who loves every individual equally treats a group of people He also desires to save? Can God save some people eternally and chose to utterly destroy certain other groups of people and still be a God who loves everyone? How do we logically package the frequently heard Christian point of view that God loves all the people of the world eternally and desires to save them all, even though He chooses to exterminate some of them?

Early on in my theological processing, when I had subjected all of God's characteristics under the one umbrella of "holiness," I did that to logically defend how God could both love some sinners in Christ and justly condemn other sinners in their sin apart from Christ, even though that superficial umbrella is something that I forced upon my theology that isn't clearly a scriptural premise.

My friend at work, on the other hand, denied that God is holy (or just and righteous) *in order to maintain* her conviction that God *only* possesses an all-pervading love or mercy for people because the *idea* that God could be loving and wrathful and would send people to hell for eternity is outside the bounds of her definition of a loving God. And what we were both doing was essentially robbing God of the glory that is due Him. God deserves glory because He is both wrathful *and* loving. He deserves glory not only because He is righteous and just in His condemnation of sin, but because He is merciful in saving some sinners and wrathful in punishing others.

To completely deny that Scripture teaches that God is wrathful because one prefers to think that the love of God bears no wrath toward anyone doesn't get us any closer to obtaining a biblical understanding of who He really is. All we wind up doing in that scenario is denying the existence of a *particular* characteristic so that it will be easier for us to have God be the way we want Him to be.

Robert Reymond, a Reformed theologian, has helped me change my perspective on this by writing:

> It is precisely in the sum total of His attributes that His essence as God finds expression...sometimes the effort is made to isolate out of the sum total of God's nature some "primary" attribute which is then said to constitute His "being" or "essence"—a *substantia* which "stands under" and unites all other varied and multiple "secondary" attributes in one unified entity...The Bible suggests the identification of God's essence with all of His attributes...*God's glory is the sum total of all of His attributes as well as any one of His attributes.* For the creature to deny Him any one of His attributes is to attack the very glory of God and to deny Him that without which He would no longer be God. Or to ascribe to Him any attribute which He himself does not expressly claim to have, which ascription can only cancel out some attribute which He does claim to have, is again to represent Him as something less than He is and thus to attack His glory.[96]

I clarified for my friend at work that Scripture does teach that God both loves the world (John 3:16) and is wrathful toward the people in it (John 3:36). One's theology needs to account for both of those characteristics. We cannot decide that we won't tolerate the wrath of God because that doesn't fit into our idea of a loving God.

My friend responded by saying, "I'll have to check, but I don't think my Bible has that translation [of John 3:36] which includes the wrath part. There is a verse that I ran across last night that says something like God causes the rain and sun both to fall on the just and unjust alike, which suggests to me that God doesn't make such distinctions."

Here we get a deeper glimpse into the gist of the problem. Rather than deal with how we can understand God in totality as He says that He is and glorify Him for *all* of His attributes and characteristics, including love and wrath, mercy and justice, we often fail to face the theological difficulty of believing in a God that loves without distinction, yet is also distinctly wrathful toward some. We somehow find more comfort and convenience in ignoring some aspect of God's character while we appeal to another aspect as more closely representing our view of the true character of God. And just as it is wrong to ignore the wrath of God because we prefer to think of God as a loving God who demonstrates no wrath of any kind, it is equally wrong, for example, for Christians to publicly decry homosexuality on the basis that God's love for individuals is always trumped by his hatred for their actions.

I couldn't help but add my thoughts to the way my friend continued to reason about this issue in her e-mail letter:

She continued: "Jesus taught us to pray, saying 'Our Father,' which suggests that Jesus is telling us that God is everyone's Father. What father would willingly and irrevocably send his child to suffer in hell for all eternity?"

My co-worker failed to ask critical questions and think systematically about what Scripture is teaching. First of all, it would be more correct to say that Jesus taught His *disciples* to pray this prayer. In context, that is who He is addressing. When my friend says "us," why does she assume that Christ is speaking to someone other than his disciples? This prayer and its contents are applicable to believers only.

Furthermore, to understand the question about God being everyone's Father, we only need to ask one other question: "Does Scripture make any distinctions about God's Fatherhood?" The answer is yes. Unbelievers are "sons of disobedience" (Ephesians 2:2). Jesus chastises the unbelieving Pharisees in John 8:44 by labeling them as people who "are of your father the devil." Only people who believe in Christ as their Savior are God's children in the biblical, spiritual sense. For many people it is easier and more convenient to simply think that because the God of heaven is a loving God and everyone's Father, He would not willingly and irrevocably send His child to suffer in hell for all eternity. It is often easier to deny God the attribute of wrath rather than struggle with how to deal with understanding Him as both loving and wrathful as the Bible actually describes Him.

She added, "I am not suggesting that everyone can do as they please and not expect consequences, only that the consequences are just that, and not punishment."

Again, we simply need to ask if the Bible ever describes the consequences that come with choices as punishment. Yes. For instance, the consequence of a life of unbelief is separation from God for eternity. That separation is both an eternal consequence and an eternal punishment. It is true that God also chastises those who are genuinely His children, not as punishment, but to discipline them and grow them up to maturity. But to believe that God will *never* punish anyone because all people are His children or because He loves them too deeply is simply wishful thinking that is outside the bounds of God's own revelation about Himself in the Bible. Again, a proper response to her statement would require us to reevaluate what Scripture teaches about whom God's children really are and on what basis they become His children, and then differentiate what Scripture teaches about consequences and punishment. To simply write off the problem entirely by suggesting that God *never* punishes anyone is robbing God of one of His characteristics that make Him the sovereign God of all glory.

She continued by asking, "As a parent, wouldn't you be there, holding out your hand, hoping that your child would turn to you and ask for your help? And if it was within your means, wouldn't you give it?"

Do you see how difficult it is to think accurately about God? My friend is clearly thinking, *It must certainly be within God's means to not punish people for eternity. After all, he is a loving God, and you'd do all you could do to help your child.* And it *is* within God's means to help. He's the Savior! But the full revelation about God is that He only saves those who believe in Him. The means of his help is to save those who believe. God will do all he needs to do to help and to save His believing children. And God will certainly do more than any human would do by saving His believing children from the spiritual consequences of their own sin.

Furthermore, she asked, "Even though your child had screwed up so bad [sic], perhaps even with eyes open to the fact that it was wrong; and even if what he had done had ticked you off, [wouldn't you give him help if he needed it]? I may be putting human character into God, but God made man in his image. If humans are capable of that kind of love, wouldn't God's love be that much greater, that [much more] perfect? There may not be a verse that says that point blank, but to my eyes, it is everywhere inferred."

The Bible clearly teaches that God's love is perfect and greater than any human love, and therefore, God would do even more than *you* would do to save someone. And we all know that we as human parents would do anything we could to save one of our children! From a human perspective, my friend is absolutely correct.

But that doesn't mean that that is necessarily the way that God would do something! If our preconceived notion of God says God *so* loves the world that He *can't* also be a God of wrath, we have robbed Him of the glory that is due His name. We cannot say that because *we* might not do something like that, God wouldn't either.

It may be easier and more comforting to believe that God is just like we are and would respond even more appropriately than we could in saving our children, but is that ultimately believing in who God is? Have we settled for believing in our own ideal version of God and not the real God because we have neglected to wrestle with the biblical revelation that God is both wrathful and loving at the same time?

How can we think correctly about God without our thinking becoming a mass of confusing and chaotic suppositions? How do we reason through the issue of just what this God is really like in His love and wrath, being fair to what Scripture teaches? How do we live with the biblical revelation of these two seeming dichotomies, love and wrath, together? The world and much of the church cannot and will not make any distinctions about God and His love, as is demonstrated in the e-mail conversation above. To most of the world, it is enough to acknowledge that God loves. We don't want to delve into anything deeper. In spite of the way the Bible describes the complexity of God's character, all we seem to want to believe is that anyone who wants to can crawl up into His lap whenever he or she wants to and just sit there and hold God's hand. What we ultimately fail to consider is that believing the wrong thing about God isn't too far from *not* believing in Him at all.

HOW SHALL WE THINK ABOUT THE PROBLEM?

Let me begin to sort this issue out by helping you think through a couple of statements:

1. Wrath cannot be unfair because God isn't unjust. Every person receives one of two things from God: justice or mercy. No one receives injustice.

Many people wrongly assume that God cannot be wrathful because that would make Him unjust. At its core, that reasoning is faulty on many levels. Sin is about inheritance. Being humans born of Adam means we cannot help but be sinners. We aren't sinners *when* we sin; we are sinners because we have inherited a sinful nature. God cannot be unfair or unjust. If he were either, he wouldn't be God any longer. It is not unfair for God to be wrathful because wrath is as much a part of His perfect character as justice is. No one receives injustice from God. He or she receives either mercy in forgiveness or justice in righteous condemnation for his or her sin from a perfect and holy God. Both forgiveness and mercy are part of God's perfect character. And so are wrath and hatred toward sin.

2. When asked on his deathbed if he knew God would forgive his sins, Heinrich Heine, a German poet and journalist, said, "Of course God will forgive me; that's His job."

Anymore it seems we have created God in our own minds rather than seek to understand Him as he has revealed Himself. We have created for ourselves a God who has no other purpose, motive, or reason for existence than to simply be forgiving and loving to the degree which we dictate and at *our* whim. We want God to be our genie. We fail often to ponder that while it is true that God forgives, it is not true that God forgives everyone under any circumstance. Nor is it true that when God does forgive he does so because He sees something forgivable in that person. In fact, it *would be* unfair for God to forgive because he found something forgivable in some but not in others. It is not God's *job* to forgive everyone equally under the parameters *we* set out for Him. It is God's nature to forgive those whom He chooses to forgive, but those he forgives are not forgiven due to something in them, but rather because of something in Him. He chooses to forgive those who believe in Christ as the Savior just like he chooses to be wrathful toward those who choose to reject Christ.

3. God loves and God is wrathful. But God never loves any unbeliever so much that His eternal wrath will not be poured out on them if they remain in unbelief.

This is a very biblical way of balancing this problem. It allows for both the wrath and love of God while not allowing either characteristic to create an improper balance in our understanding of the character of God. Both the love and wrath of God need to be kept in balance at all times when we speak about who He is. We will see that Christ's crucifixion was a result of both the wrath and love of God. God never loves any unbeliever so much that His wrath will not be poured out on him if he remains in his unbelief.

4. "God is our enemy until He is reconciled to us through Christ" (Calvin).

Rather than talking about how much God loves and desires to save every single person, we should be making it clear that the unforgiven sinner stands under God's curse in his unbelief. While he remains an unbeliever, "the wrath of God abides (or rests) on him" (John 3:36). God is our enemy until we are reconciled to Him through Christ. When it is stated that "Christ redeemed us from the curse of the law, having become a curse for us" (Galatians 3:13), not only is it implied that we were "the children of wrath" (Ephesians 2:3) and under God's curse, but it is also understood that "Christ was made a curse for *us* [who believe]." Christ became the object of divine wrath for believers, not for everyone. This is certainly the point in Romans 5. As Christians, we should be clarifying that it is in Christ that God makes the distinction about wrath and love for every person. Whether God loves or is wrathful is always and forever about one's relationship to Christ.

IS THERE A METHOD TO THE MADNESS?

Being a theologian requires that you become dissatisfied with your present level of understanding. You must desire to deepen your comprehension of the Christian faith and be committed to growing toward mature thinking about God, yourself, and the world. This dissatisfaction includes a healthy discontent with folk theology—the all-too common patchwork of unexamined clichés, slogans, stories, and half-baked notions about God that forms the thinking of many Christians today. And you must find unsatisfying the possibility of remaining at the level of accepting by sheer blind faith whatever you have been taught by your own Christian subculture. You must have such a strong desire to grow in a deepened faith that you are willing to question widely propagated yet questionable ideas and beliefs in the light of the gospel.

—Stanley Grenz and Roger Olsen

GETTING AROUND ALL THE CLICHÉS

At various times over the years I have heard pastors use some of the lamest and stalest clichés from the pulpit. Here are three examples of what should never be said from the pulpit because of the kind of confusion they tend to create when they are mentioned without clarification:

1. "God cannot love you anymore than He loves you right now."
2. "God loves everyone unconditionally."
3. "We know God wants Saddam Hussein (substitute any name here) to be saved because God loves everyone."

The problem isn't just that unbelievers are confused about the wrath and love of God. Christian pastors and teachers are also confused and add to the confusion when they fail to clarify particulars. All three of these platitudes as they are stated are troublesome theologically because they fail at a fundamental level to make any kind of distinctions about God's love. More importantly, they fail to make any theological distinction between belief in Christ and rejection of Christ as the foundation for God's love. Making statements like these from the pulpit (in particular) without any kind of contextual clarification whatsoever are juvenile and irresponsible. We as Christians have to hold our pastors and teachers accountable to making distinctions about God's love because Scripture does.

Nobody knows if God loves Saddam Hussein in a saving, eternal, or elective way until he knows that Saddam Hussein is reconciled to God in Christ! God's saving, elective love is entirely related to one's relationship to Christ. God is our enemy until he is reconciled to us through Christ. Nobody knows if God desires Saddam Hussein to be saved until he comes to saving faith in Christ! If our salvation is in Christ, how can we say that God wants Saddam Hussein saved if he remains outside of a saving relationship to Christ?

Because Scripture teaches that God loves does not necessarily mean that He loves everyone in the same way or that he is even in the process of bringing someone to Christ.

Statements like the three made above are false when applied with a huge brushstroke for those who don't believe the gospel. What could be worse than having an unbeliever sitting in the pew one Sunday, hardened in his rebellion to God's Word, rejecting Christ and living his life as a fool and as if God didn't matter one whit, only to hear some pastor babble this empty platitude, "God cannot love you any more than He loves you right now." One's natural reaction in hearing that would most likely be, "Well, I guess I don't need to believe in Jesus or change anything I am doing then if He can't love me anymore than he loves me right now, do I?"

The fact of the matter is that God *can* love you more than He loves you right now. It all depends on what you mean when you say, "God loves you." He can love you *forever* with a sovereign saving, gracious, forgiving, and elective love when you believe in Christ. And an eternal, saving love *is* more than a temporal, providential care God shows toward the good and the wicked alike who do not believe in Christ. If people think they can go on in their unbelief and rebellion and still have Him love them *unconditionally*, they are dead wrong, and the person who tells them that is either ignorant or a liar. And any pastor that implies that from the pulpit *without clarification* should receive the strongest possible rebuke. And now, we have become so careless in our thinking and biased in our theology that we have taken what is simply not true and made it the very *heart* of the gospel!

THERE ARE FIVE WAYS THE BIBLE DIFFERENTIATES GOD'S LOVE

Most often, when Christians speak about God's love, we fail to differentiate between God loving someone and God wanting to save someone. God "loving" and God "saving" are used almost interchangeably by Christians. There are five ways God demonstrates love toward people in this world, and we need to understand those distinctions clearly as we speak to people.[97]

1. *The particular love of the Father for the Son, and the Son for the Father*

God the Father loves Jesus: John 3:35; 5:20; Ephesians 1:6; Luke 3:22; and Jesus loves the Father: John 14:31. This inter-Trinitarian love has existed between the Father and Son from all eternity. There has never been a time that the Father has not loved Jesus and Jesus has not loved the Father. But this mutual love is *never* in terms of God *saving* the Son. This particular love of the Father for the Son is bound up in Christ's work of redemption for sinners. Christ is God's Beloved because he saves those God chose from eternity past. But the love the Father has for the Son is never a redemptive love. It is important to clarify that not every kind of love that the Father has, or that Jesus the Son has for the Father, is a redemptive, saving love.

2. *God's providential love over all that he has made*

My friend from work used a passage that spoke of God's providential care to argue that God makes no distinctions about whom He loves. She argued that Matthew 5:45, "for He makes His sun rise on the evil and on the good, and sends rain on the just and the unjust," means that God doesn't make any distinction between the just and the unjust; He simply loves them all. And in one sense, he does care for them all providentially and without distinction, but he also loves some, saving them *with* distinction. The fact that He loves His creation *providentially* doesn't mean that He therefore loves it *savingly.* All that He made, He pronounced "good" before sin entered the world. It is plainly taught in Scripture in many locations that God is a loving creator and is benevolent in all of His provisions toward His creation, whether or not that benevolence means He provides *us* with our daily needs or provides the *lion* who hauls down an antelope for its food or provides the *birds* of the air their food (Psalm 136:25; 145:15–16; Acts 14:17; 17:25–28; Matthew 6:25–34).

Robert Reymond writes:

> God's wise and kind providential care, benefiting the heathen physically and materially as it does and witnessing thereby to God's presence among them ultimately serves redemptive ends, and according to Romans 1:18–23, also renders men "defenseless" when they fail to acknowledge Him as God and to worship Him...In sum, God's "ordinary" works of providence disclose to men, whether they acknowledge it or not, that they are not ruled by chance or by fate but by the God who finally "lays bear [sic] his purposes of providence in the incarnation of his Son."[98]

All of God's providence toward the world He created falls under the theological notion of "common grace." But simply because God is said to provide rain and sun for the wicked through His common grace, there is no indication that this is akin to a desire to save them. Even in Job 21:4–16, God provides in a loving, providential way for the wicked that rebel against Him. Asaph argues in Psalm 73 that God is even long suffering toward the wicked, holding out His wrath against their wickedness. But the rest of Scripture urges the wicked to repent and turn to God, lest they ultimately find themselves under the eternal wrath of God.

3. *God's salvific stance toward his fallen world*

I think that John 3:16 is the most overrated and misunderstood verse in Scripture. There is a reason why Carson states that John 3:16 refers to God taking a loving *stance* toward the world in *The*

Difficult Doctrine of the Love of God. Saying that God takes a loving *stance* toward the world clarifies that God loves a wicked and condemned world by providing a Savior by whom some might be saved when they believe. There are several misconceptions here that I think should be clarified:

a. John 3:16 says, "For God so loved the world, that He gave His only begotten Son, that whoever believes in Him, should not perish, but have everlasting life."

Whoever is not in the original text; my best rendering from the original language is "For God loved the world in this manner that He gave His only begotten Son that all the *believing* one's in Him, should not perish, but have everlasting life." This is significant because most often we associate the word *whoever* with something like "anyone at all that wants to." But the key to this text is really more about sinners *believing* than God *loving.* The believing ones will not perish. Everyone else is already perishing. Everyone will not believe in Him, nor will everyone want to believe in Him. Those who do believe will not perish. Those who do not believe will not be rescued by God's love for them while they are perishing in unbelief.

b. When in the original language it says literally, "For God *so* loved the world," the "so" refers to *the manner* in which He loved the world and does not refer to *the degree* or *extent of God's love,* as we would understand in English; it refers to the fact that He gave His only begotten Son, *in order that* all *the believing* should not perish but should rather have everlasting life.

The issue here then is the *manner* in which God loved the world; He loved a wicked, unbelieving, and condemned world sacrificially and in a giving way, where He gave His most beloved Son. The purpose in doing that was so that those who believe might not perish. God never loves anyone so much that His eternal wrath will not be poured out upon him or her in his or her unbelief. His loving stance toward the world in no wise keeps Him from ultimately pouring out His wrath on the same world of unbelief that 3:16 says that He loves. John 3:16 then speaks more to the value of believing than the value of God's loving, which is much more in context with what John is saying throughout his gospel.

Many assume that simply by John's use of the word *agapao* (love) in John 3:16 that this is reference to a special love of God's for the world, indeed, the very same love in which God expresses His love for the elect in Scripture! Yet it is not the etymological study of the root word for love under consideration here that will satisfy our understanding of the meaning of the text in John 3:16. D. A. Carson, noted scholar, author, and theologian, though not discussing John 3:16 directly, points out that though it is true that different words for love in the Greek language do overlap somewhat in meaning,

> To appeal to a "root meaning" in order to discern a difference is fallacious. In 2 Samuel 13 (LXX), both *agapao* (to love) and the cognate *agape* (love) can refer to Amnon's incestuous rape of his half-sister Tamar (2 Samuel 13:15, LXX). When we read that Demas forsook Paul because he loved this present, evil world, there is no linguistic reason to be surprised that the verb is *agapao* (2 Timothy 4:10)...the false assumptions surrounding these words are ubiquitous.[99]

To say then that God's *agapao* for the world is a particularly strong or deeper or even an atoning love, is, from the standpoint of the use of this particular word alone, unsatisfactory in helping us discern the kind of love John was referring to.

John MacArthur, seminary president, pastor, and world-famous radio speaker writes:

> These two aspects of God's love—His universal love for all

> humanity and His particular love for the elect–must not be confounded. To affirm that God loves the elect with a saving love is not to suggest that He has no love for the rest of humanity. And to acknowledge that God genuinely loves even those whom He does not save is not to impute any kind of feebleness to God. In the end, none of His purposes are thwarted and every aspect of His love perfectly declares His glory.[100]

MacArthur goes on to show quite effectively through Scripture that indeed God does love the world of humanity in a way that is different from his saving, eternal love for some. He suggests that there are four ways God's love is expressed universally: common grace, compassion, admonition, and the gospel offer. Yet he concludes by summarizing that "God chooses to love those whom He chooses to love. He chooses in spite of our sin. The fact that He loves us does not mean that we are worthy. But when He chooses to love redemptively and eternally, He forgives and redeems and keeps us in the faith."[101]

God can only love you *eternally and savingly* when you believe *in Christ.* Without Christ, we have the wrath of God being poured out upon a wicked world. With Christ, we have God loving and forgiving believers. To say that God so loved the world that He gave His only Son is saying only half the gospel. Note in 3:16 that if the Son hadn't been given for us to believe in, there will be *perishing* for unbelievers, not God *loving* unbelievers! That perishing is a result of God's wrath. God will overshadow His love with wrath for all who are in unbelief.

This is why Calvin taught long ago that "God is our enemy until He is reconciled to us through Christ." Prior to our being in Christ:

- We are estranged from God through sin.
- We are heirs of wrath.

- We are subject to the curse of eternal death.
- We are excluded from all hope of salvation.
- We are beyond every eternal blessing of God.
- We are slaves of Satan, captives under the yoke of sin.
- We are destined finally for a dreadful destruction and already involved in it.

c. The word *world* in John's vocabulary is primarily the moral order in willful and culpable rebellion against God.

This is why it is just as inappropriate to suggest that the word *world* in John 3:16 (in some Reformed camps) refers to the "world of the elect," as it is to think that world means *every single existing* individual. The world is rightfully condemned for its sin and rebellion, but God rather took a stance of love toward it by the offering of His Son as its Savior for all those who believe.

4. *God's particular, effective, selecting love toward His elect*

Either the church or Israel or individuals are referred to in election. God sets His affection on His chosen ones in a way that he doesn't set it upon others; He sets His love on them *eternally.* Never are individuals or nations chosen because of their personal or national merit, but because of something within God Himself—His love for them. God's love is peculiarly, eternally, and savingly directed toward His elect. Christ is said to have loved the church. Theologically, it is wrong to see God's love in terms of desiring to save every existing individual in light of the fact that God's *salvific* love is portrayed as highly particular in choosing certain individuals.

5. *God's love is sometimes directed toward His own people in a provisional or conditional way—conditioned, that is, on obedience*

Part of the relational structure of knowing God is provisional or conditional. This has to do with our relationship with Him once we know Him. Jude 21 says, "Keep yourselves in God's love." Can someone not keep himself in God's love? This is not a reference to God's providential love. Nor is this a reference to God's yearning love that reflects the stance God took in instigating salvation for believers. Nor does this refer to God's elective or salvific love. Jesus commanded his disciples to remain in his love by obeying his commands in a provisional or conditional way (John 15:10).

Finally, wrath is not the impersonal interaction of cause and effect (i.e., we sinned, and when we did, God got mad). Someone said that God's wrath is "the relentless divine hostility toward everything that is evil." Wrath is a function of God's holiness against sin. If there were no sin, there would be no wrath. For this reason, when we speak about God's love, we should always hold it up alongside of His wrath because each characteristic clarifies the other. That's why Christianity has held that Christ on the cross is both the expression of God's love for sinners and the expression of his wrath against sin.[102]

In order for God's love to win out toward sinners, His wrath had to be poured out. *He could never love us enough to keep His wrath from being poured out on our sin, except in Christ.* But that's how much He loved us, enough to pour out His wrath so He *could* love those who are in Christ. God's love without wrath is unthinkable; love *is* pouring out wrath upon His one beloved Son so that in eternity, He could love sinners in His holiness, free from the wrath that must necessarily accompany His holiness in the presence of their sin. Once we begin to wrap our minds around this statement, we will begin to formulate correct thinking about God and His character. God's wrath must be appeased so that God can save us and love us.

The issue about wrath and love is this: God will always love. There is no appeasing of love except when the appeasing of wrath is more important. Even when he loved His Beloved (Ephesians

1:6) more than anything else that He could love, in order to love the unlovable (us), the love of God for His own Son had to become less important so that the full force of His wrath against Him would be appeased for us.

CHRISTIANITY'S FAVORITE CLICHÉS

When I was teaching a Sunday school class at a church in Eugene, Oregon, on the subject of evangelism and how we might go about preparing to be better at it, someone asked me what I thought about approaching unbelievers with the infamous Campus Crusade statement, "God loves you and has a wonderful plan for your life." What did I think about it? Not much. Spoken without any further explanation, that is certainly one of the most misleading statements about the character of God that one could ever utter to an unbeliever. It is filled with all kinds of difficulty from both a practical and a theological sense. I said that I personally would never say such a thing to anyone because frankly, I have no idea what kind of a plan God has for *anyone's* life. I don't even know what God has planned for my life! I know what God has planned for my eternity *because of the promises God has made to those who trust Christ,* but that's only because I know what Scripture says God has planned for everyone *in Christ.* If I could be sure that Bill Bright had only meant by this statement that "God has a wonderful plan for your *eternal life should you trust Christ,*" then I could muster up some enthusiasm for it, though I would still be hard-pressed to use it. If what we mean by employing that euphemism is "God has a wonderful plan for your *eternal life should you trust Christ,*" then let's say what we mean clearly and distinctly so there is no confusion about our theological perspective.

When Bill Bright first began to formulate how he could take a huge, complex issue like the love of God and fit it into a peanutshell cliché with as little theological clarification as possible, he certainly must *not* have been thinking that God has a wonderful plan for *everyone's* earthly, physical life too, could he? If he did mean that, then those "wonderful plans" must include things like car accidents, plane crashes, death from dreaded diseases, etc., that leave people crippled and mangled, who oftentimes resent God when those things happen and often ultimately ask God questions like, "Why did you let this happen to me?" God may use all kinds of things in our temporal lives to bring us to Christ to assure us of a wonderful eternity, but many of those things certainly wouldn't be considered wonderful in terms of their temporary impact on our physical life alone. That's why statements like these coined by Campus Crusade that attempt to simplify complex concepts like God's love, when spoken without explanation, are in reality, ultimately detrimental to the cause of Christ theologically.

Aside from that, three times more is said in Scripture about the judgment of God than the mercy of God. Three times more is said about hell than about heaven in Scripture. Three times more is said about judgment and hell in Scripture than there are invitations to come to Christ as Lord and Savior. That's why the random selection of God's *love* as the premier statement for the *Four Spiritual Laws* are just that—the random choosing of just one of God's characteristics in an attempt to make them more significant theologically than others. Why do we choose to highlight God's love over His perfection, or truthfulness, or unchangeableness? Why choose to elevate His love over His eternality and justice?

Unless we make the commitment in our apologetic to address individuals with their particular theological concerns and make clear distinctions about what we mean when we talk about the wrath, love, judgment, or any characteristic of God to a godless world, our evangelistic efforts will really be nothing more than the offering of mere platitudes.

I don't mean to belittle Bill Bright's efforts to evangelize here or belittle the ministerial work of Campus Crusade. I know someone will tell me that they came to Christ because he or she read a tract that had the *Four Spiritual Laws* written on it. My answer to that is that's just because God can use whatever means he wants to bring you to faith; it certainly doesn't mean that any and all ways we approach it are equally effective!

Through the years I have kept notes on some of the many really bizarre attempts people have used in evangelism. They all fall short of doing what we intended them to do because the motivation to use them is backed by wrong thinking. It's almost as if people are using these methods to outsmart God at what He does best. It's as if we've come to believe that actually talking about God theologically to an unbeliever is doomed, so we've abandoned that ship and decided that the next best tack is to come up with a more modern, random approach to doing it. Rather than see evangelism as correcting misunderstandings from a theological perspective, we've traded the mental anguish of struggling with clear theological thinking for a lame methodology that we hope will work every time with staggering results on anybody, anywhere, under any circumstance, after any experience, with any cultural background, on any creed, race, nationality, intelligence level, religious persuasion, or heart condition.

For example, don't you think it's kind of absurd to canvass the streets with a quirky little one-liner to start your apologetic spiel? Isn't it kind of odd to walk up to some stranger without any kind of other verbal engagement whatsoever, as I observed some folks in a park one day, and say, "Hey, brother, are you saved?" Just strolling up to them in the park, out of the blue? And they respond, "Saved from what?" To which you reply, "Huh? Oh well, you know—do you know if you died right now, would ya go to heaven or hell?" I get the idea, but I struggle with the methodology. It seems to me that this approach is like a fox hunt, hunting for people the way dogs hunt foxes. This is evangelism boiled down to utter basics: hunt them down and tell them it's all about your random choice of heaven or hell. How many wary pagans have well-meaning Christians tried to drag into the kingdom with this method?

Or how about what I call using the Lazy Man's Gospel method? Maybe you're a computer freak/couch potato and would rather reach the masses through a less active methodology. So in your laying around the house you come up with a really hot idea. Rather than picking up a book on theology and considering how we might apply it to the Scriptures, you use the want ads in your local newspaper to get them to flock to Jesus! To you there's nothing wrong with a little ingenuity! We could call it the new not-too-personal, when-you're-pretty-busy, why-bother-with-theology approach to evangelism. Why would anyone use personal classified ads in his local paper to appeal to the Spirit of God to do the work of evangelism for him—without ever having to learn a thread of theology—and believe that this would work? One ad I saw promises: "Copy these words precisely in your local newspaper and watch 'em come to Christ!"

> Dear God, I, in this short dialogue, want to thank you for everything and confirm once more that I never want to be separated from you no matter how great the material urges may be that have gained a vice grip in my empty spiritual life. I want to be with you and my loved ones in your perpetual glory.
>
> If you copy this prayer *exactly* as written, and post it in your local want ads for three consecutive days without asking for a request, we *guarantee* that after the third day, whatever your evangelical wish is, it will be granted, no matter how difficult it may be for God to do so!

The fact that someone would actually post this in a want ad is not only astounding to me, it's embarrassing. Not quite heretical, but certainly embarrassing.

Of course there are other methods that I've noted that really are heretical, like this one I call that old Pelagian (somewhat-antiquated-newly-resurrected-still-sure-fire) method known as the Final Vote Is Yours Gospel Method. Whoever came up with this idea must have been a politician who was thinking that evangelism is really like convincing people that their salvation is akin to voting in a voting booth. It's all about one simple truth: "Evangelism is like voting for your favorite Democrat." God casts His vote for you, the devil casts his vote against you, and all you need to do is to cast your vote for yourself to break the tie, two to one! And when you do, *Bingo!* Twenty-one! Jackpot! Winner! In this method, God may still be powerful, but obviously He's not as powerful as you are! You are the deciding factor in all this evangelism business, so make sure you cast your vote for the right candidate! Why gamble with your salvation any longer? (By the way, don't worry about those stick-in-the-mud theologians like Calvin, Luther, and Edwards, who are undoubtedly rolling over in their graves at the thought of you approaching evangelism in this manner.)

Sometimes we Christians think the best approach to reaching a lost world is to just candy-coat everything about the gospel for people. I call using this idea the Pretentious, Overly Candy-Coated Gospel Method. For some reason we think that we're going to freak folks out if we use sound theology! We're convinced before we even begin preaching the gospel that they're tired of hearing how angry God gets about sin. They're tired of all that Old Testament talk about "Fear God and keep His commandments." They're tired of hearing how God said, "Go, and utterly destroy the sinners, the Amalekites, and fight against them until they are exterminated." They're tired of hearing words like *wrath* and *judgment.* For some reason we think we can do greater wonders than God Himself by simply making God out to be the author of a pretentious, overly candy-coated gospel from our pulpits! This is one of the most patronizing evangelistic methods ever dreamed up. If you've been a Christian for any length of time, you've undoubtedly heard a spiel like this from some pulpit somewhere, and I'll bet you didn't even flinch when you heard it thrown out in the middle of some sappy sermon, "No matter who you are, no matter what you've done, no matter the depth of your hatred for truth, no matter the darkness of your wretched, unrepentant heart, no matter your obstinate hatred for God, I'm here to tell you just one thing: God cannot love you any more than He loves you right now!"

Talk about pregnant with theological problems!

Here's another one I've kept in my notes: I call it the Letting Direct Intervention Mail Do Your Evangelism for You Gospel Method.

> Recently, the Lord gave me a unique evangelism strategy. If you would take a few minutes to read the following letter (that I will soon be sending by snail mail to churches all over America) you will get an idea of what I am trying to do... Like the first-century Christians, we believe that sending letters is a natural for evangelism and discipleship. Direct mail (often called targeted marketing) is one of the effective marketing tools used by businesses in America today. If it was not effective, your mailbox would be empty. We believe it should be used to proclaim the Gospel to the people who go to their mail boxes every day, but don't go to a good church.

Just like the Apostles used letters to instruct the churches in their ministry, apparently we can garner a certain amount of success using this method. Here's what I find troubling though. This and so many of the methods I have noted above all seem to suppose that human methodology in evangelism is a better model to follow than the biblical model.

The original idea for all this evangelism business still works no matter how hard we try to avoid it with our human inventions. It's called the gospel of the cross. For some reason, Christians have come to believe that it's out of date. My guess is that nobody's using it anymore because in our flesh we don't think enough people come. Or we don't think that God has any more power to bring them to Christ other than through our methodology. Or it takes too much time to think through what the Bible teaches, and frankly we must think we're out of time! It used to be that long ago the gospel of the cross was the evangelical source of power. I don't know. Maybe we just avoid it because we've let the world dictate how we should evangelize people, and to them, the cross is just not cool, so we avoid the deep, meaningful, difficult discussions about what God was doing on the cross of Christ like we'd avoid the plague!

Talking about what God was doing on the cross forces the church to think about paradox, philosophy, and theological dilemmas. It forces us to evaluate the benefit of laying aside the human need for building up their self-esteem in place of looking at sin and God's gracious forgiveness of it. It forces us to deal with the truth that God did something to Jesus that Jesus didn't deserve instead of doing it to you. Thinking about that can lead to real difficult theological issues, and we don't want a theological mess like that on our hands! We want fruitful, long-lasting, deeply penetrating results from shallow, sugar-coated, milk toast evangelism.

BAILING THE TWENTY-FIRST-CENTURY MENTALITY ABOUT EVANGELISM

The first way we can make our evangelism more purposeful is to abandon the twenty-first-century mentality about it. We need to regain a first-century mentality of evangelism by no longer thinking of it in terms of commercial-length sound bites. This is the kind of question that twenty-first-century evangelism asks: "What can I tell someone about Jesus in a minute and a half while we're standing here waiting for the bus?"

What is our hurry? We think only in terms of commercial-length sound bites! We think we need to keep it short and sweet, pithy, not lengthy, catchy with some pizzazz, and don't forget the witty jokes! Not too deep—after all, they don't know any theology. Give them milk, preferably nonfat and powdered, thinning it down real good with water. And this is why we have churches filled with folks who are clueless about theology and the grace of God. It is this kind of methodological approach to evangelism, this wanting to deal with huge, general truths without explaining the specifics, that has made evangelism virtually ineffective for us. We seek general truths that we can tell them that won't offend them (God loves you and has a wonderful plan for your life), hoping that will be enough to stimulate some random, remote interest in Jesus no matter what roadblocks they have in their belief system.

Someone once said to me, "If I don't have a methodology in my approach to evangelism, then what can my six-year-old son say to one of his friends about Jesus while they're standing by the water fountain?" My response was, "It almost sounds like you're asking me, 'What type of canned, random statement can my son pull out of his pocket at some arbitrary time to do his evangelism duty for the day?'" Then I said, "Whoever said that evangelism is the duty of a six-year-old?" Our errors in evangelism begin when we think that we need to use some canned methodology in our approach to winning people with the truth or when we begin by making assumptions that it's everyone's duty to win the lost to Jesus the second he or she says he or she believes in Christ, even before he or she knows the gospel! First-century evangelism evangelizes people by living the gospel moment by moment in their presence.

I know that preaching the gospel means "proclaiming the good news." There needs to be proclamation. And Paul certainly does that. But what I want you to understand is that his preaching is generally within the context of his extended relationship to people. It isn't a random, methodological approach at all; Paul's emphasis asks, "What kind of permanent impact can I have on an individual's life while I live the truth of the gospel in their presence for an extended period, preferably under adverse circumstances? How will he get to see Jesus and grace more clearly in all of the many challenges he sees me facing graciously as I live in his presence day after day?" Look at the length of Paul's ministry stays: two years, three months, three weeks, one and a half years, and you begin to see his aversion to methodology.

Another difference between the first-century approach to evangelism and the twenty-first-century approach is that *first-century evangelism abandons all methodology in favor of finding the person's issue or theological misunderstanding at the moment of contact.* Paul's first-century evangelism brings some aspect of the gospel to a particular issue that the individual is struggling with and answers that particular need in hopes of getting him to think about his belief system *rather than* using a random, shotgun approach to evangelizing him.

This is the point we've missed: true evangelism should seek to correct wrong thinking about God and the world and clarify why it's wrong. Our explanations regarding theology and Christianity should attempt to clarify how someone's thinking has gone awry. This approach requires us to be quicker on our feet, to have a better understanding of theology as a whole, to be perceptive in discerning error, and to be more in tune with the issue the person we are speaking to is dealing with than being in tune with evangelizing him through some random methodology. Evangelism approached correctly necessarily requires us to abandon any kind of methodological approach. Our goal is to hear and understand the person's perspective and to show him or her how that perspective relates to a biblical worldview and theological understanding. As we'll see in the next chapter, Paul uses this simple approach repeatedly in the book of Acts.

LIFE THROUGH THE EYES OF A GUTTER SPARROW

> Indeed, the Christian life, faith, and thought that emerges from this [theological deep thinking] will be more robust, more spiritually alert, more discerning, more biblical, and more critical than it could otherwise have been. But some of the steps along the way are dangerous: work hard at integrating your entire Christian walk and commitment...fail to work hard at such integration and you invite spiritual shipwreck.
>
> —D. A. Carson

One thing becomes quite clear from studying the book of Acts as we try to determine whether or not Paul and the other early church members attempted to evangelize via some method or other. I contend that, unlike modern evangelism, the New Testament church never instituted the concept of a method of evangelism; rather, the early church was in favor of finding the person they were evangelizing. Only after a familiarity with the person he was speaking to did Paul understand what he needed to say to meet that person's need when presenting the gospel. The approach that Paul uses in bringing someone to consider the truth of the gospel changes according to the particular spiritual needs of that person. His apologetic is always based on familiarity with the person and the immediate issue he is struggling with, which changes with each particular person because each person is different.

In understanding how New Testament believers went about evangelism in the book of Acts, we see that there is no particular method to copy because the gospel is packaged and presented to meet the needs of the individual who is present. When you know what concepts and issues the person with whom you are sharing the gospel is struggling with, your *task* will be to simply bring some aspect of the truth of the gospel to *that particular issue.* Our task is to find the particular needs of the individual and package, never diluting, the gospel truth to meet that particular need. This will become clearer as we examine three passages in Acts that show that Paul was more in favor of having an intimate knowledge of the person and tailoring the gospel to meet a personal, particular truth that person was struggling with rather than some random method of evangelization.

ACTS 13:1–13

It is clear from the beginning of chapter thirteen that Luke is stressing that the Holy Spirit is at work in what he is about to record for us (13:2, 4, 9). Perhaps Luke sensed a real need to stress that God and the Holy Spirit were working in this particular presentation of the gospel because the way that Paul goes about sharing the teaching of the Lord in this particular instance is so totally foreign to modern human evangelical methods. Keep in mind that what we are concerned with illustrating is that any concept of a method of evangelizing is substituted for what the particular individual needs to hear to come to faith in Christ.

As the story in chapter thirteen unfolds, Paul, Barnabas, and John (13:2, 5), are sent by the Holy Spirit to Paphos to introduce an intelligent man, Sergius Paulus, the proconsul, to the gospel. In fact, Sergius Paulus "sought to hear the word of God" (13:7). But there was this false prophet who was with the proconsul, Bar-Jesus, translated Elymas, a sorcerer, who was "seeking to turn the proconsul away from the faith" (13: 8). Now note how Paul, filled with the Holy Spirit, addresses this false prophet: "O full of all deceit and all fraud, you son of the devil, you enemy of all righteousness, will you not cease perverting the straight ways of the Lord (13:10)?"

Now I wouldn't suggest that you use that presentation of the gospel on your employer tomorrow, unless of course the Holy Spirit leads you to do so. There is no mention of concern here in this passage by Paul about how either of these two men might respond to the truth of the gospel when it is presented in this fashion. One never senses in the story that Paul doubts the effectiveness of this particular method to reach this individual. Our modern techniques would undoubtedly teach that the use of this type of language in the presentation of the gospel would be absolutely unacceptable. It would be considered insulting and base to flatly call someone the "son of the devil." Certainly, it appears on the surface to lack compassion for the false prophet.

But what I am trying to demonstrate to you is that our modern approach to evangelism is often overly concerned with method and unconcerned with the individual. Modern methods of evangelism would insist that this approach would be at least impolite and most likely politically incorrect. I think that if any of us felt the urging of the Holy Spirit to present the gospel in this fashion to an individual, I dare say we would question the source of this urging, whether this was from the devil or the Holy Spirit. I am attempting to get you to think about some of the conventional ideas about evangelism and line them up with a biblical approach used by the apostles in the early church.

Now as it turns out, this is exactly what the proconsul would need to hear to come to faith in Jesus Christ. Imagine that, the Holy Spirit actually knowing what a particular person needed to hear so that his eyes would be opened, and he would turn from the darkness and Satan to the living God! Paul predicts immediate blindness for the false prophet as a temporary judgment, and "then the proconsul believed when he saw what had been done, being astonished at the *teaching* of the Lord" (13:12). It wasn't the miracle of blinding that he believed, but "the teaching of the Lord."

ACTS 24:22–27

Remember that Paul's evangelical concern is to abandon the method and find the individual needs of the person.

How many times, when you have shared the Gospel of Jesus Christ with someone, have you mentioned the significance of self-control as a constituent of its truth? That's not something that one would normally mention to someone when sharing the gospel, is it? Who then is Felix, and why did he need to know about self-control? Why did Paul feel that this particular concept needed to be a constituent of this particular rendition of the gospel?

Antonius Felix was procurator of Judea under Claudius and Nero, to whom Paul was brought to trial in Caesarea. Felix was described historically as someone who "thought he could do any evil act with impunity," and "exercised the power of a king with the mind of a slave."[103] He had married Drusilla, a Jewess and the youngest daughter of Herod Agrippa I. She had been given in marriage to the crown Prince of Commagene, who did not want to become a proselyte to Judaism. When she was sixteen years old, after having persuaded her to leave the king of Emesa, to whom she had been betrothed by her brother Agrippa II, Felix proceeded to persuade her to become his wife.

Paul had probably been informed by Drusilla herself about her own situation, and, in fact, it may have been Drusilla that wanted to meet Paul. When "Felix sent for Paul and heard him concerning the faith in Christ" (24:24), Paul mentioned three things to the two of them, according to the information and knowledge that he had about Felix, that would be most likely to convict him and his young Jewish wife of the truth of the Gospel of Jesus Christ.

He mentioned "righteousness, self-control, and the judgment to come." That is quite a package, which, in fact, resulted in Felix's fear of God.

Now these are not standard in Paul's seeking to evangelize the lost. There is nothing in the Bible that suggests that someone's eyes are more likely to be opened to the truth when we mention righteousness, self-control, and judgment as crucial elements of the gospel. There is nothing random or magical about these three things. Our goal is not to adopt Paul's methods but to adopt his mechanism in evangelizing.

Righteousness is attained through faith in Jesus Christ (Romans 3:22). We are not made righteous by keeping the law (Romans 3:28) or because we are good people (Romans 3:10–11). Felix obviously had a lust for young girls and set about to do whatever he could to bring about this union with Drusilla, who had no intention of maintaining any links with her Jewish heritage. The concern for Paul was to mention that the gospel had ethical implications. God is righteous, and there is a day coming when we will be judged according to righteousness.

Drusilla probably was overly concerned about wealth and political position more than her Jewish heritage. Interestingly, the law that she was undoubtedly extremely familiar with from her Jewish heritage, "Thou shalt not commit adultery," "Thou shalt not covet anything of thy neighbors,'" could only be understood by Drusilla in Paul mentioning that the gospel of Jesus Christ had ethical implications. F. F. Bruce states:

> As [Paul] talked about these, Felix and Drusilla felt that the interview had taken an uncomfortably personal turn...Paul's distinguished hearers had probably never listened to such pointed and practical teaching in their lives when he talked to them about...three subjects about which that couple specially needed to be informed.[104]

Felix had a problem with self-control, and that's why Paul mentioned it. This wasn't a hit-and-miss evangelistic conversational tool. Paul was intimate with both Drusilla and Felix and knew what was critical for them to hear. The gospel alone frees us from the power of every particular sin that enslaves us.

The important thing to note here is that this is not just a casual, five-minute, lunch-break conversation Paul has with Felix. Verses 24 through 27 of chapter 24 indicate that Felix had repeated meetings with Paul. In verse 23, Felix gave Paul considerable freedom to have friends come and go. Verses 24 through 26 suggest that it was "after some days" that he had heard about the faith in Christ, and he had probably heard about the faith often in conversation with Paul.

ACTS 17:16–34

What does a sparrow know about philosophy? The answer to that question depends on how a sparrow formulates its worldview: upon what basis does it interpret reality? How does a sparrow determine what is real and what is not true? How do sparrows logically categorize their thoughts regarding reality and establish a reasonable argument for why they think the way that they do?

Near the end of his second missionary journey, the Apostle Paul makes what appears to be a random, impromptu stop in Athens. The text says in Acts 17 that as he waited in Athens for Silas and Timothy to meet him, he realized the tremendous depth to which the Athenians were engulfed in idolatry. His spirit was provoked within him to reach these people with the truth, and he daily reasoned with them in the synagogues and in the marketplaces (17:17). It was there that he encountered two groups of people: the Stoics and the Epicureans. Only by understanding the worldview of these two philosophical groups and comprehending how they reason do we begin to sense the genius in Paul's apologetic. The basis for Paul's appeal to the truth of the gospel is based upon his knowledge of what these men believe! When he understands how they think about their world, the people in it, and their perception of its reality, it is those particular misunderstandings that he addresses with the truth of the gospel. Our approach to evangelism should be exactly the same today.

THE STOICS

The Stoics were materialists, pantheists, and empiricists. Anything that could be seen, touched, tasted, smelled, or heard (empiricism) was real. But only material things were real. This is exactly the argument that atheists pose today in justifying their reasons for unbelief, and a subject that I will discuss in detail in the next chapter. For the Stoics, there was no room for any sort of unseen, spiritual reality. They therefore necessarily discounted that spirits, angels, or a God who was a living Spirit could be real. After all, there was no empirical, material proof for such things in their notion of reality. Pantheism means literally that God is everything, and everything is God. There was this mental "Reason" that filled the whole universe, which was the "soul of the universe." But because all reality, to them, could only be realized in terms of materialism and empiricism, God, for the Stoics, was only a vague, unidentifiable mentality within the universe.

For them, God could not be distinguished from the world, nor could their view of God allow them to differentiate any of his works from anything else in the world. The thought of God creating and directing the flow of the unfolding events in time was a laugh to the Stoics. The ability to distinguish between the virtuous works of God and the sin of men hence became equally impossible.

For the Stoics, there was this sense of sheer fatalism and apathy toward all circumstances that came to pass in life. There was nothing to be done about one's circumstances except learn to grin and bear it and be unemotional in response to it. A 'stoic look' today is considered to be one that shows no emotion in the face of trials and difficulties. There was no sense of God being sovereign over circumstances and trials in life. Since God was essentially an unidentifiable, vague, esoteric aspect of the world, He could not be someone who would intervene into the events of the world.

This apathy manifested itself most in how men related to one another. There was no sense of brotherhood or unity among men. This, of course, led to a deep confusion as to the purpose of the lives of men in the world, and there were no efforts toward peace or compassion other than on an intellectual level. Interestingly, Stoicism is the seed bed for many false religions in the world today. In its philosophy of life and its worldview, we find the earliest forms of humanism, atheism, evolution, situational ethics, fatalism, New Age, Islamism, and others.

THE EPICUREANS

The Epicureans were "garden philosophers." They meditated on nature and tried to see how nature and morality interrelated. They believed that the universe was eternal and infinite, though not created by God. It came about by accident, really, due to billions of little atoms that had specific gravity and structure randomly colliding together, which happened to make all that existed. Naturally, there was no plan or design behind the universe in this mind-set. It was, after all, an accident that anything was here.

They believed in gods, but they were separate from humanity and less than remotely concerned about men. These gods were engrossed in their own cosmic interests that were of no concern to humans. In the Epicurean mind, the greatest evil was fear, particularly fear of the unknown, such as death and what the gods might do. The greatest possible achievement for men was to become completely free from any belief in the gods because the gods only brought fear into life. Once men were free from the evil associated with the fear brought about by belief in the gods, they could eat, drink, and be merry. That was the real purpose to living: "Exist in the now; that's all there is." Any kind of judgment in the afterlife could not be taken seriously since all that existed was "now."

There are multitudes of philosophical, theological, and doctrinal differences between Christianity and the philosophies of Stoicism and Epicureanism. But reading Acts 17:24–31 reveals that the Apostle Paul didn't try to wrestle with *every* detail about the differences between these two philosophies and the many doctrines of Christianity. He focused on three essential doctrines that differentiated Stoicism and Epicureanism from the doctrines of Christianity (17:19). These three major differences were in how God, man, and sin were viewed.

Foremost in our thoughts about sharing the gospel ought to be these three standard truths about Christianity: it is the one true religion that reveals the one true God and the truth about Him; it alone has the proper perspective about the nature, origin, and condition of men; and it reveals the truth about the future reality of judgment. These three errors in the thinking process of Epicureans and Stoics were foundational to their misunderstanding about all of life. Paul undoubtedly realized that delivering a deeper understanding of these doctrinal differences would help them to see the truth of Christianity more clearly and their own errors in thinking as well.

These Athenian philosophers were Gentiles. Paul does not use Old Testament prophecy or scripture with Gentiles, only with Jews. Why? Because Jews already know who the one true God is. After all, that is foundational to their heritage. They already believe, at least for the most part, the God of the Bible. What Jews needed to learn is that Jesus of Nazareth is the One who fulfills Old Testament prophecy of the biblical Messiah. It is the Gentiles who need to hear about the one true God and His relationship to men and what differentiated men from God. Paul never uses the Bible, per se (the Old Testament scriptures), to explain to Gentiles about this God either. Why should he? They don't understand that the only source of truth can be found in the true, inspired, inerrant Word of God like the Jews do.

Certainly, all that Paul explains to Gentiles is couched in the truth of the Old Testament, but he does not hold up the Old Testament as being the source of that truth because the Bible is just another book to them. You won't find Paul saying anything like "The Bible says" or "the Scriptures teach" when he is speaking to Gentiles in the book of Acts. In fact, even in the passage we are looking at, he reminds them of the writings of the Greek secular poets to suggest that what he is telling them is believable, not because it is in the Old Testament, but because it is common knowledge (17:28) even in their own culture.

GOD, MAN, AND JUDGMENT

Paul begins his conversation with these Gentiles by saying that the true God, whom the Stoics and Epicureans did not know personally, "made the world and everything in it, since He is the Lord of heaven and earth" (17:24). But Paul doesn't inform them of this only to give them correct information. He tells them this so they can distinguish the errors in their *own* thinking process. If this God made the world and everything in it, He cannot, therefore, logically be a part of the world, as pantheism suggests, since anything that anyone makes or creates must be less than and apart from the one who makes it. Furthermore, the fact that He created it suggests purpose, intent, design, and reason. It does not suggest randomness, senselessness, and fatalism as these philosophers were apt to believe.

Two of the foundational truths of the Christian doctrine of God are that He transcends the universe that He created and that He is at the same time immanent, living and operating within it. The God Paul is instructing them about is too big to be only right here, but too personal and caring to be only "out there." Since He is so much greater than we can conceive Him to be, and He is Spirit, it is ludicrous to think that He lives in these little man-made idols they think represent Him!

"Nor is He worshipped with men's hands, as though He needed anything, since He gives to all life, breath and all things" (17:25). In this statement Paul affirms that God is entirely self-sufficient. There is nothing He needs from anything or anyone to help Him exist. He is not dependent upon anything we might have or could give to Him so that He might continue living, unlike men. We, on the contrary, are utterly dependent upon Him for our life and even the breath within us, which He gives to everyone in His mercy and takes away when He sees fit. He is the creator and sustainer of life! We are daily in need of His mercy, forgiveness, strength, and love. There is a natural vacuum within us that longs for Him, yet we cannot identify it until He reveals to us that it is Him that we need.

Paul found it necessary to explain that there is no reason to be apathetic toward our fellow men either because we are all from one flesh. We have the same ancestors, and we are all in the same predicament here regarding our existence. God made the earth for our dwelling place and has in His sovereignty determined where we dwell for the express reason of seeking Him and finding Him (17:27). Furthermore, He is not so unidentifiable that He cannot be readily seen and grasped by the human mind and spirit, at least in His creation. He is not just an indistinguishable force in the universe named "Reason." He reveals Himself through the works of His creation and His immanent relationship to each person who lives. It is "in Him that we live, and move, and have our being" (17:28). He sustains our lives in His mercy. We are daily swimming in His grace, providence, mercy, power, and love. We were made in the image of God. It is our responsibility to honor Him with our worship and our understanding of His person, not with little, molded images that cannot begin to represent Him as He exists in His true majesty.

Finally, this God Who made everything is the judge of everything. He cannot be unjust, or too harsh, or uncaring, like men are. There will come a day when He will righteously judge the world by the standard of perfection established in the life of Jesus Christ. This we can be assured of because Christ was raised from the dead (17:31).

PAUL'S GRACE AND HUMILITY

At the outset, Athens appeared to have all the potential for a successful evangelical crusade. These were the most intelligent, reason-possessed philosophers of that day. If anyone was capable of coming to terms with the logic of the gospel of Jesus Christ and rationalizing its timeless truths, it was the men of Athens. But even after Paul's plea that they use their reason to see the logic of what he was saying, the mass of these philosophers utterly rejected Paul's message at Athens. Note first of all Paul's grace to these men as he responds to their rejection of him and his message.

Acts 17:18 says that when these philosophers encountered him they called him a *spermologos*. They were literally calling him something like a gutter sparrow, or a seed picker.

> Used originally as "birds picking up seed," [spermologos] came to be applied in Athenian slang to an adventurer who gains a "hand-to-mouth" living in the markets by picking up anything that falls from the loads of merchandise which are being carried about. Hence it passed into the meaning of one gathering scraps of information and retailing them at second-hand without any real knowledge of their meaning. The AV, RV "babbler," which goes back to Tindale, is thus not far from the sense, one who talks idly to no definite purpose...Amongst modern renderings we may mention—"prater" (19th century), "beggarly babbler" (Weymouth), "fellow with scraps of learning" (Moffat), "rag-picker" (Goodspeed).[105]

They were in effect saying, "Paul, your message is unreasonable! You really haven't thought this thing through very well. All you have are little pieces of different philosophies that don't fit together. You're like these little gutter sparrows all around us who flit over to those crumbs and gobble them up and then flit over to that table to gobble up some other crumbs. Your theology is a hodgepodge of bits and pieces of nonsense. Our logic will not allow us to see life through the eyes of a gutter sparrow."

But note the total grace that flows from the lips of Paul when he finally has their undivided attention. He can be totally gracious because he knows that the result of evangelism is out of his hands entirely. He bears no bitterness toward them in their rejection of the gospel. He desires no vindication. A cursory reading of the Bible explains that it is God's work to bring men to the truth. Paul sees the Athenians as lost, spiritually dead men responding the only way they know how! He doesn't panic at their rejection of the truth. He doesn't show them his Apostle's badge and say, "What's this 'gutter-sparrow' stuff? Open your eyes, guys! Idolatry is sin, and you guys are floundering in it. The real God hates sin, and according to the Hebrew Scriptures, you guys are going to fry in hell. Love God." There isn't any hint that somehow they can snap out of it if the gospel message gets laid out for them really nicely either. People don't repent because of what you say or the way you say it. They repent because God grants to them eyes with which to see the truth. The Bible teaches that if you are opposed to the gospel of Jesus Christ, you are not in the truth, and it is God alone who will grant you repentance (Romans 2:4).

Note also the humility that Paul brings with the gospel. In Acts 20:18–19, as he gets ready for one last time to speak with the elders from Ephesus, he says, "You know, from the first day that I came to Asia, in what manner I always lived among you, serving the Lord with all humility." Do you know why Paul can present the gospel with total humility? I think there are three reasons.

First, because he never lost focus from the very beginning that he was called to be a servant. There was never a question in his mind that he was doing God's work for God. He wasn't taking any credit for anyone's conversion. He never said, "I led those people to the Lord through my skills of persuasion." He never lost focus from the beginning that he was a servant doing God's work. The book of Acts closes with the Apostle Paul in a Roman prison in AD 63. His last epistle is Second Timothy, written about AD 67, shortly before his death. In 2 Timothy 2:24–26, Paul writes to Timothy, "And a servant of the Lord must not quarrel but be gentle to all, able to teach, patient, *in humility* correcting those who are in opposition, if God perhaps will grant them repentance, so that they may know the truth..." What a magnificent commentary on the grace of God in evangelism! The Greek word for *opposition, antidiatithimi,* is in the middle voice. Paul reminds Timothy that the people he was speaking about literally "place *themselves* in opposition." They are wholly accountable for their opposition because they put themselves there due to their lost and sinful condition. Yet we can be humble because God grants repentance. Lost sinners don't sort of pupate out of their sin on their own power. Paul affirms that they are not even in their right senses!

Secondly, Paul can be absolutely humble in the presentation of the gospel because he never lost focus that God is absolutely sovereign in salvation. No one fails to become a Christian because you didn't present the arguments correctly or eloquently or logically or because he or she found the weak link in your thought process. No one fails to become a Christian because we didn't make it simple enough when we talked to him or her! The reason people don't become Christians is because they love darkness rather than light (John 3:19), and in their natural state unbelievers are not only threatened by the gospel message, but they want nothing to do with God. They willingly ignore and reject the truth about themselves and God until God enables them to understand the gospel that is being presented.

Thirdly, after departing from Athens, Paul arrived in Corinth. Corinth was the same kind of city; it had the same blossoming intellectuals, all convinced of the same types of philosophy. Paul must have been thinking of Dionysius, Damaris, and the few others who came to Christ when he preached in Athens (Acts 17:34) as he strolled into Corinth. But I don't think he was wondering why it was a pitifully small number that came to Christ from the intellectual philosophers in Athens! No.

Paul had two overwhelming thoughts on his mind as he came to Corinth as the Lord's servant: power and Christ's crucifixion.

In today's huge arenas, altar calls go out to thousands upon thousands at a time in sports stadiums across the world, and even as the supposed healings of television evangelists have appealed to millions more regarding the power of the gospel, we see a completely different approach by the Apostle Paul. He wasn't thinking in terms of thousands of people coming to Christ when he wracked his brain about why the gospel could only save a few stragglers in Athens. To us, power is demonstrated by the numbers of people that respond and by great demonstrations of healing. But Paul was thinking about the few in Athens that the Lord had enabled to come! To Paul, the fact that only a handful would believe the gospel is the true demonstration of power! Because he knew that whenever *anyone* comes to Christ as a believer, it is for no other reason than the power of the gospel.

"And my speech and my preaching were not with persuasive words of human wisdom, but in demonstration of the Spirit and of power" (1 Corinthians 2:4). Paul came to the Corinthians in weakness, fear, and in much trembling because the truth was that there was power in the message that Christ had died for sinners. Paul said all he desired to know was Christ and Him crucified. He had just witnessed that the years of intellectual garbage that had been stuffed into the cerebrums of those Athenian philosophers couldn't bring any of them one inch closer to coming to the truth of Christ in faith, and all he wanted to know was Christ and His crucifixion! Everything else in evangelism is excess baggage. He trembled in weakness, not so much because he knew the message of Christ was full of power, but because there wasn't any power at all *except* God's power exhibited through the truth of the gospel and Christ's crucifixion that brought sinners to God's merciful and gracious salvation. And that salvation is an uncompromising revelation of His goodness to men.

WHAT IF IT WERE TRUE THAT GOD IS VERY GOOD?

> Indeed, it would seem very strange that Christianity should have come into the world merely to receive an explanation; as if it had been somewhat bewildered about itself, and hence entered the world to consult that wise man, the speculative philosopher, who can come to its assistance by furnishing the explanation.
>
> —Soren Kierkegaard

If God is so good, why does it look like he isn't? It seems that nothing stirs the passions of the atheist more than the fact that Christianity asks the world to believe the impossible about God. Christians might have been able to get away with simply believing that somewhere out there in the abyss of infinity there is some vague, disinterested, and impotent *something* that some people have decided to call God. The atheist could have remained dispassionate if only that *something* would have remained unfamiliar, inexplicable, and abstract enough so as not to interfere with the world's perceptions.

But enough is enough, it seems; Christianity hasn't simply asked us to believe that this God *merely* exists. It has asked us to believe that he's knowable without empirical evidence. If that isn't enough, it has asked us to believe that he's more powerful than anything we can imagine, that he can do anything at all! More importantly, it has asked us to believe that he has the best interests of this world in mind all the time. And finally, it has asked us to believe that he even cares about people and what happens to them in spite of his repeated failure to utilize his supposed attributes on their behalf.

And now that the world has clearly failed to see the enormity of this Christian proposition and the travesty of irrationality that has been perpetrated against it by this belief, the atheist has been forced to come to the world's *intellectual* rescue. Their antidote for this travesty that has been perpetrated against the world is a rational and logical explanation that can lead to only one conclusion: *If there is any kind of God that exists, it certainly cannot be the God of Christianity.* Christians have taken their faith too lightly, too illogically, too childishly, it seems, and now the speculative philosopher must come to the world's rescue and furnish it with the only reasonable explanation for this outrageous claim: no such thing exists!

B. C. Johnson, for instance, in *The Atheist Debater's Handbook* begins a chapter entitled "God and the Problem of Evil" with this illustration:

> Here is a common situation: a house catches on fire and a six-month-old baby is painfully burned to death. Could we possibly describe as "good" any person who had the power to save this child and yet refused to do so? God undoubtedly has this power and yet in many cases of this sort he has refused to help. Can we call God "good"? Are there adequate excuses for this behavior?...Certainly not. If we would not consider a mortal human being good under these circumstances, what grounds could we possibly have for continuing to assert the goodness of an all-powerful God?[106]

There are two major concerns that will be addressed in this chapter: What constitutes a reasonable proof that God exists? And, if there is any such proof, is it reasonable to assume that the God of Christianity can be *that* God? If we are assured that there is no empirical proof for the existence of a God, why does the Christian continue to believe in one? Even more astoundingly, assuming there *is* a reasonable way to hold to a belief in a God without empirical evidence, how can Christians hold to the notion of his *goodness* in light of the evil he supposedly allows if he does exist?

Interestingly, in order for this debate to take place, both the atheist and the Christian *must* assume, or at least accept as being possibly true, that God does exist and that He is some kind of real being in the universe who acts *deliberately* and *with power* in the world. Both sides must acknowledge that God is a being with particular character traits, which are the basis for the motivation of his actions; and that these actions can be scrutinized, criticized, or defended in human terms. There is no discussion that can occur for the atheist without him first acknowledging the kind of God the Christian is defending. Without both sides making these assumptions, there would be no ongoing debate on the subject of God's existence or his goodness.

The atheist desires to show that his viewpoint on the existence of a God whose existence cannot be empirically demonstrated is valid.[107] The atheist perceives the world in terms of physical reality alone and then wonders how some other reality that the Christian perceives God to exist in might better account for God's goodness. Having assumed this, the atheist then in effect says, "Provided that you can demonstrate that it is reasonable to assume that your God exists, how can you possibly suggest that your God is good when all around us we experience and bear testimony to such horrific atrocities? Doesn't the existence of these atrocities at least challenge the Christian concept of God's 'goodness' and 'righteousness'"?

At the outset, the atheist sets the parameters for understanding God by limiting his view of reality to a mere scientific, rational, materialistic, physical world which can only be understood through empirical (i.e., physically tangible) means. After all, to him, that is the only *real* world![108] The atheist believes that the Christian God can only be understood *apart* from the concept of faith. He will never be able to come to terms with the existence of the God of the Bible the way that the Christian does because of his view of reality. In the end, it is perhaps not so much that the atheist doubts the *goodness* of God in this debate, though he undoubtedly does do that. That is secondary. All of the atheist's doubts about God arise from his fundamental understanding of reality as "anti-spiritual." It is this limiting view of reality that forces the atheist to deny God's very existence and, consequently, his supposed goodness.

But the Christian also struggles at a very foundational level in this debate. If he concludes that God is indeed real in an entirely "other" sense than the mere physical reality that the atheist perceives, he must then believe in a God who is not only capable of preventing pain and suffering but also is one who picks and chooses what He does or doesn't do about it.

While the Christian believes in the literal, *spiritual* reality of the eternal, omnipotent God of the Bible, he is often incapable of debating effectively whether God remains "good" within the perspective of this spiritual reality.

The Christian must understand, ultimately, that his belief in the goodness of God comes from his reliance on the fact that Scripture alone establishes his perception of God's existence and goodness and not his experience. We cannot defend God's goodness according to what we think goodness is or in terms of how human beings understand the word 'good' if God is indeed entirely hidden.

Furthermore, what serves as fuel for the atheist's argument is the Christian conviction that even the very faith we rely on to believe in the God of the Bible is from God Himself.[109] Karl Barth wrote in *On Christian Faith:*

> Faith is a freedom; a permission. It is permitted to be, so that the believer in God's Word may hold on to this Word in everything, in spite of all that contradicts it [in reality]. It is so: we never believe "on account of," never "because of"; we awaken to faith in spite of everything...when we believe, we believe in spite of God's hiddenness. The hiddenness of God necessarily reminds us of our human limitation. We do not believe out of *our* personal reason and power (emphasis added).

Christians do not believe that God is good based upon an empirical proof that God necessarily demonstrates on a physical basis. We *awaken* to faith *in spite of* everything. We understand that whether or not God is good is not based upon the limited reality of our human comprehension of our particular experiences. Faith does not allow us to determine what "the goodness of God" *should* look like. It allows us to believe His revelation about His intrinsic goodness in spite of what our experience shows it *does* look like. Our faith in God and in his goodness cannot be scientifically tested within the bounds of this physical reality because God exists *outside* of it. It cannot be validated scientifically or empirically, and so while to the atheist it is mere nonsense to attempt to answer the questions regarding the existence or the goodness of God through some means *other than* empiricism, the Christian cannot look to empiricism as establishing its proof.

Yet both the atheist and the Christian attempt to explain the same set of facts. Both can see that there are discrepancies in our experiences that make it difficult to account for God's goodness, which is why, from the atheist's perspective it is:

> Incumbent upon the theist to provide enough reason for his belief that God is the true explanation of the universe and morality. The atheist, for his part, does not necessarily offer an explanation; he simply does not accept the theist's explanation. Therefore, the atheist need only demonstrate that the theist has failed to justify *his* position.[110]

The atheist does not offer a solution because he has none except his experience and human judgment. In the end, it is the atheist's own materialistic view of the world that has made it impossible for him to believe in a God, let alone one that is good. And we are not blaming the atheist for making that assumption; he has no other alternative! The Christian insists that this physical reality alone cannot account for our understanding of the goodness of God.

Our desire to solve the problem of the goodness of God, therefore, is at a standstill unless we ask an entirely different question than, "How does our perception of reality demonstrate that God is ultimately good?" Perhaps it might be better to arrive at some tenable solutions if we ask, "Are you so entirely dedicated to your materialistic view of reality that you will not allow for any *other* view of reality in considering the question of God's existence and goodness?"

HOW DOES CHRISTIANITY ACCOUNT FOR GOD'S GOODNESS?

Thomas Warren has written that "it is likely the case that no charge has been made with a greater frequency or with more telling force against the theism of Judeo-Christian (biblical) tradition than the complication of the existence of evil."[111] Historically, Christian theologians have insisted that God has permitted evil in order to bring about "a greater good" than would have existed had evil not been present in the world. Thomas Aquinas argued on a broad scale that "the permitting of evil tends to the good of the universe."[112]

The Christian theologian relies on the truthfulness of the biblical account to inform him of God's goodness and the existence of evil. The biblical account suggests that a good God allowed evil and sin in the world in order to bring about an immense *advantage* to men, in that, God, through the incarnation of His Son Jesus Christ, atoned for sin. This atonement for human sin is ultimately an expression of a better "good" than the "goodness" of a world that might have been without the presence of sin because the atonement for human sin is the ultimate expression of His goodness toward mankind. Philosophers have suggested that God gave "to the universe something nobler than anything that ever would have been among creatures except for this sinfulness" when He allowed sin to come into existence. [113] Therefore, in light of this biblical theological argument we cannot

> ...doubt that God does well even in the permission of what is evil, for He permits it only in the justice of His judgment. And surely all that is just is good. Although, therefore, evil, in so far as it is evil, is not a good [in and of itself]; yet the fact that evil as well as good exists, [on the whole] is a good. For if it were not a good that evil should exist, its existence would not be permitted by the omnipotent God, who without doubt can as easily refuse to permit what He does not wish, as bring about what He does wish. And if we do not believe this, the very first sentence of our creed is endangered, wherein we profess to believe in God the Father Almighty. For He is not truly called Almighty if He cannot do whatever He pleases, or if the power of His Almighty will is hindered by the will of any creature whatsoever.[114]

It is the biblical revelation of the person of God and the existence of evil that informs us of God's goodness in light of that evil, not merely our human perception of what God's goodness should look like in the world. Faith is an absolutely necessary requirement to understanding how God can be good in this world; it is not an *alternative* to answering the difficult question of His goodness; it is the solution to answering the question.

Often in speaking with people about the choices God made about the kind of world he supposedly created, they will inevitably ask, "Couldn't God have made a better choice by creating a hedonistic paradise that is free from pain and suffering? Isn't a world free from pain and suffering better than this world? Because God did not create such a hedonistic paradise, is He not therefore lacking in the qualities of love, goodness, and power?"

The remainder of this essay will attempt to address these questions. We recognize that the Christian, theistic conception of God not only grants that there is evil in the world that God created, it believes that God has ordained its existence (using this word *ordained* in the normal dictionary usage of "commanded, ordered, established, or intended") to demonstrate how good He is. Scripture teaches that not only has God created the whole earth and all that dwells within it but that He remains good in spite of the choices He made to create it as He did and to govern it as He does.

B. C. Johnson has written of this formidable and difficult problem that "throughout history God has allowed numerous atrocities to occur. No one can have justifiable faith in the goodness of such a God."[115] Yet there are literally millions of people who *do* have justifiable faith in the goodness of the God of Scripture who has not only allowed evil atrocities to exist, but has in His sovereignty decreed that they be so without negatively impacting their view of God's goodness.

According to biblical theology, an infinitely good God *demonstrated* His goodness in spite of His allowing evil to exist. Romans 8:28 says, "And we know that all things work together for good to those who love God, to those who are called according to His purpose." Note, however, that this verse does not teach that all events in life are "good" from the human perspective *in spite of the fact* that some of them may actually be evil! Nor does this verse teach that the good and evil events alike work together within God's providence for the benefit of both the Christian and atheist.

This verse, however, does teach that as Christians we know that God's ordaining of all events, regardless of how they appear in this physical reality, work together for an ultimate good to those who love God, because God is ultimately good. Christians must keep in mind this decisive end in their understanding of God's goodness. There appears to be nothing in Scripture to indicate that all things *also* work together for good to those who hate or deny the existence of God.

WHICH KINDS OF CHOICES DEMONSTRATE GOODNESS?

Now, if we suppose for a moment that Scripture is true in terms of its declaration that God remains infinitely good while permitting the existence of evil *and* apparently fails to remedy each instance of it from a human perspective, then does the existence of evil in the world demonstrate God's goodness or negate it? In other words, if God is truly good, would He *allow* evil to exist because He is good, or would He *destroy* evil because He is good?

Furthermore, would there even be an atheist in existence to question the goodness of God if God were intent upon eliminating *every* evil?[116] This, of course, only requires two things. First, the atheist must necessarily admit to the possibility of possessing a single evil thought in his mind for at least one second during his lifetime. We ask that if the atheist would acknowledge the possibility that for one second during his lifetime he has had a thought that was evil, or merely not good, is the fact that God allows him to exist in spite of his evil thought, a demonstration of God's goodness? Or would the fact that he did not destroy the atheist the second he had an evil thought demonstrate that God is evil?[117]

Scripture is replete with examples of the apparent thriving of the wicked in their wickedness. "For I was envious of the boastful, when I saw the prosperity of the wicked. For there are no pangs in their death, but their strength is firm. They are not in trouble as other men, nor are they plagued like other men" (Psalm 73:3–5).

"Because the sentence against an evil work is not executed speedily, therefore the heart of the sons of men is fully set in them to do evil" (Ecclesiastes 8:11).

The prophet Habakkuk wrote of his confusion about the thriving of the wicked while the righteous God-fearer suffers: "You [God] are of purer eyes than to behold evil, and cannot look on wickedness. Why do You look on those who deal treacherously, and hold your tongue when the wicked devours?" (1:13). In Judges

6:13, Gideon complains with wonder that "if the Lord is with us, why then has all this [hardship] befallen us?"

The question remains for us to consider: Which action on God's part demonstrates His goodness? Is God good because He allows evil to exist? Or can His "goodness" only be demonstrated by His elimination of evil as the atheist suggests? Who determines the degree of evil that must be present before God eliminates it? This issue is especially difficult for the atheist. B. C. Johnson states:

> A very large disaster could have been avoided simply by producing in Hitler a miraculous heart attack—and no one would have known it was a miracle...No one is requesting that God interfere all of the time. He should, however, intervene to prevent especially horrible disasters. Of course, the question arises: where does one draw the line? Well, certainly the line should be drawn somewhere this side of infants burning to death. To argue that we do not know where the line should be drawn is no excuse for failing to interfere in those instances that would be called clear cases of evil.[118]

The atheist must obviously perceive that premeditated murder is a relative "goodness," which leads to several serious problems. For instance, how does murdering Hitler demonstrate God's goodness? Furthermore, how do we know that God *didn't* interfere in Hitler's actions, for example, by preventing *every* Jew from being exterminated? Which is the greater good: allowing only some Jews to live or murdering Hitler?

Furthermore, how would anyone prove that it was *God* who gave Hitler a heart attack were he to have died from one rather than that his heart naturally stopped beating apart from any intervention by God?[119]

Who decides what is ultimately "good"? Should it be the atheist? If so, on what grounds will he suggest that he knows best what is good or not good in every circumstance? He cannot claim eternal omniscience. Perhaps he would claim this knowledge on the grounds of his own goodness. Furthermore, it is intriguing that the atheist is not requesting that God interfere *all* the time but just when the atheist says so. Perhaps the atheist imagines that the Christian God should be available to intervene at every beck and call that the atheist determines He should.

The atheist apparently knows as well that a line *should* be drawn in some cases that require the knowledge of "goodness." Apparently unbeknownst to God, it is before the death of innocent children. But we wonder, if all children are innocent in the atheist's perspective, wasn't Hitler once an *innocent* child as well? How is it that the atheist can label as good the murdering of innocent children if they turn out to be like Hitler and still use God's failure to rescue innocent children from burning as a demonstration that God is *not* good? Who knows whether or not one of those children that God allows to burn in a fire will not grow up to be the next Hitler?

Furthermore, on what basis does the atheist determine the innocence of children? Certainly not on his understanding of what they will do thirty or forty years after their birth! For even the atheist would have to agree that though Hitler may have been innocent as a child, that innocence certainly left prior to his choosing to murder several million Jews! And if we compare the supposed innocence of children to a perfectly holy and just God, what more can we say then of their innocence than that it is only a relative one?

Won't the atheist agree that even humans allow for degrees of evil when they make "good" choices? Does not a general in the army prefer a slight wound accompanied by great victory to no wound at all and no victory? Certainly goodness is relative even in the light of evil choices.

Winston Churchill allowed the Nazi bombing of the city of Coventry, England, during World War II even though he knew ahead of time that the Nazis were preparing to do so and could have prevented the deaths of innocent people. Through various spy networks and the obtaining of a Nazi book of codes, Churchill had learned of the Nazi plan to destroy the non-military site of Coventry. Yet he reasoned that if he were to evacuate all of the citizens from Coventry prior to the bombing (thereby sparing the loss of innocent life), the Nazis would have known the British had broken their secret codes, thereby endangering the future good that would come from being able to determine the war plans of the Nazis more thoroughly and gain the ultimate victory in the war. The difficult choice was to allow some innocent people to die at Coventry for the greater good of eventually defeating the Nazis once and for all. Did Churchill make a "good" choice? Or would it have been better to save Coventry, yet be defeated by the Nazis in World War II? Perhaps that is a something only God can determine.

THE PROBLEM OF THE VALUE OF PLEASURE AND PAIN

The atheist often supposes that if God is ultimately "good," then He could have demonstrated that goodness more effectively through the creation of a hedonistic-like paradise where only pleasure or pleasant consequences exist. The question of whether human beings might always be capable of only choosing the good in a paradise of pleasure is virtually incapable of being determined in light of our current perspectives of reality. [120] The Christian biblical perspective is that a perfectly good God allows evil to exist while He Himself remains good. Christians admit that evil is endemic to the world and to those of us who live here because of the presence of sin. The atheist's argument that all that God needed to do to have made a better choice when He created was to change the *environment* to one that is hedonistic is essentially flawed if it does not take into consideration how our present world is affected by sin.

For we see that even in our world that now exists, pleasure does not always lead to good. In fact, the physical pleasures that we now experience can just as easily lead human beings to jealously, envy, addiction, and hatred as they can lead to good (assuming of course that the atheist would agree that these previous things are not good). I believe it can be demonstrated that injecting heroin into one's veins, for example, is one of the most pleasurable sensations that humans can experience in the flesh. Yet there are limits to the goodness of these pleasurable sensations. For a little too much heroin can lead to death. And unless the atheist is willing to agree that death is a possible "good" that results from living in a hedonistic paradise of pleasure, we cannot say that the presence of that pleasurable environment alone guarantees "good" results if human beings, as they now are, were to live there.

Furthermore, we could even question whether we could experience *more* pleasure in a "hedonistic" world than we are capable of experiencing in the world in which we now live. More importantly, has anyone experienced not only *every* possible pleasure to its fullest extent in this world, but every possible *extent* and *avenue* of *every* pleasure in the human body we have in this world that contains evil? It is utter speculation on the part of the atheist to assume that we could experience more pleasure than we are currently able to experience and without negative (evil) consequences while remaining the human beings that we now are.[121]

We grant the atheist his case that he is not necessarily arguing for a world where *no* pain exists, but perhaps only for a world where less of it exists. B. C. Johnson, for example, does not necessarily require a *completely* hedonistic world where no suffering of any kind at all might exist as the only possible alternative to this one. "[The atheist] need only claim that there is suffering which is in excess of that needed for the production of various virtues (which virtues, according to the theist, produce courage, sympathy, etc)."[122] It is interesting, isn't it, that the atheist suggests that suffering might bring virtue to humanity? One would gather by his arguments that suffering would not be considered a relative good but rather something that God in his goodness would necessarily remedy if indeed he were good. Huston Smith has written that Hinduism, for example, accepts the existence of pain in reality "when it has a purpose, as a person welcomes the return of life and feeling, even painful feeling, to a frozen arm."[123] Yet, is it not with difficulty that anyone accepts the notion of purposeless pain? What function would useless pain have in the physical world? Apparently even the atheist doubts the possibility of the existence of purposeless pain when he suggests that some suffering might be necessary to produce virtue.

Now, we need not look far to see that at least certain kinds of pain *do* serve a good purpose in this world. Scientists have explained that lepers experience the mangling and deterioration of their flesh because they are no longer able to sense pain in the extremities of their bodies. Because they cannot feel the pain that would normally caution them to be attentive to their own actions, lepers cannot determine whether or not they are incurring any detriment to their flesh. Pain in one's extremities protects the person from incurring more damage to them.

Even the atheist can easily see that pain in the world in which we now exist is necessary and that it actually serves a "good" purpose in our world. And even though we agree with the atheist that pain in certain excesses is most often considered to be evil and *appears* to be of no use to us in this world, God had a purpose and use for it in the world that He created. Does our world not function better in some degrees because of the existence of pain in it?

Though it remains difficult to assimilate the excesses of pain and evil that appear in this world, the Bible teaches further that God uses physical pain and suffering to chastise His own "for their own good" (rather than plant them into an imaginary world of hedonism and pleasure which is free from pain). King David wrote, "It was *good* for me to be afflicted so that I might learn your decrees...I know, oh Lord, that your laws are righteous, and in faithfulness *you* have afflicted me (Psalm 119:71, 75, emphasis added).

Charles Haddon Spurgeon, London's greatest preacher, was afflicted with gout for most of his adult life. His response to that affliction demonstrates a Christian conviction that in spite of pain and suffering, God uses it toward our ultimate good.

> The result of [being in the melting pot of pain] is that we arrive at a true valuation of things [and] we are poured out into a new and better fashion. And, oh, we may almost wish for the melting-pot if we may but get rid of the dross, if we may be but pure, if we may but be fashioned more completely like our Lord.[124]

The response of the greatest apostle in the New Testament to God's goodness and the struggle he had as God formed him toward the pattern of Christ through pain and suffering is clearly laid out for us in 2 Corinthians 12:9b, 10: "Therefore, I will boast all the more gladly about my weaknesses, so that Christ's power may rest on me. That is why, for Christ's sake, I delight in weakness, in insults, in hardships, in persecutions, in difficulties. For when I am weak, then I am strong."

DOES GOD DEMONSTRATE THE GREATEST GOOD BY ALLOWING THE GREATEST EVIL?

Is it possible that in our desire to answer these difficult questions regarding the place of good and evil in this world that we have failed to ask the most important question of all? *Could God have demonstrated the greatest good by allowing the greatest evil?*

Our tendency to question whether God should have made a world other than He did is worth serious reconsideration. After all, though it is fun to speculate, this *is* the world we live in.[125] We all experience both good and evil here, some of us to a greater or lesser degree than others. Yet if God did not create this world with the intention of it being a hedonistic paradise but rather created it to be, as one man suggests, a "scene of history in which human personality may be formed toward the pattern of Christ," how shall we go about reaching that end while we live in a world that is evil?

First, the Christian theist must acknowledge his own responsibility for his own evil and cannot fault the world's Creator for it because he believes that Scripture is true when it says that God is perfect.

The Westminster Confession of Faith has stated the biblical truth that "God from all eternity did, by the most wise and holy counsel of his own will, freely and unchangeably ordain whatsoever comes to pass" (WCF 3:1). But what Christians often fail to understand is that *in His perfection there exists a mysterious element that defies human comprehension.* God being perfect does not mean that his choices are *perfectly* understandable.

From our finite perceptions of reality, humans are too willing to challenge the concept of whether God is entirely good. We critique His wondrous ways, faulting Him for what appears to us to be haphazard carelessness in His creation without any trepidation. We so arrogantly dispute His power and ability by suggesting that He could have done it better "if only." We see murder, rape, greed, and death all around us and do not hesitate to shake our fists in the air and say, "Why have *You* allowed this?" Why do we remain so thoroughly blind to the extent of His goodness in light of our own evil? Would any of us be alive for a second longer if God were to eliminate all evil because of His goodness?

This issue is at the heart of the mystery of the Gospel: This God who is good, who created human beings with a huge propensity toward evil, chose the greatest good for them by experiencing the greatest evil for them. This God, in demonstrating His goodness, by His grace alone saves believing men from their evil rather than destroying them for it. In doing this, God demonstrated for those who believe that though they are worthy of nothing more than to pay for their own wickedness with their own lives, He paid the price for their evil for them with the life of His only begotten, perfect Son.

Perhaps rather than challenging God's goodness, we might become inclined to see how it can be that Scripture explains to us that while God is free from any evil in and of Himself and would remain holy and just even if He held us accountable for each of our sins, He has chosen rather to demonstrate His goodness toward mankind in that "God was in Christ reconciling the world to Himself, not imputing their trespasses to them" (2 Corinthians 5:19). He chose the greater good of allowing the world to become what it is so that we could experience the *greatest* demonstration of His goodness toward the great number of us who are evil. And that greatest good was to reconcile wicked sinners to Himself, not at the cost of our lives, but at the cost of Christ's life.

This mystery is the gospel that defies human comprehension. The *mystery* lies in the fact that God's goodness is demonstrated to us through the explanation in Scripture that instead of a perfectly holy God obliterating humanity because of its sin, God did the most *in*humanly incomprehensible thing to remedy that situation. This remedy is a mystery precisely because His solution is, at the same time, a horrible demonstration of the extent our own evil and an incomprehensible demonstration of the extent of His goodness toward us. Even the goodness of God's solution for our wickedness is incomprehensible in that God poured out His wrath against evil upon His own Son, who was the only person to have ever existed who was free from any evil whatsoever, so that he wouldn't pour it out on us!

I urge the reader to consider 1 Corinthians 1:18–31. The gospel message of God pouring out His wrath upon His own Son is a message that is absolutely foolish to those who are perishing in their unbelief (1 Corinthians 1:18). Yet that very same message has the power to save those who believe it. God, in His mysterious wisdom, has made what the world believes to be true about "goodness" foolish. The gospel is foolish to the unbeliever because the world can never understand God's goodness unless it understands God through faith and the wisdom of the cross of Christ. In fact, not only can the world not know God through its own kind of wisdom, it was *pleasing* to God to save those who believe the very same message that the rest of the world rejects as foolishness (1 Corinthians 1:21).

Scripture records that "it pleased the Lord to bruise Him [Christ]; He has put *Him* to grief. When You make His soul an offering for sin, He shall see *His* seed, He shall prolong *His* days, and the pleasure of the Lord shall prosper in His hand. He shall see the travail of His soul, *and* be satisfied. By His knowledge My righteous Servant shall justify many, for He shall bear their iniquities" (Isaiah 53:10–11). That message of forgiveness of sin by the pouring out of God's holy wrath against His perfect, sinless Son is a message that cannot be understood apart from faith.

The very idea of God putting His own sinless Son on a cross to pay the penalty of sin for every person who would ever believe that message is impossible for the human mind to accept as logical or rational. The unbelieving world asks, "How can that message demonstrate God's goodness, when, for all intents and purposes, that message describes one of the most horrific absurdities capable of being conceived?" And even to begin to grasp that message in faith requires of the believer that he acknowledge that the greatest good could only come about through what appears to us to be nothing short of an atrocity. God's gracious forgiveness speaks volumes not only of our inability to save ourselves but begs the question, "What if God demonstrated the supremacy of his goodness by allowing the greatest evil to occur?"

PART 3

EMPOWERING THE SOVEREIGN GRACE OF GOD IN THEOLOGY

DOING THEOLOGY WITHOUT A LABEL?

> "But," says someone, "He foresaw that you would have faith; and therefore, He loved you." What did He foresee about my faith? Did He foresee that I should get that faith myself, and that I should believe on Him of myself? No; Christ could not foresee that, because no Christian man will ever say that faith came of itself without the gift and without the working of the Holy Spirit.
>
> —Charles Spurgeon, *The Early Years*

Calvinism thrives in spite of the fact that it has taken a serious theological beating throughout the years. The name itself conjures up all kinds of menacing thoughts. For example, I remember speaking with a Seventh Day Adventist nurse one day on the phone, whom I had never met, about my general health and she was explaining to me about how she felt led of the Lord to minister to people's health problems in such a way that would take into consideration their spiritual condition as well as their physical condition in determining the overall status of their health. She said she was implementing this idea because the Bible taught that God not only loved everyone in the world but was concerned about their spiritual health. She felt motivated to express God's love for everyone by reminding them of the importance of taking care of both their spiritual and physical health.

In an honest desire to understand her theological position that motivated her sense of mission, I asked, "In what way do you feel God *demonstrates* His love for everyone in the world?" Her immediate response was, "You're not into that Calvinism stuff are you?" From her point of view, only a Calvinist would want to know how God *demonstrates* His love to everyone—to everyone else it was apparently patently clear! An Arminian theologian wouldn't need to explain how it was demonstrated because he would be equally committed to biblical truth, which to him plainly taught that indeed God did love everyone in the world, though explaining that in practical terms might be difficult.

Needless to say, our conversation took a turn for the worse at that point, but I don't believe either one of us really wanted it to! Before we had even realized it, by virtue of some vague, human instinctual need to clarify another's theological position and compare it to our own (or perhaps justify it in light of our own), we had become adamant about what we understood our labels to represent. We had identified and qualified the other person's theology because of the label that we had attached to what we believed their theological position represented from our own point of view.

Though I'm sure she had little more than a surface understanding of all that lay behind what Calvinism meant to *me,* what she had attached to the label called Calvinism, from her perspective, was enough of a reason for her to stuff all that the label meant to her into a big box marked, "Calvinism: Discard All Contents." She had indeed made a value judgment on all of my theology based on my request for further clarification of her one statement about how God demonstrated His love for everyone. And I had not been able to comfortably fit her statement about God's love for everyone into my box of practical theology because of the way that I had restricted what the label Calvinism might and might not tolerate in its definition.

Now, I grant you that a theology that teaches predestination and that man's faith is not generated from within himself, as classic Calvinism has been advocating since the beginning, but is given to him as a free and gracious gift from the Holy Spirit at the whim of God's foresight, doesn't sit well with theologians of the opposite camp. This doctrine of predestination has been up against some very strong competition from theologians and preachers throughout history (to say nothing of the devil himself). A. M. Hills, a prolific author, pastor, and counselor of the Nazarene persuasion, wrote that "[Charles Finney] declared that [Calvinism] was as vile a calumny against the holy God as was ever vomited out of hell."[126] Hills further admonishes that statements from the Calvinistic Catechism "are the most God-dishonoring and blasphemous theology that was ever put in the human language."[127] And the reason Calvinism is so intolerable to these theologians is because it denies the function and power of man's will in the process of salvation.

I kid you not, I once received a phone call from a man who was interested in finding out whether two stories that were related to him in a Sunday school class were true or not. He asked for some kind of input from me in answering two questions: "Is it true that John Calvin once cut off the head of a child for stealing a loaf of bread?" and "Was it true that Calvin routinely took people out onto a river in a boat and threatened them to verbally acknowledge the biblical truth in his TULIP acronym about predestination, and depending on their response, let them try to swim to shore or drown if they chose not to believe in it?"

The fact that an adult Sunday school teacher in an evangelical church in the twentieth century would make such statements about Calvin in an effort to destroy the Christian historical view of predestination and ask his class to accept this character assassination without possessing any kind of historical or legal validation whatsoever is absolutely staggering. In this teacher's eagerness to eliminate from the minds of his students any trace of the biblical doctrine of election and grace that he obviously fervently despised in his failure to understand biblical theology, he made two outlandish comments that not only could not be validated but were also completely contrary to the nature of the doctrines of grace and election upon which Calvin based the whole of his theology!

To suggest that Calvin would try to *force* someone to believe in the doctrine of divine sovereignty and predestination by either confessing it as biblically true or paying the penalty of death by drowning for denying it is poignantly absurd. Could a man like Calvin, who rested all of his theology, hope, and Christian values on the two doctrines that see salvation inextricably connected to the sovereign God of a tiny universe, really teach or believe such a thing? Calvinism has taken a theological beating because no one can do theology without a label.

Hopefully now you will begin to sense the emotional depth of the struggle between these two theological points of view. Calvinists expect Arminians to see theological things differently. And please understand that I'm not advocating that you should try to fit yourself within the man-made confines of one or the other of these labels. I can't help the baggage that is tagged on to the labels of each of these two views. I couldn't care less if you ever *say* that you are a Calvinist or an Arminian. What I care about is how you think through theological concepts. I care about how you process Scripture. And I ask you to reflect on one single issue: "When you interpret Scripture and the work of God in salvation, do you believe it is correct to perceive salvation and God's sovereignty in the saving of souls from any other theological position than a biblical one?"

The clashing of these two ideological systems has been in process since the two systems of biblical thought were labeled as such!

Interestingly, Calvinists readily agreed that, had a man succumbed to the Arminian persuasion at the time of the Puritans, had he betrayed the true gospel message by teaching that man somehow musters up from his spiritually dead corpse a faith in the living God, he would have been branded, as Spurgeon wrote, "the vilest heretic breathing, but now *we* are looked upon as the heretics, and they as the orthodox." But heresy and orthodoxy were not only struggles that theologians had centuries ago!

How can the Christian lay community be held accountable to recognize the faults in Arminian theology when its seminaries, teachers, evangelists, talk-radio hosts, and authors not only do not recognize it, they actually teach it as though it were soundly biblical! How did this teaching find a home alongside Christian doctrine when the term *Arminian* had for centuries referred to the teaching of a party or sect outside the orthodox doctrine of the Christian church? How did we stray so far from what we once considered to be the truth?

We no longer see theology from the perspective that our eternal God sees it. We see it from the perspective that theology revolves around finite men and their choices and desires and not from the perspective that God is sovereignly bringing all things to pass to bring glory to Himself.

UNTWISTING THE THEOLOGY OF THE SECOND EPISTLE OF PETER

Someone asked me in the middle of a class that I was teaching on Calvinism, "How do we reconcile the Calvinist doctrine of unconditional election [which states that God freely chooses some from the mass of sinners for salvation, while passing over others on no condition that they met], with such apparent contradictions as 2 Peter 3:9: 'The Lord is not slack concerning His promise, as some count slackness, but is long-suffering toward us, not willing that any should perish but that all should come to repentance'?"

That person went on to ask, "Isn't it quite obvious from this verse that God does not desire that any [single individual] perish, but that every single person would come to repentance? How then can we even tolerate for one moment this nonsense about election with a plain verse like this that obviously contradicts the idea of sovereign election?"

I think this verse is probably one of the most misunderstood verses in all of Scripture. Ironically however, no one supporting the Calvinist view could ask for a better opportunity to explain the principle of election than in the context of this verse. When understood in its full context, it is clear that in this verse Peter is teaching, in a most staggering revelation, the truth of God's sovereign choice of individuals in election.

Yet on the surface, this is perhaps one of the most misinterpreted and misrepresented texts in all of the New Testament. How many times has someone used this verse to attempt to prove and justify the belief that God desires that everyone be saved? Nothing could be farther from the heart of God, and we shall see momentarily how this verse has been hermeneutically wrenched from its context to distort the view that what God really wants is to save everyone.

THE PRACTICAL MISREPRESENTATION

First of all, let's see how this verse has been used by at least one Christian publication to make it mean something God never intended it to mean. The following question appeared in an issue of *Focus on the Family,* as well as in Dr. Dobson's book, *When God Doesn't Make Sense.* [128]

A woman wrote in to Dr. Dobson that her daughter was living a life of rebellion and had chosen to reject the faith by living with a twice-divorced man whom she had no intention of marrying; and furthermore, she had had at least two abortions and was exhibiting disgraceful language when she spoke. She apparently showed no interest in returning to the church. The mother expressed anger at God for allowing this terrible thing to occur. She wrote that she had wept until there were no more tears, and she was writing to

Dobson seeking any kind of encouragement that Dobson could offer. In response, Dobson explains by writing:

> Often, this anger at the Lord results from a misunderstanding of what He will and won't do in the lives of those for whom we intercede. The key question is this: Will God require our offspring to serve Him if they choose a path of rebellion?

The biblical answer to that question is no; God will not require our offspring to serve Him while they remain in their natural state of rebellion simply because they are the offspring of believers.[129] We must clearly repeat that God will do whatever He wishes, with whomever He wishes, for as long as He wishes, whenever He wishes. That's what *sovereign* means. He is under no obligation ever to do what we wish He would do.

The key question then is not so much whether God will require our offspring to serve Him if they choose a path of rebellion. Just because God has changed our stony, wicked heart to enable us to believe the gospel does not mean that he desires that the children of all believers necessarily come to Him in faith. God may require certain people to serve Him. The ones that He desires to serve Him are the ones that will serve Him. No others will serve Him because they cannot escape their natural, rebellious, sinful wills until God is pleased to change it for them. Until He changes their hearts, they can choose to do nothing else as free moral agents but rebel against Him. However, God can choose to use a rebellious unbelieving person to do His will should He so will it, and that person will do what God chooses that he does, whether or not he thinks he is doing God's will.

Anyone who now serves Him was also once in rebellion, just as this lady's daughter is. The reason that those Christians who serve Him aren't in rebellion any longer is because God has changed their wicked, rebellious heart into a heart that loves and desires to serve Him. Did those people who now serve God freely choose to serve Him? Yes, they did but not while they were in rebellion to Him. When they were in rebellion, they chose the only thing that they really freely wanted: to run from God. They freely chose to serve Him when they were enabled to see that He alone is worthy of service. But at that time they were no longer in rebellion; they were new creatures.

Dobson went on to say:

> The answer...is that God will not force Himself on anyone. If that was His inclination, no person would ever be lost. Second Peter 3:9 says, "He is patient with you, not wanting anyone to perish, but everyone to come to repentance." To claim this great salvation, there is a condition. An individual must reach out and take it. He or she must repent of sins and believe on the name of the Lord Jesus Christ. Without that step of faith, the gift of forgiveness and eternal life is impossible.

Now follow the logic. There is a certain degree of truth to this response, though you will see that at its core it is highly questionable as to whether or not it is scriptural. It is true that if God's inclination was to save everyone by "forcing Himself" on them, then indeed everyone would be saved. But, as we shall see in a moment that certainly is not what 2 Peter 3:9 is teaching. It is obviously not the case that God desires to save everyone in the world, as hell will one day prove. Either that or we need to specify that God is not capable of fulfilling His own desires. He does not will that all men be saved, nor does He desire it. If He either willed it or desired it, everyone would be saved. Even the Arminian view acknowledges this truth.

The Arminian view that Dr. Dobson has expressed here is pleading with us to see that, from their perspective, God does not desire that a single person perish, but if you do perish, it's your own fault. You could have come to God on your own, but you didn't will it. God didn't want you to perish as much as you wanted yourself to perish, and what you wanted won over what God wanted. But to say that "God will not force Himself on anyone" is somewhat misleading because it implies that He will not *in any way* interfere with someone who will not willingly come to Him! In other words, the choice to come really belongs strictly to every wicked, unregenerate sinner alike, regardless of God choosing you! The implication is that the sinner in his rebellion is capable of choosing between the good of coming to God *or* the evil of rebelling against Him before God does a work on his obstinate and sinful heart to change his will to come.

The fact of the matter is that Scripture teaches that God *must* interfere in that person's life if he is ever going to come to God, because left to his own way, he will only choose that which is wicked, hateful, rebellious, and sinful because that's all he *can* choose.

Furthermore, this Arminian view clearly demonstrates that salvation has a condition. Dr. Dobson has excelled at laying open the huge theological chasm between Arminianism and Calvinism for us. The Scriptures teach that our election is not based on *any* condition or merit of ourselves. It is unconditional, without condition. Under the premise offered here, what would ever keep us from saying that we played a part in our salvation? What prevents us from saying that "I met the condition for salvation by choosing to come? If I meet the condition, it is God who is robbed of His sovereign rule. What *I* will is what God *must* do. I will to repent, and I meet the condition of salvation, and God has no alternative left but to save me. I reached out from my own free will and repented of my God-hating nature and took salvation because I clearly saw that that was better than eternal hell with the devil and his minions."

This theological position teaches that I must first take the step of faith before the gift (which is obviously not free) of forgiveness and eternal life is mine. If I don't take that step, it is impossible for me to be saved. God can't save me, and He won't save me until I make myself savable by believing the gospel on my own.

> Said another way, God will not save a person against his will, but He has a thousand ways of making him more willing. Our prayers unleash the power of God in the life of another individual...[God] makes the all-important choices crystal clear to that individual and brings positive influences into his or her life to maximize the probability of doing what is right. Beyond that, He will not go.

Of course Dr. Dobson's statements, in an effort to comfort the mother here, have exceeded all logic and scriptural basis. Apparently, if what he has written is true, God will only save me if it's my will to be saved. God will not save me unless I will that it be so. The sovereign power of the Creator of the universe is bound by our prayers for the lost soul. It is our prayers that actually unleash His power.

Now think about the last two sentences in the above quote for a moment. Does God really make the all-important choices crystal clear to everyone? Of course He doesn't! What is the very best choice? Isn't it eternal salvation? No other choice compares to that for anyone. If He so clearly lays out the options of heaven and hell, why are the gates of hell being so overcrowded with lost sinners? Or are the options of eternal hell and heaven only made crystal clear to those who God, in His absolute sovereignty and perfect will, effectively calls from eternity past as His elect to spend eternity with Him? To suggest that God is only willing to maximize the probability of doing what is right really leaves a lot of room for error, doesn't it?

According to Dr. Dobson's theological point of view, God apparently only positively influences us into a more likely probability of doing what is right. If He were just a little more sovereign, though, He could bring about His choices. But beyond positive influence, God will apparently not venture.

Do you see the tremendous difference in how the sovereignty of God is viewed between Arminianism and Calvinism? The reason we struggle so much with the concept of election and predestination is because we do not have a proper perspective on the sovereignty of God. In the Arminian teaching, which has engulfed evangelical society, we have a tiny, little, powerless God that can't run the details of a universe without being bound by the choices of apostate sinners.

Some of you may wonder what other choice is available as we counsel others in this kind of situation? How can we come alongside and encourage someone who is suffering as they watch their wayward child rebel against God, without robbing God of His sovereignty? Is the only avenue of comfort open to us to rob God of His glory and sovereignty? Is there no biblical counsel we can give them that can help them through this time of suffering and despair that they feel as they watch their rebellious child move farther and farther away from God, without making God some sheepish, little wimp who isn't in control?

There are some ways that we can biblically counsel others in times of suffering about lost and rebellious children. Perhaps the greatest comfort can be expressed by reassuring the person that the God he or she believes in and trusts is in absolute control of all events that occur. Nothing anyone does takes Him by surprise! Perhaps God is leading them into a dark valley so they might see Him more clearly after all the trials they have run into.

Of course, an Arminian could never comfort a lost person with these words. If God is not in control, how can we ever confide in what He does or find any rest in Him? Our genuine comfort does not come in what God or we might do but in the fact that He is sovereign and in control. He is able to bring to Himself whomever He wishes, and He will bring to Himself all those whom He has chosen to save in His own good time. It is only because He is absolutely sovereign that we can trust in Him in all things that occur. And the fact that God does not choose some does not in any way deprive Him of His righteousness, justice, and mercy. Whether or not God chooses to bring a rebellious child to Himself or not, every single decision and carrying out of His will is perfect and righteous.

Doesn't the Bible teach that God uses our rebelliousness, wickedness, and backslidings to correct us and reprove us (Jeremiah 2:17–19)? The prodigal son had every opportunity to remain in the good graces of his father's mercy, yet only after seeing his own emptiness and misery after leaving the goodness of his father did he come to his senses and run back to him in repentance. As long as a child seeks what only God can give from some source other than God Himself, there is not much more we can do but be prayerful and hopeful that God will bring that person to Himself.

Now let's look at how the context of 2 Peter clearly teaches that Dr. Dobson's view of the sovereignty of God, and the will of God in the election of lost souls, is utterly untenable in his interpretation of 2 Peter 3:9.

Clearly from the salutation in 1:1 and in 3:1, Peter is writing the epistle to believers. He begins in 1:1 with "to those who have obtained like precious faith with us by the righteousness of our God and Savior Jesus Christ."

The word translated as "obtained" is from the Greek word *lagchano,* which appears this one time in 2 Peter and a total of four times in the New Testament, being used only once in the Septuagint. All five examples clearly demonstrate the meaning of the term.

In Luke 1:9, Zacharias was chosen to burn incense in the temple by the casting of a lot; in John 19:24, the soldiers guarding the cross cast lots for Jesus's garments. *Lagchano* has the distinct idea and translation, "to receive or be determined by allotment."

In Acts 1:17 it carries the idea that Judas the deceiver "was numbered with the disciples, and *obtained* a part in the ministry" of the twelve. More importantly however, for our purposes, it is the Apostle Peter who uses this same word here in Acts 1:17, as he does

in his second epistle, to describe how Judas obtained a part in the ministry of the twelve. The idea is the same as in 2 Peter 1:1, "to obtain a post or position by divine allotment." Judas was divinely chosen by God.

In the Septuagint, the Greek translation of the Hebrew Old Testament, *lagchano* appears one time only in 1 Samuel 14:47 (called 1 Kings in the Septuagint). The NKJV translates that word in the verse as, "So Saul established his sovereignty over Israel." The English translation of the Septuagint reads, "And Saul received the kingdom, by lot he inherits the office of ruling over Israel."

The word from Homer down in classical Greek had the sense of "to have a post assigned by fate; to obtain by inheritance; to obtain something by casting lots; to fall to one's share by lot."[130]

It is clear in 2 Peter that those who have obtained like precious faith have obtained it through no merit or attempt of their own. Rather, they have obtained their faith because God threw down the lots at random and they fell where they fell or, more precisely, they fell upon whom He chose. If they fell on you, you are one of the elect, destined to believe, and if they didn't, you aren't. There is nothing that you could have done to merit this gracious gift. It was obtained by grace. And if grace is a free gift that means there is nothing you must do to receive it.

Examining the intent of the text, isn't that clearly the way Peter intended to describe how faith was obtained? Nowhere is it indicated in the New Testament that the lots of faith were cast in favor of those would first reach out and take it or who were first able to choose to believe the gospel (see Acts 13:48). Isn't that the reality of unconditional election that Calvin was so adamant about, that there is no condition by which we have been elected, that our election is all God's work, every last speck of it, and none of ours? Our election, if truly unconditional, is based on nothing other than the random choices of a sovereign God!

We already know by what Peter wrote in 2 Peter 3:7 ("until the day of judgment of ungodly men"), that some men will remain

ungodly and suffer judgment for it, namely by not being saved! How can those of the Arminian persuasion say that Christ died for all in terms of atoning for their sin when clearly Peter informs us that some men will remain ungodly until judgment day and suffer the penalty for that ungodliness?

When Peter writes in (3:9) that God is "long-suffering toward us, not willing that any should perish, but that all should come to repentance," the use of the word *all* must mean some qualified group other than every single individual alive on earth (seeing as how some men will clearly not be saved because they remain not only ungodly but unrepentant, as he already said!)

The only thing that makes sense within the context, whether it is popular or not, is that Peter means, "God is long-suffering toward us (believers, the elect, those to whom the lot of election has been cast in favor of being saved), not willing that any (future believers who are among the elect) should perish, but that all (elect believers) should come to repentance." If God grants faith to us without us meeting any condition first, and God must bring those who are to be saved to Christ, and in order to see the kingdom of heaven, we must first be "passively" born from above, then the only *all* Peter could be talking about here are all those God has chosen to elect. [131]

How many times has this verse been butchered and wrenched from out of its context simply because people have an incorrect view of God's sovereignty? How many times must we listen to a missionary say, "God does not desire that a single soul be lost?" If that was what He truly desired, then not one soul would be lost! Why then do we constantly assume that God cannot do what He really desires?

In response to the scoffers (3:3), Peter is saying that God does not procrastinate as to the fulfillment of His promise (which is that He will return for judgment). The delay in question is not whether God can *ever* make the promise that He will return in judgment good, but, seeing as how time means nothing to Him who is eter-

nal, the delay is so that all who are elected to repentance in the plan of God *will* repent! He is holding out because He is long-suffering toward the elect!

Why should God be long-suffering toward those whose lives are futile and incapable of bringing glory to Him in salvation, who will never repent, who are not willing to come to Christ? Surely Peter is not suggesting that God is holding out for all those ungodly men who will receive judgment for their ungodliness (2 Peter 3:7)! For the Calvinist, it can surely be affirmed that God knows who it is that will believe and who will not! Why would God hold out for that group of ungodly men that will never repent? If He were holding out for them, He'd never return.[132]

Peter writes in 2 Peter 3:10 that the day of judgment will come quickly, bringing destruction. But surely not for those whose sin has been forgiven! Therefore, what manner of persons ought you (who have had your sins forgiven) be? Holy and godly! Can the unregenerate, non-elect ever be holy and godly? Not if they are dead in trespasses and sins! Likewise, the ungodly and unrepentant are not looking for the coming day of wrath that God has promised. They are scoffing at that notion of God returning for judgment, "saying all things continue as they were from the beginning of creation" (3:4).

Likewise in 3:13, we (elect) are the only ones looking for a new heaven and new earth where righteousness dwells. Certainly some of the non-elect might look for that world as well. And some believe that they will deserve to be there! But who but the elect can possibly be found by God to be living in peace without spot and blameless (3:14)? Not the spiritually dead who are totally depraved, who elsewhere Peter suggests have the opposite inheritance of the elect, one that is corruptible, defiled, and fading away (1 Peter 1:4).

Finally, we see in 3:15 that the reason that the long-suffering of our Lord is salvation is not because He is waiting to save every single man, but rather His delay is because He is waiting for the elect to come to repentance so that they will be saved! The long-suffering of our Lord is also doom, but only for those who remain apostate and unregenerate (3:7).

Clearly, the 2 Peter 3:9 passage in its context teaches that God delays His return in judgment to await the fruition of the faith of all the elect. He does not desire that any of us should perish, though He will certainly return in judgment where many ungodly men will perish.

THE SMALLER THE WORD, THE BIGGER THE PROBLEM

> Theology should arise out of persevering prayer, sustained study of the substance, thrust, and flow of the biblical text, and uncompromising fidelity to the truths thus discovered, whatever the costs.
>
> —Martin Luther

THE ISSUE OF GOD "DESIRING" TO SAVE *ALL* MEN

As I was beginning to reflect on some of the things I had been taught in seminary, I wrote a letter to one of my theology professors (and the head of the theology department of the seminary from which I graduated) to ask if we could briefly meet to discuss some of the issues that I was struggling with. Upon my arrival there, he immediately asked me to turn to 1Timothy 2:3–4 and read what that verse said. I read, "For this is good and acceptable in the sight of God our Savior, who desires all men to be saved and to come to the knowledge of the truth." Then he asked me what that meant. I said that I understood it to mean that God desired that all *types* of men be saved and come to the knowledge of the truth—men from every walk, background, and heritage of life, whether kings, slaves, rich, poor, etc. But, I said, I was struggling with how that verse could mean that God desired that every single man on the planet be saved and come to the knowledge of the truth simply because that interpretation would bring with it too many other theological problems.

At that point my theology professor wanted more clarification. He said, "So then, verse six does not mean that Christ gave Himself a ransom for all men, like it clearly and plainly says?" I said that that verse by itself read that Christ gave Himself a ransom for all (it did not say all men in verse six, though it did say men in verses one, four, and five), but that the word 'all' could not mean every single person unless the concept of God's sovereignty in election were mutilated or His ability to do so were somehow rendered impossible. He said, "Do you know who was king at the time this letter was written? It was Nero, one of the wickedest, most insidiously guileful humans who ever lived. Do you mean to suggest that this verse is saying that in some way, Christ did not pay the ransom price for Nero?" I said that that was most definitely what I was suggesting. He then very flatly stated, "In some way, Christ had to have ransomed Nero from sin. In some way, Christ's shed blood covered his sins as well."

Now remember, this is a conversation with the head of the theology department at a major conservative Baptist seminary! Having great respect for this professor, but perhaps possessing not quite as much timidity as I possessed while a student in his classroom, I was compelled to say, "When do I get to hear you tell me what way He ransomed Nero from sin? Do you mean that Christ *sort of* ransomed him? *Completely* ransomed him? *Could have* ransomed him, had Nero only believed first? There are too many passages in the Bible that refute that He ransomed all men. Therefore, Paul couldn't have meant all in the sense of every single individual here in this passage and have the rest of Scripture be true. If Christ did pay some vague, indefinable, and unknown ransom price for every man, as you are asking me to consider, it could not have been a very effective ransom, as hell will one day verify. More significantly, it could not have been a biblical ransom."

Furthermore, I said, "If He did die for every individual and ransom them from the marketplace of sin, you must necessarily thoroughly change the meaning of *ransom* in the New Testament to mean something it does not mean anywhere in Scripture. Equally troubling, of course, is the problem that in stating that He in some way or other ransomed every person from sin by His death and covered his sin with His shed blood, there remains the scriptural fact that many souls will obviously spend their eternity in hell; there, they will be unable to escape because their sins were never forgiven, in particular, their sin of unbelief, from which they were never ransomed. Anyone who is spending eternity in hell is paying for his own sin; otherwise he would not need to be there! It just will not do to simply state that men like Nero were ransomed by Christ's shed blood. I think you should reconsider what Paul must have meant when he used the word *all* in this passage."

Perhaps it is best to quote the writings of J. K. Grider, a professor at an Arminian theological seminary, to see that the problem in either theology, Arminian or Calvinistic, is not ever related to Christ dying for all people. In fact, that position is not even a theological tenet in either Arminian or Calvinistic theology! Grider writes:

> Yet such a view [that Christ paid the penalty for our sins, shed His blood for their sins] is foreign to Arminianism, which teaches instead that Christ *suffered* for us...what Christ did He did for every person; therefore what He did could not have been to pay the penalty, since no one would then ever go into eternal perdition. Arminianism teaches that Christ suffered for everyone so that the Father could forgive the ones who repent and believe [italics mine].[133]

You can see now that the struggle to correctly define the nature of Christ's death is difficult for Arminians. Acknowledging the validity of the Calvinist's argument, Grider affirms that Christ couldn't have paid the penalty for the sin of every man because then there would be no need for hell. If on the cross Christ paid the ransom for the sin of every man, including Nero, then no one would need to spend eternity separated from God, to which the Calvinist says, "Thank you for proving my point that that could not have been what Christ accomplished." The Calvinist would agree that Christ suffered for us (yet qualifying the "us" as the elect), but only as an example for believers to follow (1 Peter 2:21), never suggesting that the suffering was a payment held out until man chose to believe.

Clearly we have seen that the crux of the issues remaining for Arminians is whether or not people believe and repent on their own. But the illogical thrust of Arminian doctrine evades the sense of all of soteriology, including how we think of God's sovereignty in election, what eternal life and regeneration really are, and whether Christ merely suffered for men so that the Father could forgive them when they finally got around to choosing to repent. The Calvinist would say that the elect were redeemed from sin, that is, *actually saved,* through the precious blood of Christ that He shed on their behalf, yet "through Him believe in God" (1 Peter 1:21).

The Calvinist does not need to confuse Christ's suffering with His redemptive work. If it is true, as the great Greek scholar and Arminian commentator R. C. H. Lenski suggests, that Christ atoned for all and expiated the sin of all, why does Paul still refer to some as "sons of disobedience" (Ephesians 2:2)? Why is the wrath of God coming upon them (Ephesians 2:3)? What ever is the purpose of hell?

Seeing as how hell is a reality, and only those whose sins are not forgiven wind up there, it is preposterous to suggest that Christ's death paid the penalty for all sinners. For again, this is neither true of Calvinistic thought nor Arminian thought! On this issue, Douglas Wilson writes:

> The key question we must ask ourselves is, what exactly does the cross of Christ do for sinners? Christians have adopted two basic answers to this question. The popular answer is that the cross creates the possibility of saving everyone, while the biblical answer is that the cross actually saves those who believe in Christ. The popular answer holds that those who are saved can attribute their salvation to the cross plus their decision to apply for its benefits, while the biblical answer holds that those who are saved can attribute their salvation to the cross alone.[134]

Even some Arminians are astute enough to grasp how absurd it is to suggest that Christ's death ransomed everyone, which is exactly why Arminian theologians change the effect of His dying from "paying the penalty" to merely "suffering" for us.

AN UNREASONABLE PLEADING FOR CONSISTENCY

One thing that will become obvious to you as you grow in your knowledge of Scripture and the way people defend it is that many Christians make an enormous plea for *consistent* interpretation. For example, they insist that the word *all* should always be interpreted as "each and every existing individual" and never anything else because the word *all* means the same thing no matter where it occurs! To them it always means "everyone."

Commenting on 2 Corinthians 5:14 ("One died for all, therefore they all died"), R. C. H. Lenski, an otherwise careful exegete, demonstrates how important the Arminian concept of universalism is to properly exegete their theological perspective when he writes:

> The Calvinistic effort to limit this word [all] to "all the elect" constitutes one of the saddest chapters in exegesis. The Scriptures shine with the "all" of universality, but Calvinists

> do not see it. Their one effort is to find something that would justify them to reduce "all" to "some." Calvin himself says that all = all kinds, all classes, rich and poor, high and low, rejecting no class, taking some of each, but not all in the sense of every individual.[135]

I am bringing this to your attention to further demonstrate how Arminianism has virtually eliminated the concept of the sovereignty of God in election. It is my hope that it will become clear to you by further exposing more roots of this theological position that the real trouble for the above writer and other Arminian translators is not in the way Calvin or the Reformers understood the words *all, each,* and *every* in Scripture. The real problem is that Arminian theology tries to explain the true sense of Scripture by making Scripture thoroughly *inconsistent* in its meaning. For surely a scholar such as the one quoted above can readily see that their arguments hold no water at all when there are countless examples in the Bible where the use of *all* and *every* obviously does not mean "every single individual." (One need only look at the following passages to know that that is true: Mark 1:5; Luke 21:17; Acts 21:28; John 12:32; Acts 22:15; John 1:7; Acts 19:27; Colossians 1:23).

Let's just look at John 12:32 more carefully as an example. It surely cannot be said even by Arminian scholars that Jesus was in the habit of contradicting Himself. We have already shown how extensive Jesus's teaching on particular election is in the Gospel of John, especially in chapter six. Are we now to think that somehow Jesus forgot what He said in chapter six, and in chapter twelve, verse thirty-two is teaching that when He is crucified, He will draw every single person to Himself? Surely it is obvious to even the staunchest Arminian that Jesus has no intention of drawing *every single man* to Himself, especially the ones that the Father has not given to Him. Or does Jesus mean that when He is crucified that He will draw all different kinds of people to Himself, from all walks of life and from every continent on the earth, but not every single individual? This must surely express Christ's intention or else He is suffering from amnesia.

The real problem for the Arminian position is adequately articulated by this great scholar elsewhere when he attempts to clarify further the fairness of God from man's perspective. "The real assurance for me that Christ died for me is this alone, that He died for absolutely all. If He omitted any, knowing what a fearful sinner I am, I must come to the judgment that He surely passed by also me."[136]

Bible interpretation cannot rely on consistency; it must rely on context. Context always determines the sense of meaning in Scripture, never consistency. To say that if *all* means "every single person" *here in this particular text,* then it must mean "every single person" *in every other text* is almost humorous in light of Romans 5:12–21. Approaching the text like that is sort of like shooting yourself in the foot. It is setting up a false method of securing the correct interpretation that you hope will guarantee absolute understanding, which, in reality, guarantees that you won't understand the meaning of the text if you apply it with broad strokes. In fact, taking that approach to interpretation leads to utter chaos.

Regarding the use of the word *all* in the 1 Timothy passage above, "For this is good and acceptable in the sight of God our Savior, who desires all men to be saved and to come to the knowledge of the truth," I would suggest that people approach understanding it like this: Start asking more questions about the text than just, "Who does the *all* refer to?" Here's how I have proceeded to think through the issues in this 1 Timothy passage.

Obviously, if Scripture is trying to teach that God "desires" to save everyone, then the good Bible student must ask: Why doesn't God *do* what He apparently *desires* to do in 1 Timothy 2 and elsewhere, namely, save everyone? If He's the God of Scripture, he certainly must be able to at least do what He wants to do. Clearly, even a bad theologian will admit that God does not save everyone. Why then doesn't He do what Scripture suggests that he wants to do? I propose that there are only four possible ways of dealing with this:

1. He *can't* do what he wants to do; or
2. He *won't* do what he wants to do; or
3. He *doesn't want to do* what he wants to do; or
4. He has no intention of desiring to save every single individual when Scripture says He desires to save all men because Scripture uses *all* in many different ways, one of which means "some only." And in this passage it seems quite clear that what God desires to do, and does do, is to save "all kinds of men."

a. If we say God cannot do what He genuinely wants to do, then what kind of a God are we left with?

Does the Bible teach that we have an omnipotent, sovereign God, who supposedly cannot do what He wants to do? That is not the God of the Bible. The next question is: Why would God want to do something that He knows He can't do? What is the benefit to that predicament for God? Surely this can't be a rational way to understand this passage.

b. Is it reasonable to say that God *won't* do what he wants to do?

He wants to save everyone, but He doesn't save everyone, not because He can't, but because he won't! The further we take this, the more absurd it becomes!

c. There are too many instances where Scripture says God does do what he wants to do, so why doesn't he save everyone if that's what he really wants to do?

Scripture suggests that God does *exactly* what he pleases to do when he wants to do it in several clear and unchallengeable statements.

All that God *does* brings Him pleasure and all that He is *pleased* to do, he does. Compare Isaiah 46:9, 10; 44:28; 48:14; Jonah 1:14; Psalm 115:3; Psalm 135:6. The Hebrew word in these verses translated as "pleasure" or "being pleased" means "to be mindful of, be attentive to, keep, protect," with the idea being more of eagerness or zealousness in the attention, where the end notion is one of "excited or delighted attention." It carries the notion of both emotion and feeling great favor toward something. God is said to have this attentive or excited delight toward people, matters, activities, and things.

For instance, God is said to delight in certain people, like Israel, His chosen; He delights in the Sabbath being kept; He is pleased by His law being observed; He is pleased by demonstrating mercy toward people; He is pleased by Israel's knowledge of God and truth. He is pleased in making the universe as a kind of spin-off of his overflowing delight in His own glory.[137]

Every activity that God is engaged in gives Him delight! Again and again in Scripture we read that he acts for the sake of his Name. His great goal is to magnify his fame and to manifest the renown and the honor of his Name in all that he does. When Psalm 115:3 says, "But our God is in heaven, He does whatever He pleases," we find that the English versions translate the word *pleases* with a variety of words like *desire, wish, want, pleases, purposes, wills,* and *determines.* This is significant. When this Hebrew word for *pleases* is used of God, it is translated to include not only His wanting and determining but wishing and purposing and desiring and doing.

1. Psalm 115:3 says, "Our God is in heaven; He does whatever He pleases."
2. Isaiah 46:9, 10: "I am God, and there is none like Me, Declaring the end from the beginning, And from ancient times *things* that are not *yet* done, Saying, 'My counsel shall stand, And I will do all My pleasure.'"

3. Jonah 1:14: "Therefore they cried out to the Lord and said, "We pray, O Lord, please do not let us perish for this man's life, and do not charge us with innocent blood; for You, O Lord, have done as it pleased You."

4. Again, Psalm 135:6: "Whatever the Lord pleases, He does, in heaven and in earth, in the seas and in all deep places." Psalm 115:3 says, "But our God *is* in heaven; He does whatever He pleases." Here in Psalm 135 we have, "Whatever the Lord pleases, He does." It is what pleases Him that is the motivation for His action. And all of His actions please Him. There is nothing that God does that displeases Him.

Clearly, the Bible teaches that God does all that He pleases. And all that He does pleases Him. Therefore, what do we do with a verse that implies that God desires to do something, but clearly doesn't do what He desires, in light of the fact that other verses clearly teach that God does do what He desires, and everything he does pleases Him?

Considering these options may seem silly, but after we explore them we see that the only reasonable way to look at 1 Timothy 2 is to reevaluate the meaning of *all.* Strangely enough, it seems to be the Arminian preference to teach that God wants to save everyone, but He won't because of our apostate free wills; or that God won't save us because *we* don't will it so! Somehow it's more satisfying to the Arminian theologian that the wills of pagans in rebellion to God's wishes are able to do what *they* want to, but the sovereign, directing, providential God of the universe isn't able to do what he wants to do.

Amazingly, for some theologians this is a better option logically than to just rethink how Paul must have intended the word *all* to be used in this context. He says, "Therefore, I exhort first of all that supplications, prayers, intercessions, and giving of thanks be made for all men," in 1 Timothy 2:1. But if he meant each and every existing individual when he wrote "all men," why not leave it at that instead of qualifying it in verse two by saying "for kings and all who are in authority"? If "kings and all who are in authority" are a part of the "all men" in verse one, there wouldn't be any need to qualify who he meant. Kings and all who are in authority are not *all* men; they are some part of all men. Likewise, in verse four, the statement "who desires *all* men to be saved," must not mean "each and every existing individual"; it must mean all *kinds* of men; kings, those in authority, those who are not, etc. The truth about the gospel is that it saves *all kinds of men* from every tribe and tongue and in every nation. The gospel does not save every single existing individual. It saves every single individual who believes it.

CHRIST DIED FOR A PURPOSE —NOT A POSSIBILITY

Let's look at another passage of Scripture that helps further elucidate this discussion. Paul is clearly making a comparison in Romans 5:12–21 between what happened to Adam (and consequently mankind, as a result of Adam's disobedience) and what happened to those who believe in Christ as a result of His obedience. What happened *theologically* to mankind through Adam's disobedience and sin, namely, condemnation and judgment to *all* men, is being compared to what happened *theologically* through Christ's obedience and death, namely, righteousness and grace to *all* who believe. By using these phrases of comparison between 5:12–21, "just as" (12), "as through" (18), "even so" (18), "so also" (19), "so that" (21), Paul is teaching that just as *this* condemnation and death happened to every man in Adam due to Adam's disobedience, *this* justification and life happened to every man in Christ due to His obedience.

Now, this is an unusual way to make comparison for this reason: Paul is not using these comparative phrases as a one-to-one *numerical* comparison. He is not saying that because death affected every single man through Adam's disobedience, *even so, just like that, as through that,* now every single man has been made righteous because of Christ's death. Even though the comparison appears to be numerical in some sense because Paul uses words like *all* or *every,* the context reveals that it is plainly not intended to be numerical. He is clearly not saying that Christ's atoning death was on behalf of every man.

For instance, when we read Romans 5:18, even though the word *all* is used, evidently the comparison is not intended to imply all men across the board numerically in both instances but only in one instance.

> Therefore, as through one man's offense *judgment* came to all men, resulting in condemnation, even so through one Man's righteous act *the free gift came* to all men, resulting in justification of life.
>
> Romans 5:18

Paul is summarizing that, in reality, when Adam committed his offense of disobedience, sin and its natural consequence entered the world: death happened physically and literally to Adam and all of his descendents. And with that came God's condemnation toward all men who had sinned because all men are sinners in Adam. He is their representative head.

Now, it wasn't the *possibility* of death that entered the world when Adam sinned but actual, literal death. It was the *inevitability* of death for each and every man that entered the world. No man who would ever live after that would be able to avoid death, the consequence of sin. The entrance of sin into the world *is* the cause of the entrance of the inevitability of death into the world.

Now, just as actual, literal death happened to those who are in Adam, resulting in the condemnation of all men, Paul is saying that *even so, just like that, as through that,* actual, literal justification of life came to all men through one Man's (Christ's) righteous act of obedience to God. It wasn't the *possibility of life and righteousness* that came to men in Christ's death; it was the actual righteousness of Christ and eternal life that came to them.

But Paul cannot mean that the comparison is to be understood numerically, that is, that every single living man has now received this justification of life, *just as* every single man has received the death that entered the world because of Adam's sin, in spite of the fact that he uses *all* in both instances. He has already clarified in the first verse of Romans 5 that righteousness is procured by men *only* by faith in Christ. Paul opens his entire argument in Romans 5:1 by stating, "Therefore, having been justified by faith, *we (who are of faith)* have peace with God through our Lord Jesus Christ."

The righteousness procured by Christ that results in freedom from condemnation belongs only to those who now believe in Christ. That freedom belongs to every single man *of faith,* not every single man in existence. This freedom from condemnation does not belong to all men indiscriminately, including atheists, Christ haters, and unrepentant sinners across the board. These have not been assured of their freedom from the just condemnation, which can only be removed by actual, genuine faith. Christ's death, therefore, can*not* be said to be atonement for every man who ever lived because every man is not justified before God; only men of faith are justified before God.

So Paul's use of *all* in verse 18 where he writes, "*The free gift came* to all men, resulting in justification of life," does not mean each and every single man, as it would if he were making a simple numerical comparison, but rather *all men of faith.* That's why he adds the qualifying statement at the end of 18 that the result of that faith is a justified life, a life made right before a holy God by faith in Christ.

Following Paul's line of reasoning, Christ couldn't have died for the sins of every human being, as some Arminian theologians are so prone to say. Paul makes it very clear in his comparison that Christ's obedience resulted in *actual justification of life* for believers. It didn't result in the *possibility* of justification, any more than

Adam's sin resulted in the *possibility* of death and judgment. Men inevitably face God's condemnation as a result of sin entering the world. They don't face the *possibility* of condemnation; they *are condemned* as a result of Adam's sin. In exactly this way, Paul is saying Christ's death did not make atonement *possible;* it actually resulted in atonement for those who believe. Christ atoned for and made justification of life a reality only for particular individuals, those who have genuine faith in Him, not all men.

Below is an overview of the verses in Romans chapter five and what they demonstrate about the two Adams.

THROUGH THE FIRST ADAM:

- Disobedience came into the world (19)
- Sin entered the world (12)
- Death entered through sin (12)
- All men died because all sinned (12)
- Death reigned (14, 17)
- Many died by one offense (15, 19)
- Judgment came by one offense (16, 18)
- Condemnation came by one offense (16, 18)
- Many were made sinners (19)

THROUGH THE SECOND ADAM:

- Obedience came into the world (19)
- The free gift (of the grace of God) abounded to many believers (15)
- The free gift came as a result of many trespasses (16)

- The free gift resulted in justification (16)
- Abundant grace and righteousness reign in life (17)
- The righteous act came to all men resulting in justification of life (18)
- Many made righteous by one act of obedience (19)

The issue in Romans 5 is that Paul clearly uses *many* to mean both *many* and *all.* And he uses *all* to mean both *all* and *some.* If one pleads for a consistent interpretation for the word *all* here, it only guarantees failure because it ignores the only genuine key to interpretation: context.

I would suggest to anyone struggling with this issue that he first abandon the idea of consistency as his method of interpretation if it costs him a normal, reasonable understanding of the context. And I think that is what people want. We want to read the Bible with a sense of normalcy in understanding the language, with the end result being to understand what God has intended to say.

THE T.U.L.I.P ACRONYM EXPLAINED

> He who believes in God without reserve, and is determined that God shall be God to him in all intellectual, moral, spiritual (pursuits), throughout all his individual, social, religious relations, is, by the force of that strictest of all logic which presides over the outworking of principles into thought and life, by the very necessity of the case, a Calvinist.
>
> —Benjamin B. Warfield

Calvinism and Arminianism are two theological viewpoints that are diametrically opposed to each other, each attempting to garner its support from its view of Scripture. What these two tenets represent today is not necessarily represented explicitly in the writings of these men. For instance, Calvin did not commit to the notion of limited atonement anywhere in his writings. It is quite present in his thought process by inference, however.

a. All for whom Christ died are saved;

b. Not all men are saved.

c. Therefore, Christ did not die for all men (and therefore the atonement is limited in design and function, but not in its efficacy).

When Calvin died in 1564, Jacob Arminius was four years old. Though the TULIP acronym references the five points known today as Calvinism, it is not correct to think that Calvin devised this acronym. These five points (Total depravity, Unconditional election, Limited atonement, Irresistible grace, and Perseverance of the saints) are simply the Calvinistic theological answer to a five-point manifesto put together by a group of Arminian theologians in the early seventeenth century that made certain declarations of how they understood Scripture. These Arminian theologians wrongly held two theological suppositions in principle, which the TULIP acronym corrected:

1. Divine sovereignty is not compatible with human responsibility; and

2. Ability necessarily limits obligation (i.e., if we are not able to respond or come on our own, we cannot be held accountable for not coming or responding). This would be unfair of God to hold us so accountable.

From these two principles, the followers of Jacob Arminius drew two incorrect deductions:

1. Since the Bible regards faith as a free and responsible *human* act, they thought, faith cannot be caused by God and must be exercised independently of Him; and

2. Since the Bible regards faith as mandatory on the part of all who hear the gospel, *ability* to believe must be universal among all men.

The TULIP acronym we associate with Calvinism today was a Reformed theological response to the five principles proposed by these Arminian theologians to demonstrate that the Arminian deductions and principles were biblically *incorrect*. The five points of Calvinism are also referred to as the Doctrines of Grace. Following is a brief explanation of those Doctrines of Grace.

TOTAL DEPRAVITY:

Man's corruption due to original sin is all pervasive. Man is a spiritual corpse before the spiritual life is bestowed upon him, having lost any and all ability of *will* to any spiritual good accompanying salvation. "From this original corruption, whereby we are utterly indisposed, disabled, and made opposite to all good, and wholly inclined to evil, do proceed all transgressions" (WCF). Original sin is the reason for the condition of sin in men. The only *true* freedom we have as sinners is freedom *from* righteousness. Following this reasoning, man cannot convert himself by his own strength or prepare himself for conversion. He cannot respond to any offer of grace in this state due to his moral corruption and liability to guilt. No aspect of man is untouched by sin:

- intellect (can't think rightly about God);
- sensibilities (all his loves and desires are tainted by sin);
- will (men do not will themselves to seek after God; rather they seek His benefits while fleeing from Him).

"Seeker-sensitive worship" misses the boat theologically then because it doesn't correctly understand man's sin problem. The Arminian opposite to total depravity is Free Will: Man's sinful condition has disabled him, but he must be morally able to "believe." Man may be sick and near-sighted but still able to believe and obey; otherwise, God is not just if he condemns man after the fall without giving him the chance to be saved. A just condemnation must include an innate and moral ability (freedom of will) to believe the gospel.

UNCONDITIONAL ELECTION:

God's selection of individuals for salvation is wholly without condition. God's sovereignty and man's inability are intrinsic in the Calvinistic doctrine of election. God is free to do as He pleases. In fact, doing what he pleases is the motivation for all of His actions! Not only does God do what He pleases, but all of His actions are just and righteous. In Calvinism, God chooses solely on the basis of His free grace and not on any condition met by the sinner such as his faith. God does not foresee any faith in the sinner except as He himself bestows it on those whom He unconditionally elects. If God's election is from eternity past, it cannot *also* be based upon the temporal choice to believe. The sinner's election is the cause of his faith, not the result of it.

REPROBATION

Reprobation is not a part of the TULIP acronym, but it is fitting to insert it here as a corollary to the explanation of unconditional election. Just as election is not passive from God's perspective, neither is His choice to not choose to elect certain individuals. God has a special love (salvific) for the elect, manifested in giving them eternal life, and leaves the rest to be damned for their own sins and wickedness. Election, then, is a foreordination of some corpses to life. Reprobation is the foreordination for some to remain spiritually dead. Calvin clearly and precisely set forth this doctrine, and though he abhorred it, he refused to deny it in the Scriptures (Romans 9:10ff, 18ff). This is not just a passive *passing over* the non-elect but an actual hardening of the heart to resist the gospel. Calvin reasoned that because we cannot comprehend God's counsel and will, it must simply be believed, leaving the matter in God's hands. Furthermore, this doctrine is to be handled carefully so as not to give unbelievers an opportunity for using it as an excuse for rejecting the gospel.

The Arminian opposite to unconditional election (being elected due to nothing in us) is conditional election (election conditioned upon one's faith). God elects on the basis of the sinner's *foreseen* faith in Arminian theology. God looks down the corridors of time, sees which ones will believe, and chooses them once they do believe. This makes sense in Arminian theology because God loves all men equally, demonstrated by giving all men an equal chance to be saved. Faith then is acquired by the effort of the individual and is not a gracious gift of God to us.

Loraine Boettner quotes Dr. Benjamin Warfield in *The Reformed Doctrine of Predestination:*

> The removal of the elect by the pure grace of God, not merely from a state of condemnation, but out of the company of the condemned—a company on whom the grace of God has no saving effect, and who are therefore left without hope in their sins; and the positive just reprobation of the impenitent for their sins is repeatedly explicitly taught in sharp contrast with the gratuitous salvation of the elect despite their sins.[138]

LIMITED ATONEMENT:

Christ's death was a particular atonement for the sins of believers and procured their salvation only. Christ's death atones for a definite number of people by design, the elect, to whom the atonement is limited. The atonement of the Son was designed for the salvation of those whom the Father had elected unconditionally. If Christ forgives *all* sin on the cross by His atoning death, then He also forgives the sin of unbelief. If the sin of unbelief is forgiven, then no one deserves to go to hell.

Christ's death only made redemption *possible* from the Arminian perspective. Christ died for all persons indiscriminately. Christ's blood does not accomplish pardon unless man freely wills to accept the pardon.

IRRESISTIBLE GRACE:

The effectual calling of the Spirit is just that: effectual; it cannot be resisted by the elect; otherwise, they wouldn't be elect. The Holy Spirit regenerates those whom the Father chose and for whom the Son died, their faith following God's regeneration. The crucial issue here is not whether or not we sinners *ever* resist the Spirit's calling. We do! The issue is whether or not we *ultimately* resist the Spirit's calling. If the Arminian says that we do have the ability and will to ultimately resist the Holy Spirit, then the Calvinist's concern is that God is not omnipotent and sovereign in bestowing His grace to men as Scripture clearly teaches.

The Arminian view that God's grace is resistible and that salvation is man-centered is a very prevalent theological perspective today and is clearly demonstrated in these quotes of Billy Graham's from *Decision* magazine:

- "The new birth is something that God does for man when man is willing to yield to God."[139]
- "Any person who is willing to trust Jesus Christ as His personal Savior can receive the new birth now."[140]
- "The Holy Spirit will do everything possible to disturb you, draw you, love you, but finally it is your personal decision...make it happen now."[141]

PERSEVERANCE OF THE SAINTS:

It is God who perseveres in the elect saint to the end. The Spirit continues to work faith in the regenerate, and they therein persevere in good works, always struggling against the remnants of their original sin whose guilt is pardoned but whose power is decreasingly felt until it is destroyed at death. The sinner's perseverance in grace to the end then depends not upon him but upon the decree of the immutability of their election that flows from the free and unchangeable love of God the Father.

The Arminian response to perseverance of the saints is that sinners can also fall from God's gracious, saving grace. It is man who keeps himself saved by his own continuing faith and obedience. He can surely fall from grace because he willed his own salvation.

INROADS TO A FAITH PROFANED

> If anyone should ask me what I mean by a Calvinist, I should reply, "He is one who says, 'Salvation is of the Lord.'" I cannot find in Scripture any other doctrine than this. It is the essence of the Bible. "He only is my rock and my salvation." Tell me anything contrary to this truth, and it will be a heresy; tell me a heresy and I shall find its essence here, that it has departed from this great, this fundamental, this rock-truth, "God is my rock and my salvation." What is the heresy of Rome, but the addition of something to the perfect merits of Jesus Christ–the bringing in of the works of the flesh, to assist in our justification? And what is the heresy of Arminianism but the addition of something to the work of the Redeemer? Every heresy, if brought to the touchstone, will discover itself here.
>
> —Charles Spurgeon

Charles Spurgeon converted to Christianity more than 145 years ago. He had a simple, clear biblical understanding of what it meant to have faith in our sovereign God. And he believed the truth about

God's sovereignty just as mighty men of God before him had. As all Calvinists of his day, Spurgeon maintained a bold assertion that faith springs from the heart of the believer through the work of the Holy Spirit. Before Spurgeon, the great Baptist preacher Dr. John Gill, a valiant proponent for the sovereignty of God in salvation, believed that all the work of a man's salvation, "the work of regeneration, conversion, sanctification and faith is not an act of man's free will and power, but of the mighty, efficacious and irresistible grace of God."[142]

For anyone who might think that Spurgeon and Gill do not speak for modern theologians, consider this quote from another modern scholar: "The cause of any person believing is the will of God; and the outward sound of the gospel strikes the ear but in vain until God is pleased to touch the heart within."[143]

Yet sometime in the last century and a half, Christian theologians, pastors, and laymen began to subtly reinterpret this simple, clear Reformed understanding of our God-given faith in the sovereignty of God to mean that sinners come to believe in Him by themselves.

This heterodoxy has been rampaging into almost every seminary throughout the country like a stampeding garrison, hoping to crush its enemy, the sovereign grace of God in salvation. It is rampant, and there is nothing we want to do to change it. What the Christian church must finally be challenged to deny is that it not only believes but teaches that anyone and everyone who wants to be a Christian can be one whenever he or she chooses to become one.

Do we not now find that a good part of the Christian church currently reasons that man (in his natural state of spiritual death and apostasy) is capable of believing in Christ through his own endeavors when he wants to? According to this theological proposition, all a man has to do is search his (not so desperately, wicked, evil) heart for some latent desire to come to Christ, which the church has become convinced everyone possesses! Once he musters up this desire, he himself then shreds the garments of sin that have fettered his heart, mind, and soul, and through this sudden, mysterious unveiled desire and longing for Christ, he transforms his own heart, formerly dead in trespasses and sins, into a spiritually regenerated muscle. Then the Holy Spirit, longingly, anxiously, initially resisting the temptation to rescue the depraved sinner, is finally enabled to applaud the life-changing transformation he found within his heart because the final component in his salvation has been set in place: self-generated faith.

This opinion is formulated upon the deliberate denial of revealed truth that has become coupled with the acceptance of error. Scripture teaches that "man, by his fall into a state of sin, hath wholly lost all ability of will to any spiritual good accompanying salvation: so as, a natural man, being altogether averse from that good, and dead in sin, is not able, by his own strength, to convert himself, or to prepare himself thereunto."[144]

The theological tragedy in modern evangelicalism is that the church is appalled by a theology that teaches that God is absolutely sovereign in choosing who will and who will not come to Him.

REFLECTIONS ON HERESY

These are some of the adjectives that were conjured up in the minds of the early sixteenth-century evangelicals when they reflected on the word heresy: blasphemous, scandalous, venomous, abomination, infectious. In fact, these were just a few of the words used to describe the *opinions* of a man who, failing to acknowledge that his beliefs were filled with theological errors, was to be tied to a stake and burned alive for his transgressions.

Miguel Servetus was led outside the city of Geneva on October 23, 1553, and burned alive for the crime of heresy. As he walked to his death that day, these fateful words fell from his lips, "Jesus, thou son of the eternal God, deliver me!" And but for the transposition of a single adjective in that sentence, his life would have been spared! How careful and exacting were the theologians of old!

Yet Servetus would not renounce his theological premise that the church's view of the Trinity was a three-headed dog that guarded the gates of Hades in Greek and Roman mythology. He rejected the mystery of the Trinity in his final breath by meaning that Jesus was not Eternal Son; he was merely a human and became divine. His adamant grip on this theological misconception would not allow him to rescind and say that Jesus Christ is the Son of God *from all eternity!*

It was said of Servetus by the judges in his trial:

> You have promulgated false and thoroughly heretical doctrine, despising all remonstrances and corrections...and with malicious and perverse obstinacy sown and divulged...opinions against God the Father, the Son and the Holy Spirit, in a word against the fundamentals of the Christian religion, and that you had tried to make a schism and trouble the Church of God by which many souls may have been ruined and lost...you have neither shame nor horror of setting yourself against the divine Majesty and the Holy Trinity...For these and other reasons, desiring to purge the church of God of such infection and cut off the rotten member...we now condemn you...to be burned with your books to ashes. And so you shall finish your days and give an example to others who would commit the like.[145]

Clearly, the judges believed that the extent to which his theological opinion had strayed from Christian theology could indeed potentially pollute the thinking of the church. And so to stop the spread of this heresy, there seemed to be no other solution than to burn him alive with his writings.

Note the reasons again for the charges of heresy: "...sown and divulged opinions against the Trinity...against the fundamentals of the Christian religion...tried to make a schism and trouble the church...setting yourself against the divine majesty."

It was said that even while the now-famous theologian and prosecuting attorney John Calvin pleaded with him at the end to renounce his "rhapsody patched together from the impious ravings of all the ages," remarkably, there remained the hint of a question as to whether or not he should be executed among those who witnessed the ensuing travesty. How could "[Servetus], a man so far from orthodoxy, be, nevertheless, fundamentally pious and earnest in the quest for truth?"[146]

What does it mean to be a heretic in the twentieth century? How do we define heresy now, and what parameters do we insist its definition be limited by? According to the American Heritage Dictionary of the English Language, a heretic is one who "adheres to a controversial or unorthodox opinion or doctrine in some field." In this definition, there is no taking into account the degree of one's sincerity or piety or depth of knowledge or scholastic training prior to holding to this unorthodox opinion. Heresy is about one's opinions alone, not one's character. Heresy in terms of religion is about one's theological opinions, and how they differ from mainstream theology.

And just as it is fitting that the avoidance of the errors and consequences that accompany heresy should always have been the aim of the church, this same careful purpose was the very reason for the signing of the Westminster Confession of Faith on August 27, 1647. The signers of the confession agree that it was for

> ...a principal part of the intended uniformity in religion, and as a special means for the more effectual suppressing of the many dangerous errors and heresies of these times; the General Assembly doth therefore, after mature deliberation, agree unto, and approve the said Confession, as to the truth of the matter (judging it to be most orthodox, and grounded upon the Word of God).[147]

Servetus was burned alive as a result of the desire to crush his theology. No one cared that he might be sincere in his in error! No matter how pious he might have appeared to be to some or how diligent he was in his quest for truth or how sincerely honest he was while in error, it was his adherence to an unbiblical doctrine that led to his being put to death.

But one is no longer a religious heretic because of what one believes about theology. It has been my intention to show you that heterodoxy has engulfed the sleepy, careless minds of the sons of God primarily by allowing ourselves the privilege of interpreting Scripture from a perspective that refuses to empower God in His sovereignty. Heresy has ever so carefully and gradually been defacing and hewing that stalwart banner of Christianity, the sovereign grace of God. Volumes of the literature we produce and read verify that fact. Have you ever wondered why Christian people have such a bitter distaste and total lack of discipline to study doctrine? Could the reason for our utter lack of concern for interpreting Scripture with a view to the doctrine of the sovereignty of God be because the foundation of God's sovereignty has departed from every thought that surrounds our theology?

Oh, yes, I know how well we have learned to parrot, "We believe in the sovereignty of God!" Yet even the reference notes that are printed in our Bibles (to assist us, no doubt, in gaining a better understanding of the mystery of God) prove that we do not believe that He is really sovereign in every area of life. Feeling somewhat threatened, we'll say louder than we mean, "We *insist* that we believe that God is all-powerful." But our scholarly commentaries and Bible tracts deny it fervently. In fact, they ridicule the idea by teaching that God has no power other than the power we grant to Him to change and redirect a callused heart to come to Him only when that person says, "Now You may change me." A bit louder now, we retort in total assurance that "We teach the lost sinner that God is sovereign in His gracious salvation." Yet all the while we deny the very essence of the truth and wonder of grace and sovereign choice by teaching unbelievers that He is equally merciful to all alike as soon as they decide to believe. Angrier now, we stand adamantly, and clamor, "We would *never* stand for heresy because it's a lie, and we love the truth!" Yet the words that appear on the pages of our Christian books are tainted all about with the error that God is not sovereign. Our sermons and seminaries are no longer capable of piercing the dark chasm we have cut away from the truth: that sovereign grace is of God alone.

While we continue to grow more accustomed to believing heterodoxy rather than truth, we find it practically unbearable to hear the truth. As we befriend laziness and careless thinking, we can no longer grasp with the slightest apprehension that we are, all the while, stuffing our minds with volumes of sacrilege that belittles the sovereign glory of God.

I personally stand to gain nothing from persuading you of the logic and brilliance of the view that God is sovereign in every area of life. But it is there, in truth, that He is lifted high above the simple and trite concepts so many of us have come to imagine about Him. Few modern-day theologians have the audacity to go to the extremes that the early Reformers did to eliminate the impertinence of error from our presence. In retrospect, the early Reformers did have one thing going for them that we no longer do. They were at least able to recognize heresy when it reared its ugly head.

No, I am not asking anyone to take a stand beside Calvin's position on heresy. Few scholars in the twenty-first century believe that the glory of God is maintained by the burning of heretics because they know that burning heretics doesn't defend the glory of God; it kills people. How unfortunate though that the modern twenty-first century evangelical church now believes it is free from serious controversy or doctrinal aberration when, in reality, it has grown more and more tolerant to heretical doctrine, clearly being unable, in most instances, to differentiate heresy from biblical truth. As important as it is to remain certain that heretical doctrine does not infiltrate Christian doctrine and pollute biblical theology, it is crucial to remember that from the inception of the church, heresy was considered to be that which is in opposition to Christian theology. Being a heretic meant adhering to doctrines that were in contradiction to the biblical perspectives of truth. Yet, as we have seen, heresy exists very unobtrusively alongside Christian theological doctrines in the evangelical church today and, for the most part, without its members and leaders either knowing or caring about it.

If heresy has been so potentially detrimental to historical Christian doctrine because of its corruption of the truth, what has changed our attitude about it in the last few hundred years? It was easy to spot a heretic like Servetus. Today's heretics do a better job of blending in, or at least, keeping quiet. Lorraine Boettner writes:

> Schaff declares that Servetus was "proud, defiant, quarrelsome, revengeful, irreverent in the use of language, deceitful, and mendacious"...Bullinger declares that if Satan himself should come out of hell, he could use no more blasphemous language against the Trinity than this Spaniard.[148]

A man of this stature and infamy would be easily recognized even today. Servetus just happened to be a heretic who had a lot of character flaws. It shouldn't take us long to question one's theology if he were described as a blasphemer against the Trinity. But what if his blasphemy were much more subtle than that? What if his heretical view was no longer judged to be a threat to Christian doctrine even by modern scholars because the scholars themselves taught heresy? What if a heretic were someone who was well-liked and a friend to Christendom? Can a man be publicly acknowledged as a godly man in every conceivable sense *except* in his opinions about theology? Could heresy ever come out of the mouth of such a one? Can the fledgling seeds of heresy be that subtle?

Even if we were to find that there was indeed a subtle heresy that had encroached Christian theology today from the inside, by very famous Christian men or organizations, I believe that most of us would just continue to tolerate it rather than take the necessary first steps to challenge it. That is, unless we were enabled to see the severity of the damage it could do. Once we understood the potential damage heresy could do, what we would hopefully at least begin to do is question our own theology.

Perhaps the greatest single reason we would be least motivated to unseat heresy today is because it would require us to relearn, rethink, and reanalyze our understanding of theology, and quite frankly, that is just too much work for lazy Christians. We have been spoon-fed little baby bites of the Bible for so long and have had delivered from the pulpits and Sunday schools so much strained theology that we are incapable of thinking theologically for ourselves. When Sunday school teachers and elders and pastors refuse to teach doctrine that they have struggled with and prayed about and thought through, what can we possibly expect our congregations to swallow but little thimblefuls of Bible food?

Anyone who has been in the twenty-first century Christian church for any length of time knows that controversy is to be avoided at all costs—apparently, even at the cost of tolerating heretical doctrine. Controversy is disconcerting. Controversy ruffles feathers. Ruffled feathers make for very nervous Christians. And a whole community of ruffle-feathered Christians is a very unsightly and unnerving mess.

Heterodoxy is being written, preached, and unabashedly proclaimed over the radio waves of the world, by renowned men of God with utmost assurance that what they are saying is true, and no one questions a word they say because we are no longer even capable of knowing what heresy is! Our opinions about what wrong opinions are have changed. And one reason is because we have abandoned the study of doctrine because doctrine is boring to most Christians. They want sermons that make them feel good, not challenge them to grow in the knowledge of God from God's perspective.

But true doctrine has its source in the Living God who inspired Scripture. All other doctrine is either from man or from demons. If studying, thinking through, and learning about doctrine ruffles your feathers, it's time to find out why! If it bores you and does not meet your needs, you may be in serious trouble. If listening to someone speak about doctrinal issues in sermons and Sunday school makes you uncomfortable or bores you or overloads your thimble, it's time to be reminded about what heresy is and the historical struggle Christianity has endured in spite of it. It is precisely because we are no longer able to discern sound doctrine that we are unable to separate truth from falsehood. It is my hope that we become lovers once again of doctrinal truth that sees God as the sovereign Lord of salvation. Though few of us can praise the fervency with which the church desired to rid itself of heresy a little more than five hundred years ago, one wonders how so much accord could have been reached since that time regarding our inability to discern heresy.

AFTERWORD

When my good friend and pastor of the church I attended formerly for a number of years initially read some of the statements I had written in this book, he commented, "You have shown that the conclusions to much of our theology are wrong. Are you going to help fix it?" At one other point he wrote, "Point out the solid stuff because all I'm reading is negative."

I realize that I might have alienated the reader somewhat by the extent of my negativity and, undoubtedly, I have been asking you to be challenged by a lot of theology that you may not be too comfortable with. But if you find that you are not comfortable with the things written here, I want you to ask yourself why you aren't comfortable with them?

I also realize that the stones of controversy I am quarrying can be painful. They are not easy things to deal with, particularly if your thought processes have been accustomed to accepting most of what you read without serious concern for whether or not it lines up with biblical theology. As you continue to think through some of these issues, you will find that acknowledging these stones of controversy will require you to rethink how you view most of Scripture and evangelism. Whether or not you are willing to rethink your views of Scripture will depend greatly upon how you now view it. Is it sacred to you? Is it holy? Is it truthful and free from error? Is it absolutely sufficient to give us all that we need to live the life of faith? If you have answered yes to all of these questions, let me ask you a few more questions.

Is it worth whatever price you need to pay to interpret it and understand it as correctly as possible? Is Scripture worth re-evaluating and questioning on a continuous basis, to understand how you *are arriving* at your theological conclusions? If it is, then it is worth bailing a theology that is shallow, unbiblical, and perhaps even heretical to make sure you have the proper perspective on the issues we have raised.

I remember as I first started to struggle with some of these concepts and began to reexamine some of my theological views, I called a pastor of a Reformed Church (I had graduated from a Dispensational seminary) to talk through some of the questions that I was struggling with. As our conversation continued, I realized that if I began taking these ideas seriously and to their obvious conclusion, it would require me to do three things.

First, it would require me to continuously reevaluate and reformulate my theological positions in the light of Scripture as I studied and learned. It would require me to ask myself, "Why do I hold to any particular tenet? What is the emotional attraction to any particular position? Is the reason I believe something because someone else said that it was true? Do I believe something because that's what my teacher taught me to think or because that's what he taught me to say?"

I remember that while I was teaching a class on Calvin and Reformed theology at church, a member's mother was visiting for one of the classes in the series. You could pretty much tell that halfway through the class, she really wanted to get out of there. She was about as uncomfortable as someone could be without standing up and screaming, "Hearing you talk about these things is driving me nuts. I'm getting out of here!" As soon as I had finished praying at the end of the class, she virtually ran out of the sanctuary. Her son came up and said one sentence that clarified the heart of the situation. He said, "She loves the person about whose theology you were asking us to reevaluate." She was so emotionally tied to the person whose theology she had been consuming and jamming into her cerebrum for so long that it had, at least for the time being, won out over my logical appeal to reconsider his theological propositions.

When I first began to struggle with many of these same issues I have been asking you to consider, it came right down to the fact that there was a lot of illogical stuff in my brain that needed to get recycled, which ultimately meant that I would need to throw out a lot of useless debris that had gotten stuffed into my cerebrum before I had the chance to thoroughly evaluate how it related to the whole of Scripture. Maybe that's why so many jokingly refer to seminary as "cemetery."

Secondly, I'm not sure if one can hold to theological tenets without being adamant about their truths. I never personally imagined how often I would find myself being absolutely convinced about their truthfulness while at the same time being challenged to communicate them in love to someone else (Ephesians 4:15). It gradually became quite clear that while holding to these views might be theologically sound and scripturally accurate, they were still far from being mainstream in the theological thinking of other Christians, even in Baptist congregations. In fact, most of the views I have asked you to reevaluate are so staggeringly prevalent that it's frightening to think of the degree to which we have failed all along to consider what Scripture and historical theology teach.

Once you endeavor to walk this path, it may begin to seem that every book you pick up, every article you read, every commentary you study, and every pastor you talk to is tainted with bad theology. After a while, you really begin to wonder if perhaps you are not the only one in a crowd of thousands who sees things differently. And then you open the Scriptures again and start comparing verses and doing word studies and digging deeper and deeper and reading more theology and you realize that it's not entirely you at all; it's that most of the Christian church and the material it publishes are devoid of the concept of the total sovereignty of God. And when we get right down to it, it is a frightening thought to think that we promulgate so much literature that teaches that our God is not really sovereign in the lives of men at all.

Thirdly, holding to these tenets could become an obsessive and laborious mental task. My caution would be that there might be a tendency to be so concerned with the sifting out of these difficult concepts that the practical implications of how these truths we are tenaciously holding on to no longer work themselves out in our every day walk with the Lord. If you begin to see how much of our thinking has been wrong, unbiblical, perhaps even heretical, the tendency might be for you to make this whole arena of policing scriptural and non-scriptural writings your theological vocation.

There is still much of evangelical Christianity that teaches and cherishes the truth. And there is much, as we have suggested here, that does not. My friend and pastor, whom I cherish more and more, had cautioned me to look carefully at whether or not the result of this sifting and challenging of evangelical Christian thinking had revealed any bitterness in my own life. And I believe that it had. But the bitterness is not with any particular group of people, although some might question that in reading this book. My bitterness didn't arrive because I had been fed plateful after plateful of Arminian thought in seminary that never helped me to discern the subtle differences when it should have. My bitterness and frustration arrived with the recognition that I had read and reread passages in Scripture but had personally failed to really see Scripture for what it says and then was not forthright enough to believe and proclaim it. For so long I had been packing away information into my brain that was not only illogical and errant but downright foolish. If any bitterness was revealed, it was due to my own frustration with my failure to grasp and think through some of these theological issues before I walked into their tunnel without bringing a flashlight.

In other words, throughout all of this catharsis there needs to be a constant evaluating of one's walk with Christ and one's theological positions. Having said these things, I also assumed that reason and wisdom would eventually win over my previous state of ignorance and confusion, so while the process may be painful and challenging, as it has been for me, I am hoping that with whatever surgery is necessary, there will be a successful reconsideration of your theological perspective, knowing as well that it takes a long time to heal from radical surgery.

WHO NEEDS TO HAVE THEIR THEOLOGY CORRECT?

Getting it to be "correct" means knowing what the Word teaches. I think we should expect that men who are as godly and committed to Christ as Billy Graham is ought to be able to make critical distinctions in their theological understanding, don't you? If we don't expect men of his caliber to have their theology right, what on earth will we ever do about the man who sits next to us in the pew on Sunday morning? Shall we just sit there and let them say, "Oh well, doctrine never meant much to me anyway."

Knowing what the Word teaches means careful, diligent study and reflection on what God means in His Word, regardless of whether or not that's what we think the Word *should* say! Diligent study and reflection means putting the pieces together so that the whole of God's Word speaks more clearly than any single part. If we put together the pieces of the whole and it doesn't wind up saying, "Our God is absolutely sovereign in every detail of salvation," then we ought to start wondering just what god we're talking about, because that doesn't sound like the God of the Bible.

Having it be "correct" also means taking a stand on those truths, no matter how deeply entrenched we find our mistakes have become while working our way back out of them through thorough and thoughtful reflection. All of God's truth for us is in His Word. We have to be more thoughtful about what He is saying and more careful to be true to His Word and better students of it. That's what He's expecting from us! And that can't be accomplished without a solid theological foundation that begins with the sovereignty of God.

I am suggesting that we begin again to reexamine very carefully what our understanding and biblical perspective has said about God and how He works and the state of men's hearts and how they respond to the Holy Spirit. Because, my friends, if there is no real problem with saying that there is nothing else the Holy Spirit can do if you decide to reject Him, then there is nothing wrong with saying that God hasn't got a clue who the elect are. And if there's no real problem with saying that God hasn't got a clue who the elect are, you can kiss whatever concept of assurance in salvation you thought you had good-bye! And if there is no real problem with whether or not you are genuinely saved from the pit of eternal agony because of something you did or because of something God did, then there is no real problem with saying that Jesus was mistaken; everyone is going to spend eternity in heaven. And if that is true, you can hang up your evangelism shoes!

Some of you might be thinking, "*Well, look how many people have come forward at Billy Graham crusades. Don't those kinds of results say something about a theology that teaches that man chooses for God instead of God choosing men?*" Some will say, "People are coming to Christ; that's all that matters." But the Christian church should not be looking to put another notch on its evangelism belt, or say, "We led him or her to make a decision for Christ." The church is looking for people to come to Christ who never stop coming to Christ!

We are attempting to share the "whole counsel of God" with lost sinners in hopes that God will use His gospel to change a heart so that heart can respond to the truth. We are looking for committed Christians who are in it until the very last day. And if the decision to be saved is up to the sinner and not God, you can be sure they won't make it because it's just too long a haul! The church is looking for genuine converts, not people who were temporarily swayed by some silly pamphlet or untruth about the import of their decision or some weird notion of the sovereignty of God that happened to have met their own fancy and approval one Sunday morning after a weekend binge.

Only those who God brings to himself will stay with Him forever. No fleshly method of evangelism has ever succeeded in accomplishing what only the Holy Spirit is capable of accomplishing—raising Lazarus from the spiritual pit of death. May God be glorified in all that we say and think about His wonderful Person, and may we never be ashamed of our utter lack of commitment to the study of the Person of God. Because if we are committed to His Word and truth, we just might find that through the mess we've made of who God is we were able to chisel away at some of the controversies just enough to begin to see who He really is.

APPENDIX

BIBLICAL VERSES SUPPORTING THE ORDER OF SALVATION

Predestination

Romans 8:29–30; Romans 9:1–25; Eph 1:3–14; 2 Thessalonians 2:12–13

Election

Ephesians 1:4, 9, 11; Romans 8:28–30; 1 Peter 1:2; 2 Thessalonians 2:13

Effectual Calling; Inward Call (Regeneration)

John 1:12–13; John 3:1–10; John 6:44, 45, 63–65; Ephesians 2:1–5; Titus 3:3–6; Romans 8:30

Regeneration Conversion: Faith-Repentance

Acts 20:21

(Faith)

Ephesians 2:8–9; Philippians 1:29; Acts 13:48, 16:14, 18:27; James 2:14

(Repentance)

Acts 5:31, 11:18; 2 Corinthians 7:10–11

Justification (Legal Declaration)

Deuteronomy 25:1; Acts 10:43; Proverbs 17:15; Romans 3:21;
Romans 4:8; Romans 5:1–2; Romans 5:12–18; 8:32;
Galatians 2:16; 3:1–13; 2 Corinthians 5:21; Philippians 3:9

Adoption

Romans 8:15–17, 23–25; 9:4; Galatians 4:1–5; Ephesians 1:5;
John 1:12–13; 1 John 3:1–2; John 8:40 to end

Union with Christ

1 Corinthians 12:13; Galatians 3:27; John 14:20; 15:1–6;
Ephesians 1:22–23; 4:12–16; 5:23–32

Definitive Sanctification

John 10:26–30; Romans 6; 1 Corinthians 1:2, 6:9–12

Progressive Sanctification

Leviticus 11:44; Matthew 5–7; Romans 13; Ephesians 4–5;
Philippians 2:1–13; 1 Corinthians 13; Galatians 5: 16–23;
1 Peter 1:15–16; 2 Peter 1:1–10, 3:18

Perseverance of the Saints

Jeremiah 32:40; John 6:37–40, 10:26–30; Romans 8:30-end; Philippians 1:6; 1 John 3:9

Glorification

Matthew 25; 1 Thessalonians 4:13-end; 2 Corinthians 5:1–8; Philippians 1:23, 3:20–21; 1 John 3:1–3; Revelation 6:9–10

ENDNOTES

1 J. I. Packer, "Regeneration," Walter A. Elwell, ed., in Evangelical Dictionary of Theology (Michigan: Baker Book House, 1989), 924–926.

2 Compare these Biblical passages for more on regeneration: Ezekiel 11:19; John 1:13; Acts 16:14; Philippians 2:13.

3 See Appendix for the Bible verses associated with each step of the Order of Salvation.

4 The inference is thus drawn: The only thing that can ever come from nothing is nothing. If in the beginning of time we started with nothing, nothing is all we would have now. The fact that *something* is here now must lead one to the conclusion that there has always been something that has been in existence.

5 J. I. Packer, Knowing God (Grand Rapids: Intervarsity Press, 1973), 13–14.

6 F. A. Filby, Creation Revealed: A Study of Genesis Chapter One in the Light of Modern Science (New Jersey: Fleming H. Revell Co., 1963), 15.

7 The Greek word translated 'interpretation' in verse 20 is (epiluseos). It occurs only here in all of the New Testament. It was an accountant's term which literally meant to "loose, untie, release, set free." It later came to mean "explain, disclose." See Joseph Henry Thayer, A Greek-English Lexicon of the New Testament (New York: American Book Company, 1886), 240.

8 Frederic Louis Godet, Commentary on Romans (Grand Rapids: Kregel Publications, 1977), 430.

9 To call on His name is to recognize what His name expresses, the One Eternal God.

10 For Thayer's excellent discussion of the use of this word and all its implications in the New Testament, see Thayer, Greek-Lexicon, 511–512.

11 Daniel B. Wallace, Greek Grammar Beyond the Basics: An Exegetical Syntax of the New Testament (The Libronix Digital Library System, 1996), 572–582. See his extensive comments on the use and meaning of the perfect tense in Greek.

12 In Galatians 5:1–6, Paul makes the argument that to believe that circumcision is a necessary adjunct to faith in Christ for salvation is anathema.

13 B. A. Demerest, "Analogy of Faith," in Evangelical Dictionary of Theology, 43–44.

14 This section has been greatly influenced by Loraine Boettner's chapter on The Sovereignty of God. Loraine Boettner, The Reformed Doctrine of Predestination (New Jersey: Presbyterian and Reformed Publishing Co., 1932), 30–34.

15 Erwin Lutzer, Ten Lies about God: 'And how you might already be deceived' (W Publishing Group: Nashville, 1973), 105.

16 Duane Edward Spencer, TULIP: The Five Points of Calvinism in the Light of Scripture (Grand Rapids: Baker Book House, 1979), 24–28.

17 Compare the following passages: John 5:42; 6:44; 8:34; 15:4, 5; Romans 5:18; 7:18, 24; 6:23; 8:7; Ephesians 4:18; 2 Timothy 3:2–4; Hebrews 11:6.

18 G. Herbert Livingston, "'āwen," R. Laird Harris, ed., et al., in Theological Wordbook of the Old Testament [TWOT] (Chicago: Moody Press, 1980), I, 23–24.

19 Robert Shaw, An Exposition of The Westminster Confession of Faith (Great Britain: Christian Focus Publication, Reprinted 1992), 116.

20 Charles Ryrie, A Survey of Bible Doctrine (Chicago: Moody Press, 1972), 118.

21 "The divine *pneuma* [spirit], has imparted to man the gift of life, but this life is experienced on the level of the human *pneuma*....made alive in Christ...means that [men] were spiritually dead, i.e., their spirits did not enjoy a living relationship with God. To be made alive means to be quickened in spirit so that men enter into living fellowship with God." George Eldon Ladd, A Theology of the New Testament (Grand Rapids: William B. Eerdmans, 1974), 463.

22 John 6:44–45 says, "No one can come to Me unless the Father Who sent Me draws him...therefore, everyone who has heard and learned from the Father comes to Me."

23 Reprobation is the eternal and sovereign decree of God to determine some men to be vessels of wrath fitted unto destruction in the way of sin so that the glory of God's justice may be shown in them. Romans 9:22–24; 11:9; 1 Peter 2:8–9; Matthew 10:16; John 15:16.

24 Boettner, The Reformed Doctrine of Predestination, 114.

25 William Ames, The Marrow of Theology (Grand Rapids: Baker Books, 1968), 152–153.

26 Thayer, Liddell-Scott, Louw-Nida, United Bible Studies and Friberg Greek lexicons.

27 Ames, Marrow, 33.

28 "But the true meaning of election is designating certain men to partake in this salvation: specific love, Romans 9:13; love relating to supernatural and chief good, Jeremiah 31:3; Ephesians 5:25; love involving a setting apart from others in which, in a comparative or relative manner, there is contained a certain real intention to love, Romans 9:13; John 17:6; 1 Corinthians 1:27, 28." [Ames, Marrow, 154].

29 John Calvin, Institutes of the Christian Religion, ed. John T. McNeil (Philadelphia: The Westminster Press, MCMLX), Book III, chapter 22, section 7.

30 Gordon H. Clark, Predestination, 'The Combined edition of Biblical Predestination and Predestination in the Old Testament' (New Jersey: Presbyterian and Reformed Publishing Company, 1969), 149.

31 The Westminster Confession of Faith (1647), Chapter III 'Of God's Eternal Decree;' The Savoy Declaration of Faith and Order (1680), Chapter III, 'Of God's Eternal Decree;' The London Confession of Baptist Faith (1688), Chapter III, 'Of God's Decree.'

32 The Belgic Confession of Faith (1561), Article XVI, Eternal Election; The Second Helvetic Confession (1566)–Chapter X, 'Of the Predestination of God and the Election of the Saints;' The French Confession (1571), Article XII; The Thirty-nine Articles of Religion (1801), Article XVII, 'Of Predestination and Election.'

33 William Klempa, "Supralapsarianism," in The Westminster Handbook to Reformed Theology, Donald K. McKim, ed. (Louisville: Westminster John Knox Press, 2001), 214–215. Klempa's final comment in this article is "it appears that on the question of the place of the fall of man in the electing purposes of God, a reverent agnosticism is advisable."

34 John H. Leith, An Introduction to the Reformed Tradition: A Way of Being the Christian Community (Atlanta: John Knox Press, 1981), 103–105.

35 Ames, Marrow, 27.

36 F. H. Klooster, "Elect, Election" in Evangelical Dictionary of Theology, 348–349. Man's common misery means that state of sin by which all men commonly suffer. Perhaps the most descriptive portion of Scripture that explains this 'common misery' is Romans 3:10–18.

37 Acts 13:48 clearly says, "And as many as had been appointed to eternal life believed." Our appointment to eternal life did not come about because we believed in Christ. Our faith came about because of our appointment to eternal life.

38 Francois Wendel, Calvin: 'Origins and Development of his Religious Thought,' trans. by Philip Mairet (Grand Rapids: Baker Books, 1950), 281.

39 Klooster, "Elect, Election," in Evangelical Dictionary of Theology, 348–349.

40 Thayer, Greek-English Lexicon, 538.

41 John N. Oswalt, "bāhar," Harris, et. al. TWOT, I, 100.

42 In 2 Peter 1:1, the NKJV states that Peter's letter is addressed to "those who have obtained like precious faith with us." The word translated *obtained* is from the Greek word *lagchano* meaning to "obtain by lot; to receive by divine allotment, obtain." The use of this particular word implies randomness in selection. But randomness does not necessarily imply purposelessness.

43 J. I. Packer, "Call, Calling," in Evangelical Dictionary of Theology, 184.

44 Spencer, TULIP, 45 ff.

45 There are three voices in Greek: active, middle and passive. The voice of this word "begotten from above" in John 3:3 is passive, just like the voice of "begotten us again" in 1 Peter 1:3. In the passive voice the subject *is acted upon* or *receives the action* expressed by the verb.

46 In the Parable of the Soils, Luke writes that there are four types of ground which refer to four kinds of hearts that are impacted by the word of God. The good (regenerated) hearts "are those who, having heard the word...keep it and bear fruit with patience (8:14)."

47 Joseph Agar Beet, A Commentary on St. Paul's Epistles to the Corinthians (London: Hodder and Stoughton, 1902), 264.

48 Thayer, Greek-English Lexicon, 36.

49 Thayer, Greek-English Lexicon, 32.

50 Louis Berkhof, Systematic Theology (Edinburgh: The Banner of Truth Trust, reprinted 2003), 468–469.

51 Anthony Hoekema, Created in God's Image (Grand Rapids: Wm. B. Erdmann's Publishing Co., 1986), 86.

52 The Westminster Confession of Faith, Chapter X, "Of Effectual Calling."

53 Scripture repeatedly speaks of *only* two groups of people, for example: regenerate and unregenerate, converted and unconverted, sheep and goats, Christians and unbelievers, those in Christ and those outside of Christ, saved and unsaved, repentant and unrepentant, tares and wheat, sons of God and sons of disobedience.

54 Iain H. Murray, Evangelicalism Divided: A Record of Crucial Change in the Years 1950 to 2000 (Edinburgh: Banner of Truth, 2000), 3–6, 32.

55 J. I. Packer, A Quest for Godliness: The Puritan Vision of the Christian Life (Crossway Books: Wheaton, Illinois, 1990), 200.

56 Acts 11:21; 14:15; 15:3, 19; 26:18, 20; Luke 1:16; James 5:19; 1 Peter 2:25; 2 Corinthians 3:16; John 12:40; 1 Thessalonians 1:9.

57 D.G. Bloesch, 'Conversion,' in Evangelical Dictionary of Theology, 272–273.

58 William J. Bouwsma, John Calvin: A Sixteenth Century Portrait (Oxford: Oxford University Press, 1988), 9.

59 Bouwsma, John Calvin, 11. From Calvin's commentary on Jeremiah 31:18.

60 J. I. Packer, Keeping in Step with the Spirit (New Jersey: Fleming H. Revell, 1984), 104.

61 The many different references to Paul's experience on the road to Damascus in the book of Acts are never described by the word 'conversion' in the Bible. Even in Acts 2:41, which certainly would imply that three thousand were "converted" to Christianity after Peter's sermon, Luke never mentions the word converted.

62 Frederick Field, Notes on the Translation of the New Testament (n.c.: Hendrickson Publishers, 1994, Reprint from 1899 edition), 251.

63 Wendel, Calvin, 236–239.

64 Wendel, Calvin, 238–239.

65 Thayer, Greek-English Lexicon, 379.

66 Joseph Smith, *History of the Church* (Shadow Mountain), 4, 535–541.

67 James Edward Talmadge, The Articles of Faith: A Series of Lectures on the Principle Doctrines of the Church of Jesus Christ of Latter-day Saints, (Salt Lake City: Deseret News, 1899), 78–79.

68 Catechism of the Catholic Church, Part Three: Life in Christ, Article Two: Grace and Justification. Accessed December 28, 2010. http://www.vatican.va/archive/catechism/p3s1c3a2.htm.

69 We must never let the gospel truth of "imputation" and the Catholic notion of "imparting or infusing" the righteousness of Christ meet. In Scripture, imputed righteousness alone justifies; imparted righteousness does not play any role in our justification. There can be no moderation. The antithesis between imparted or infused righteousness and imputed righteousness must always exist. To confuse the two is to disguise Roman Catholicism in Protestant garb. See Rev. Mark Herzer, "Arminianism Exposed ver.1.1," accessed January 3, 2011. http://www.the-highway.com/Arminianism_Exposed2.html.

70 Thayer, Greek-English Lexicon, 634.

71 P. H. Davids, 'Adoption,' in Evangelical Dictionary of Theology, 13.

72 Examples of the English sense of perfect would be I have loved, we have been loving, you have stood.

73 Ames, Marrow, 35.

74 Wendel, Calvin, 258–259.

75 Charles G. Finney, Finney's Systematic Theology (Grand Rapids: Bethany House, 1976), 320–322.

76 "Is sanctification also monergistic?" an email reply on line found at http: //www.monergism.com /the threshold /articles/questions/sanctification01.html.

77 Dieter, et al., Five Views on Sanctification (Grand Rapids: Zondervan House, 1987), 189–190.

78 The Westminster Confession of Faith, Chapter XVII: Of the Perseverance of the Saints.

79 Robert Shaw, An Exposition of The Westminster Confession of Faith, 180–181.

80 Note that the Parable of the Soils refers to those who immediately stumble when tribulation or persecution arises because of the word (Matthew 13:21).

81 The sin of unbelief is the only sin that cannot be forgiven. That is why it is theologically incorrect to say that Christ's death atoned for *every* sin. It is correct to say that Christ's death atoned for every sin of the believer. To suggest that Christ's atonement covered even the sin of unbelief in unbelievers is incorrect.

82 Thayer, Greek-English Lexicon, 156.

83 J. K. Grider, 'Glorification' in Evangelical Dictionary of Theology, 442–443.

84 Jay Smith, 'Dare We Confront?' A call for a new Paradigm in Muslim Evangelism (The Jay Smith Papers, September 1999), 3.

85 J. I. Packer, A Quest For Godliness, 307.

86 Nicolas Pioch, http://www.ibilio.org/wm/paint/auth/bosch/fools/. The paintings of Hieronymus Bosch can be accessed at http://en.wikipedia.org/wiki/List_of_paintings_by_Hieronymus_Bosch.

87 Louis Goldberg, "kāsal" Harris, et. al., TWOT, 1, 449.

88 Louis Goldberg, "'ēwil" Harris, et. al., TWOT, 1, 19.

89 Louis Goldberg, "k^{e}sil" Harris, et. al., TWOT, 1, 449.

90 Henry Howard, Earl of Surrey, sonnet from *Tottel's Miscellany*, 1557.

91 J. P. Lange, The Gospel According to Matthew, trans. Philip Schaff (New York: Charles Scribner's Sons, 1864), 160.

92 The devil is not himself "the spirit that now works in the sons of disobedience." [If the word 'prince' were in apposition to 'spirit' in Greek (placed alongside it to further qualify it, i.e., prince = spirit), they would both be in the genitive case. 'Prince' is accusative, and 'spirit' is genitive]. Here, the devil is called the prince or ruler *over* that spirit, that ruler whose authority is exercised in the realm of the air. *Spirit* is not in a personal sense here--it is "a spirit of this age" concept. Paul implies that Satan is controlling that *spirit of the age* which is continuously working in the unbeliever until God makes the disobedient son "alive in Christ." See F.F. Bruce, The Epistle to the Ephesians (Pickering & Inglis Ltd.: London, 1961), 48.

93 Martyn McGeown, "The Notion of Preparatory Grace in the Puritans," Protestant Reformed Theological Journal 41 (2007): 77–78.

94 Though many modern commentators are more apt to avoid this specific interpretation because of the theological implications and further difficulties that may ensue from it, it certainly is a feasible translation of the original. Even if it was interpreted to be "they might return to their senses [and escape] from the snare of the devil, after having been captured by him to [do] the will of that [dreaded] one [the devil]," as is equally viable, no Christian theology allows us to believe that Satan does *anything* in his own will and power that is not already permitted by God for him to do! After all, as Luther

said, "The Devil is still *God's* devil." For the various possible interpretations of these verses, see Daniel B. Wallace's Greek Grammar Beyond the Basics: An Exegetical Syntax of the New Testament, (Texas: Galaxie Software, 1996), 390. See also Newport J. D. White, "The Second Epistle to Timothy," W. Robertson Nicoll, ed., The Expositor's Greek Testament, (Grand Rapids: Eerdmans, 1988) 4, 169.

95 Richard G. Moulton, Ecclesiastes: The Wisdom of Solomon (New York: MacMillan and Company, 1898), xix-xxii.

96 Robert L. Reymond, A New Systematic Theology of the Christian Faith, second edition (Nashville: Thomas Nelson, 1998), 161–165.

97 These five points are highlighted and expanded upon from D. A Carson, The Difficult Doctrine of the Love of God (Wheaton: Crossway Books, 2000), 16–21.

98 Reymond, A New Systematic Theology of the Christian Faith, 401–402.

99 D. A. Carson, Exegetical Fallacies (Grand Rapids: Baker Book House,1984), 22.

100 John MacArthur, Jr., The Love of God (Dallas: Word Publishing, 1996), 95.

101 MacArthur, The Love of God, 146.

102 "Apart from God's act of reconciliation through the atoning death of His Son, the cross reveals nothing but wrath and judgment. It is the condemnation of the world. Besides, how could the cross be a demonstration of the love of God unless God was in Christ reconciling the world unto himself through the death of the Son of God (2 Corinthians 5:19)..." Herman Hoeksema, Reformed Dogmatics (Grandville: Reformed Free Publishing Association, 2004), 1, 550.

103 F. F. Bruce, The Book of the Acts: The New International Commentary on the New Testament (Grand Rapids: Wm. B. Eerdmans, 1988), 437.

104 Bruce, The Book of The Acts, 448.

105 James H. Moulton & George Milligan, The Vocabulary of the Greek New Testament: 'Illustrated from the Papyri and other non-literary Sources' (Grand Rapids: Eerdmans Publishing Co., 1930), 583.

106 B. C. Johnson, The Atheist Debater's Handbook (Amherst: New York, 1983), 99–100.

107 On what basis does the atheist come to the conclusion that there is no spiritual reality? On what basis does he come to the conclusion that empiricism is the only valid source for determining all that is real?

108 One cannot prove what does *not* exist through any means, empirical (see, hear, touch, taste, smell) or otherwise. Using empirical means as a scientific proof can only prove what *does* exist. If atheism is certain that God does *not* exist, there would be no empirical proofs available to prove it. So why make any effort to do the impossible?

109 This short paper cannot consider all of the implications about faith. We are only considering here that faith does not arise within ourselves through our own efforts.

110 Johnson, The Atheist Debater's Handbook, 12.

111 Thomas B. Warren, Have Atheists Proved There Is No God? (Nashville: Gospel Advocate Co., 1972), vii.

112 Gottfried Wilhelm Freiherr von Leibniz, "The Best of all Possible Worlds," John A. Mourant, ed., Readings in the Philosophy of Religion (New York: Thomas Y. Crowell, 1954), 384.

113 Leibniz, Readings, 384

114 St. Augustine, "Evil as Privation of the Good," Readings, 391. The reference is to the Apostle's Creed, which begins with the words, "I believe in God the Father Almighty, Maker of heaven and earth...."

115 Johnson, The Atheist Debater's Handbook, 106.

116 A friend of mine made a good point here. We are not suggesting that *questioning* God's goodness is an evil in and of itself. Nor are we suggesting that having a single evil thought makes the whole person evil. What we are suggesting however, is that all humans have at times thoughts that are essentially evil, and we are assuming that evil thoughts arise from an innate evilness. That God does not destroy us for this innate evil is a good thing.

117 Perhaps at this juncture, the atheist might consider it a 'good' compromise if God were to only erase the evil thought that came to the mind of the atheist the second that he had it, rather than eliminate the atheist altogether.

118 Johnson, The Atheist Debater's Handbook, 104.

119 It is curious that the atheist suddenly and conveniently argues for a "God-produced miracle" in his belief system. We wonder if a miracle certainly *would* be the atheist's contention, were he to discover that *God* had actually produced a heart attack in Hitler.

120 By this I mean human beings as they now are. Neither the Christian nor the atheist can speak reasonably or explain what might be involved in speaking of some other kind of human being that exists in a different kind of world. In this imaginary utopia of pleasure, where the divinity apparently demonstrates His love and goodness by providing nothing but pleasure to human beings, yet no evil consequences to any of those pleasures whatsoever, do humans have the same

bodies they have now? Are they still sinful? Would all other things in the world be equal? How would they need to be different to live in that world and experience more pleasure?

121 It might be reasonable to ask here whether or not the evil consequences can be deemed good in that they might restrain the participant from a complete abandonment to utter hedonism to the neglect of other necessary considerations in life.

122 Johnson, The Atheist Debater's Handbook, 102–103.

123 Huston Smith, The World's Religions (New York: Harper San Francisco, 1991), 22.

124 Hank Hanegraaff, Christianity in Crisis (Eugene, OR.: Harvest House, 1993), 266.

125 On what basis does the atheist make the assumption that a 'safe and peaceful world' is a better world than this one? Certainly it is not on the basis of his omniscience. On what basis does the atheist make the assumption that he knows what would make this world a better world? If this is the only world he has experienced, how could he know?

126 A. M. Hills, Homiletics and Pastoral Theology (Missouri: Nazarene Publication House, 1929), 356.

127 Hills, Homiletics, 363.

128 James Dobson, Focus on the Family, December 1994, 18, No. 12. I have tremendous respect for the ministry that Focus on the Family has maintained since its beginning, and this is no more than a reflection on the typical types of theological misunderstanding that many ministries continue to demonstrate.

129 However, I do not mean to imply here that God cannot use an unregenerate sinner to do His will. That is not a Scriptural concept. God certainly did use Cyrus to accomplish His will. Cf. Isaiah 45 ff.

130 J. M. Whiton, Greek English Lexicon Abridged from Liddell and Scott's Greek-English Lexicon (New York: American Book Co., 1871), 404.

131 The Greek word in John 6:44, "No one can come to Me unless the Father *draws* him...," is *elko,* and means 'to draw by inward power, lead, impel; properly: to drag ships down into the sea,' or 'to drag' along a dead body. See Thayer's Greek Lexicon at *elko,* 204–205. See also Bauer, Arndt and Gingrich, A Greek Lexicon of the New Testament and Other Early Christian Literature (Chicago: The University of Chicago Press, 1979), 251.

132 This statement is actually a tremendous stumbling block for Arminian theologians. Most Arminian theologians suggest that God does not truly know who is going to repent, because men are "free" to choose God or not choose Him, and God will not interfere in their free-will choices. But if God doesn't interfere in their choices, how will He ever be able to return in judgment? If it is true that man freely chooses God, and because, in Arminianism, men are free to choose, and God will not interfere in those choices, then God would never know when to return in judgment, because He might errantly come and bring judgment upon someone who was only seconds away from freely choosing repentance. It seems fairly inconsistent to me to suggest that God would have given everyone free will if indeed He wanted to save them all.

133 J. K. Grider, 'Arminianism,' in Evangelical Dictionary of Theology, 80.

134 David C. Hagopian, et al., Back to Basics: Rediscovering the Richness of the Reformed Faith (Phillipsburg: Presbyterian and Reformed, 1996), 44.

135 R. C. H. Lenski, The Interpretation of St. Paul's First and Second Epistles to the Corinthians, (Minnesota: Augsbury Publishing House, 1963), 1029.

136 Lenski, Corinthians, 1029.

137 Leon J. Wood, "hāpēs" Harris, ed., et al. TWOT, I, 311.

138 Loraine Boettner, The Reformed Doctrine of Predestination (Phillipsburg: Presbyterian and Reformed Publishing Company, 1932), 107.

139 Rev. Eric Kampen, "Is Arminianism a Different Gospel"? Accessed on January 1, 2011. http://www.mountainretreatorg.net/articles/arminianism.html. Billy Graham, How to Be Born Again, quoted from (Word Publishers, 1989), 15.

140 Billy Graham, How to Be Born Again, 182.

141 Billy Graham, How to Be Born Again, 194.

142 C. H. Spurgeon, C. H. Spurgeon Autobiography, Volume 1: The Early Years 1834 -1859 (Edinburgh: The Banner of Truth Trust, 1962), 552.

143 Loraine Boettner, The Reformed Doctrine of Predestination, 359.

144 The Westminster Confession of Faith, Chapter IX, Of Free Will.

145 Hans Hillebrand, ed., The Reformation (Grand Rapids: Baker Book House, 1994), 290. Quoted from Hunted Heretic, Roland Bainton, p. 207–209.

146 John T. McNeill, The History and Character of Calvinism (Oxford: Oxford University Press, 1954), 176.

147 Robert Shaw, An Exposition of The Westminster Confession of Faith, v.

148 Loraine Boettner, The Reformed Doctrine of Predestination, 415

BIBLIOGRAPHY

Ames, William. The Marrow of Theology. Grand Rapids: Baker Books, 1968.

Bauer, Arndt and Gingrich, A Greek Lexicon of the New Testament and Other Early Christian Literature (Chicago: The University of Chicago Press, 1979), 251.

Beet, Joseph Agar. A Commentary on St. Paul's Epistles to the Corinthians. London: Hodder and Stoughton, 1902.

Berkhof, Louis. Systematic Theology. Edinburgh: The Banner of Truth Trust, reprinted 2003.

Boettner, Loraine. The Reformed Doctrine of Predestination. New Jersey: Presbyterian and Reformed Publishing Co., 1932.

Bouwsma, William J. John Calvin: A Sixteenth Century Portrait. Oxford: Oxford University Press, 1988.

Bruce, F. F. The Book of the Acts. The New International Commentary on the New Testament. Grand Rapids: Wm. B. Eerdmans, 1988.

Bruce, F. F. The Epistle to the Ephesians. Pickering & Inglis Ltd.: London, 1961.

Calvin, John. Institutes of the Christian Religion. Editor John T. McNeill. Philadelphia: West Minster Press, MCMLX.

Carson, D. A. Exegetical Fallacies. Grand Rapids: Baker Book House, 1984.

Carson, D. A. The Difficult Doctrine of the Love of God. Wheaton: Crossway Books, 2000.

Clark, Gordon H. Predestination: The Combined Edition of Biblical Predestination and Predestination in the Old Testament. New Jersey: Presbyterian and Reformed Publishing Company, 1969.

Dieter, Melvin E., Anthony A. Hoekema, Stanley M. Horton, J. Robertson McQuilkin, John F. Walvoord, editors. Five Views on Sanctification. Grand Rapids: Zondervan House, 1987.

Elwell, Walter A., editor. Evangelical Dictionary of Theology. Michigan: Baker Book House, 1989.

Field, Frederick. Notes on the Translation of the New Testament. n.c.: Hendrickson Publishers, 1994, Reprint from 1899 edition.

Filby, F. A. Creation Revealed: A Study of Genesis Chapter One in the Light of Modern Science. New Jersey: Fleming H. Revell Co., 1963.

Finney, Charles G. Finney's Systematic Theology. Grand Rapids: Bethany House, 1976. .

Godet, Frederic Louis. Commentary on Romans. Grand Rapids: Kregel Publications, 1977.

Graham, Billy. How to Be Born Again. Word Publishers, 1989.

Hagopian, David C., editor. Douglas J. Wilson, Douglas M. Jones III, Robert Wagner, contributers. Back to Basics: Rediscovering the Richness of the Reformed Faith Phillipsburg: Presbyterian and Reformed, 1996.

Hanegraaff, Hank. Christianity in Crisis. Eugene, OR.: Harvest House, 1993.

Hans Hillebrand, ed., The Reformation. Grand Rapids: Baker Book House, 1994.

Harris, R. Laird, Gleason L. Archer, Bruce K. Waltke, editors. Theological Wordbook of the Old Testament. Chicago: Moody Press, 1980, vol. I & II.

Hills, A. M. Homiletics and Pastoral Theology. Missouri: Nazarene Publication House, 1929.

Hoekema, Anthony. Created in God's Image. Grand Rapids: Wm. B. Erdmann's Publishing Co., 1986.

Hoeksema, Herman. Reformed Dogmatics. Grandville: Reformed Free Publishing Association, 2004, vol. I.

Johnson, B. C. The Atheist Debater's Handbook. Amherst: New York, 1983.

Ladd, George Eldon. A Theology of the New Testament. Grand Rapids: William B. Eerdmans, 1974.

Lange, J. P. The Gospel According to Matthew. Translated by Philip Schaff. New York: Charles Scribner's Sons, 1864.

Leith, John H. An Introduction to the Reformed Tradition: A Way of Being the Christian Community Atlanta: John Knox Press, 1981.

Lenski, R. C. H. The Interpretation of St. Paul's First and Second Epistles to the Corinthians. Minnesota: Augsbury Publishing House, 1963.

Lutzer, Erwin. Ten Lies about God: And how you might already be deceived. W Publishing Group: Nashville, 1973.

MacArthur, John Jr. The Love of God. Dallas: Word Publishing, 1996.

McGeown, Martyn. The Notion of Preparatory Grace in the Puritans: Protestant Reformed Theological Journal 41 2007.

McKim, Donald K., ed. The Westminster Handbook to Reformed Theology. Louisville: Westminster John Knox Press, 2001.

McNeill, John T. The History and Character of Calvinism. Oxford: Oxford University Press, 1954.

Moulton, James H., and George Milligan. The Vocabulary of the Greek New Testament: Illustrated from the Papyri and other non-literary Sources. Grand Rapids: Eerdmans Publishing Co., 1930.

Moulton, Richard G. Ecclesiastes: The Wisdom of Solomon. New York: MacMillan and Company, 1898.

Mourant, John A., ed. Readings in the Philosophy of Religion. New York: Thomas Y. Crowell, 1954.

Murray, Iain H. Evangelicalism Divided: A Record of Crucial Change in the Years 1950 to 2000. Edinburgh: Banner of Truth, 2000.

Packer, J. I. A Quest for Godliness: The Puritan Vision of the Christian Life. Crossway Books: Wheaton, Illinois, 1990.

Packer, J. I. Knowing God. Grand Rapids: Intervarsity Press, 1973.

Packer, J. I. Keeping in Step with the Spirit. New Jersey: Fleming H. Revell, 1984.

Reymond, Robert L. A New Systematic Theology of the Christian Faith. Nashville: Thomas Nelson, Second edition 1998.

Ryrie, Charles. A Survey of Bible Doctrine. Chicago: Moody Press, 1972.

Shaw, Robert. An Exposition of The Westminster Confession of Faith. Great Britain: Christian Focus Publication, Reprinted 1992.

Smith, Huston. The World's Religions. New York: Harper San Francisco, 1991.

Smith, Jay. Dare We Confront?: A call for a new Paradigm in Muslim Evangelism. The Jay Smith Papers, September 1999.

Smith, Joseph. History of the Church. Shadow Mountain, vol. 4.

Spencer, Duane Edward .TULIP: The Five Points of Calvinism in the Light of Scripture. Grand Rapids: Baker Book House, 1979.

Spurgeon, C. H. C. H. Spurgeon Autobiography, Volume 1: The Early Years 1834-1859. Edinburgh: The Banner of Truth Trust, 1962.

Talmadge, James Edward. The Articles of Faith: A Series of Lectures on the Principle Doctrines of the Church of Jesus Christ of Latter-day Saints. Salt Lake City: Deseret News, 1899.

Thayer, Joseph Henry. A Greek-English Lexicon of the New Testament. New York: American Book Company, 1886.

Wallace, Daniel B. Greek Grammar Beyond the Basics: An Exegetical Syntax of the New Testament. The Libronix Digital Library System, 1996.

Warren, Thomas B. Have Atheists Proved There Is No God? Nashville: Gospel Advocate Co., 1972.

Wendel, Francois. Calvin: Origins and Development of his Religious Thought. Translated by Philip Mairet. Grand Rapids: Baker Books, 1950.

White, Newport J. D. The Second Epistle to Timothy. Editor, W. Robertson Nicoll. The Expositor's Greek Testament. Grand Rapids: Eerdmans, 1988, vol. 4.

Whiton, J. M. Greek English Lexicon Abridged from Liddell and Scott's Greek-English Lexicon. New York: American Book Co., 1871.